PHOTOGRAPHING YOUR FAMILY

PHOTOGRAPHING YOUR FAMILY

by Greg Lewis

AMPHOTO

American Photographic Book Publishing
An Imprint of Watson-Guptill Publications
1515 Broadway, New York, NY 10036

To my family:
Mary Ann, Ian, and Elizabeth
I love you all.

First published 1981 in New York by American Photographic Book Publishing: an imprint of Watson-Guptill Publications, a division of Billboard Publications, Inc., 1515 Broadway
New York, NY 10036

Library of Congress Cataloging in Publication Data

Lewis, Greg, 1945-
Photographing your family

1. Photography of families. I. Title.
TR681.F28L48 778.9′2 81-10956
ISBN 0-8174-5473-X AACR2
ISBN 0-8174-5474-8

Manufactured in the United States of America

1 2 3 4 5 6 7 8 9/86 85 84 83 82 81

CONTENTS

CHAPTER ONE

PHOTOGRAPHY AND YOUR FAMILY

Capturing those special moments forever

Photography is magic. It is a process that captures light, time, place, and detail. It is a magic that brings joy, excitement and discovery to our lives. When taking photographs, our primary tool is the camera, and our most frequent subjects are our families—the people who make up our happiest memories.

There seems to be little question about the importance of family photographs. We save them all, regardless of their technical faults, and few people would think of discarding an old family album or of including it among the odds and ends in a garage sale. In fact, family photos become more valuable as time passes, serving as memory triggers to those days that somehow seemed to go by so quickly. It is no surprise, therefore, that family albums are among the first items people try to save when their homes are threatened by fire or flood.

Often, however, the photos we take are inaccurate reflections. Pictures are out of focus, or they are too light or too dark, or they simply do not capture the feeling of the moment. This book is intended to help you with those problems and to show you how to produce photos you will enjoy and be proud of. The simple and practical techniques discussed will help you regardless of your skill. They can also be used with any camera. Laboratory procedures, detailed discussions of optical theory, and complicated techniques will not be discussed. This is a straightforward how-to book for people who want to photograph people they love.

In the next chapter, we will discuss types of cameras and how to choose lenses and film. In order to improve your photos, you will need a basic understanding of these tools. If you are an advanced photographer, you may want to skip this material.

In Chapter 3 you will be given important tips on how to improve family photos. Fancier, more expensive cameras will not give your photos meaning any more than an expensive typewriter will contribute to the creation of a good story.

Good photos serve as memory triggers to those days which pass by so quickly. Photograph by Betty Rosenzweig.

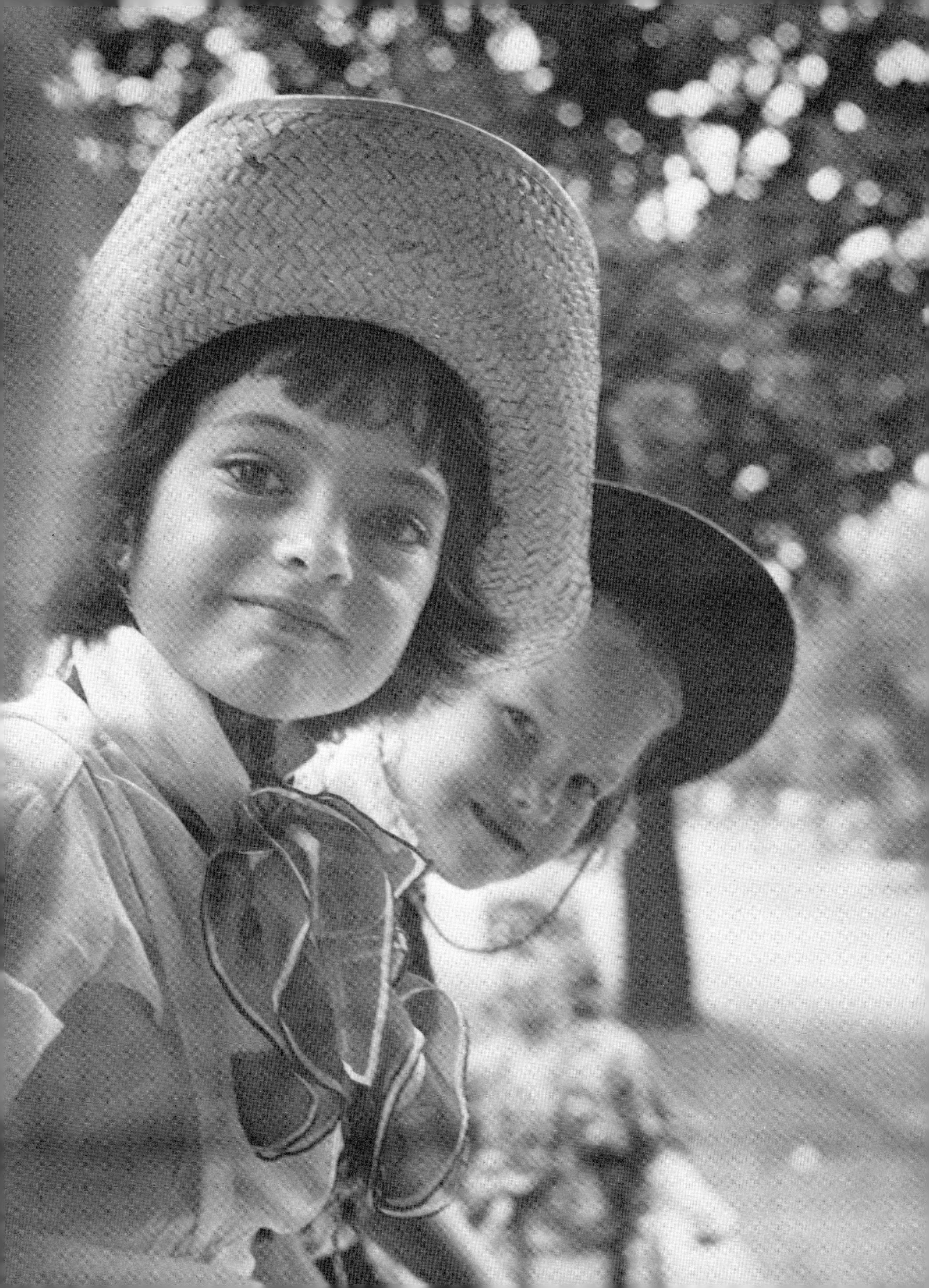

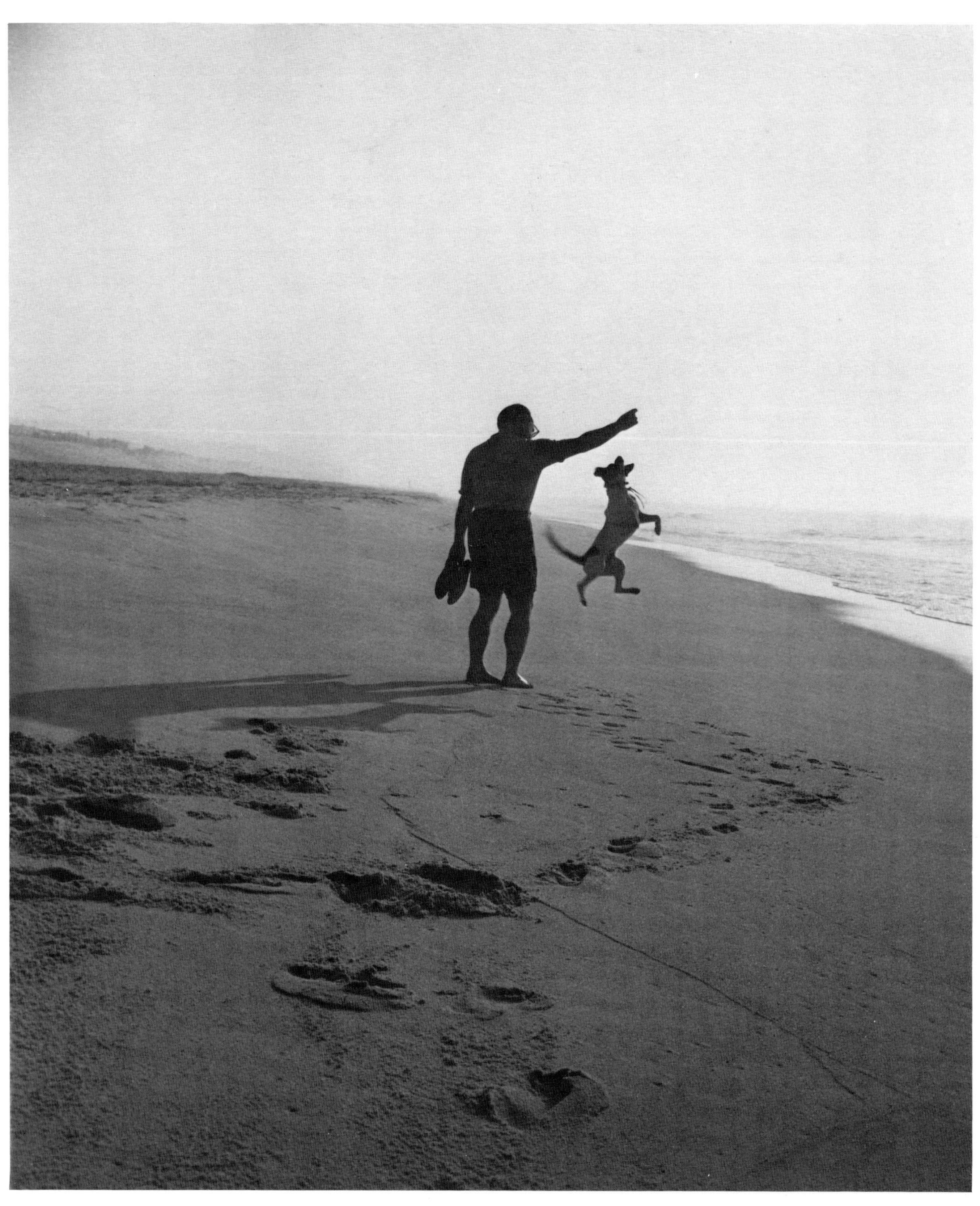

A quiet moment captured forever. Photograph by Betty Rosenzweig.

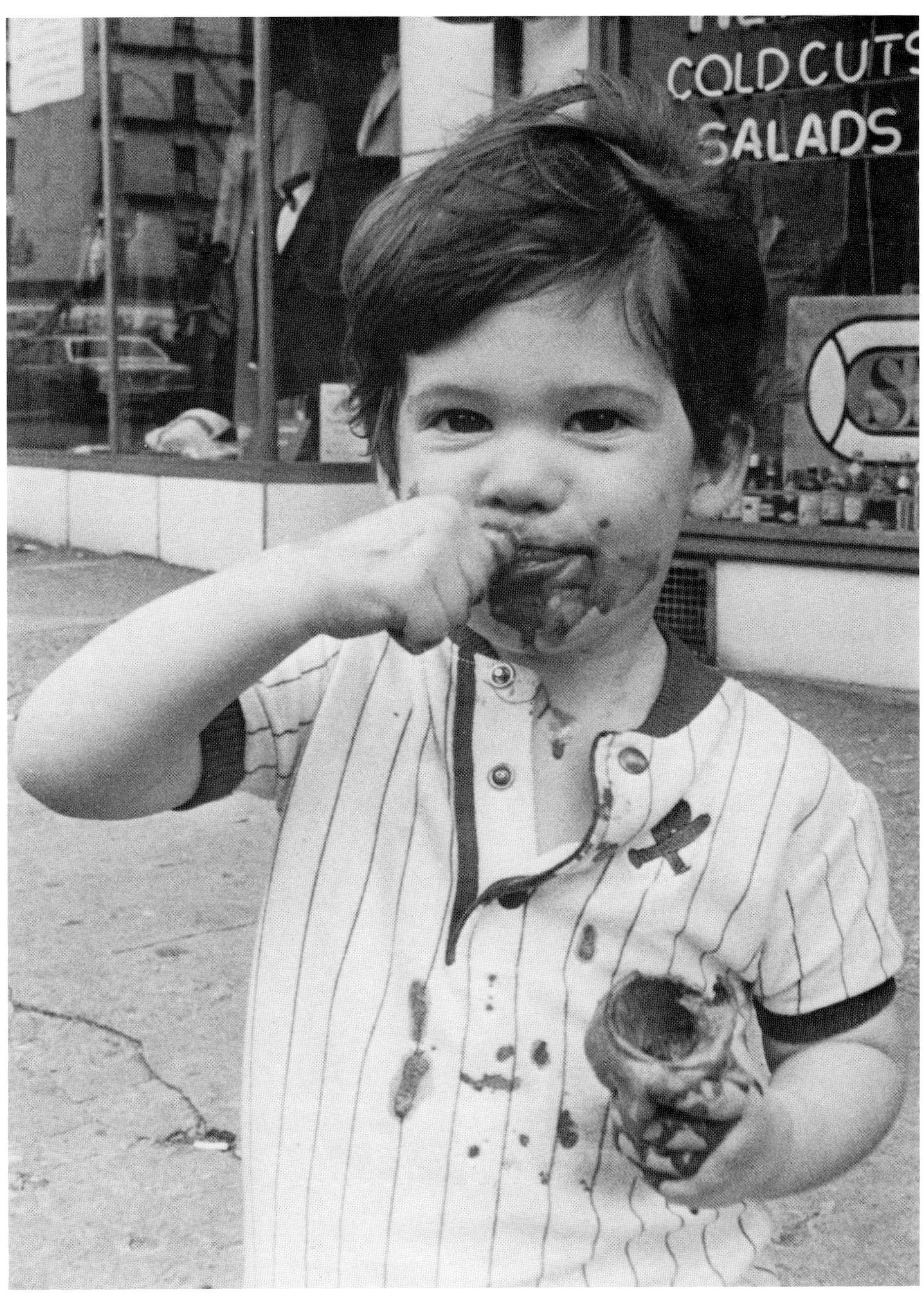

Give a child an ice cream cone, then get your camera ready–you're sure to get interesting results. Photograph by Michael O'Connor.

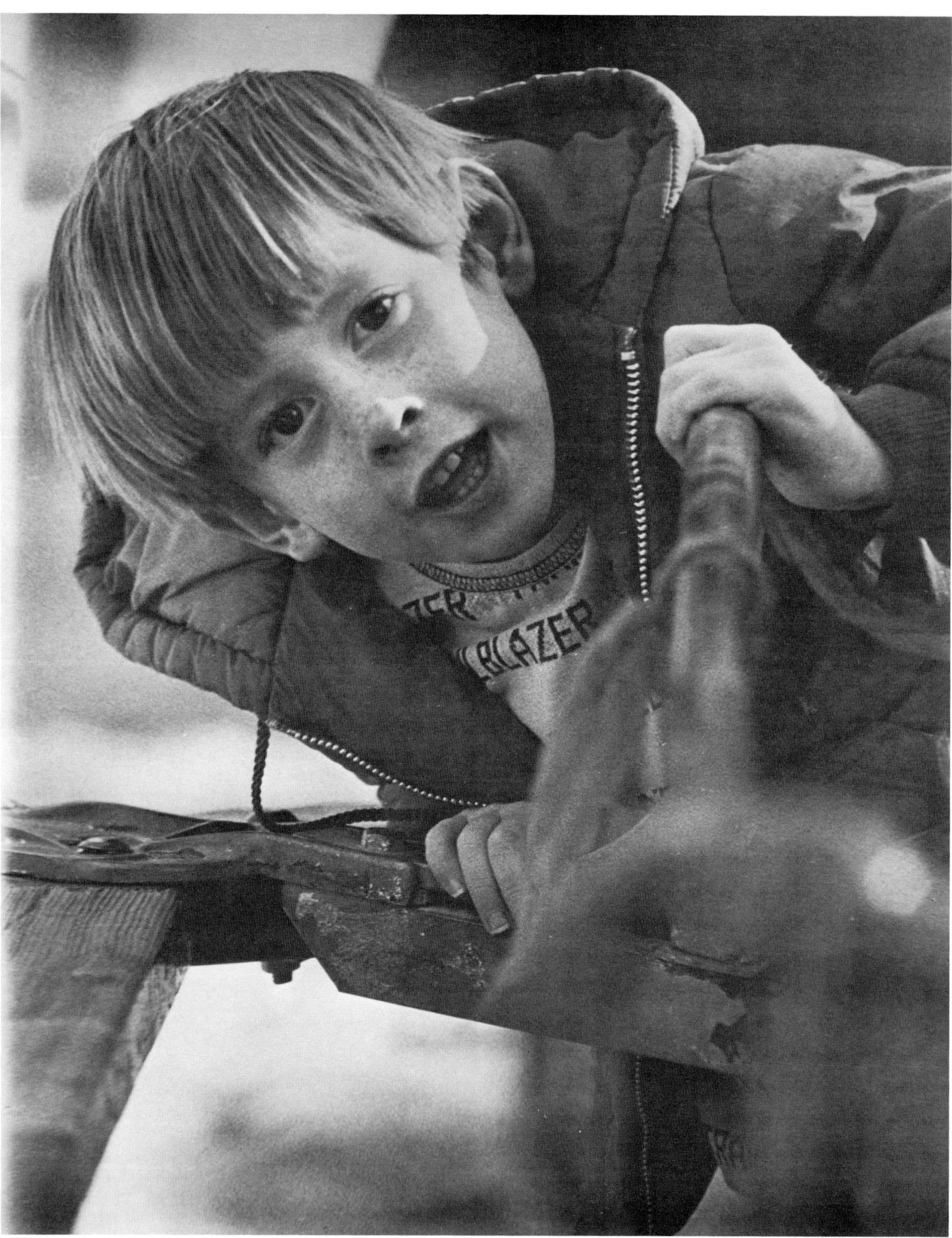
BLAZER

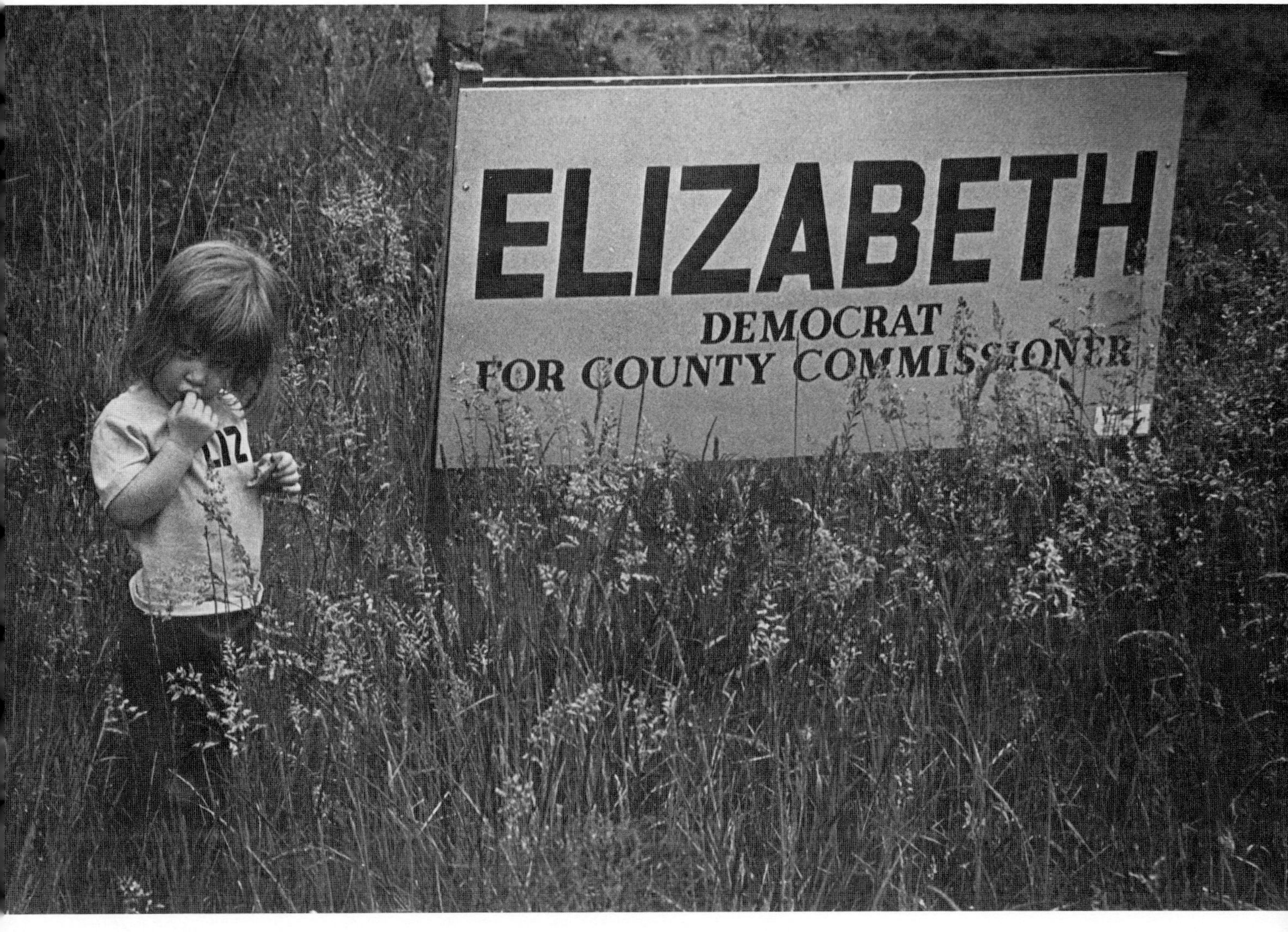

This chapter will therefore concentrate on improving the visual message of your photos. These methods will work with all cameras, simple or complex.

Children are the next topic discussed. They are natural, exciting, and compelling subjects, and because they are such an important part of family life, cameras often turn in their direction. You will learn how to encourage their cooperation and capture those charming moments that race by.

Light is essential to photography. In Chapter 5 you will learn how to use it to control the mood and impact of your photos. Beginning photographers can make powerful images with the simplest cameras if they know how to use light.

Chapter 6 covers techniques that will help you capture the excitement and spontaneity of events. These techniques will also help you avoid photographic problems on special occasions, such as on weddings, graduations, and holidays. You will also find tips on taking action photos of family athletes and actors.

Above: Have fun with names. If you see a store, street sign, or campaign poster bearing the name of a family member, make a picture like this.

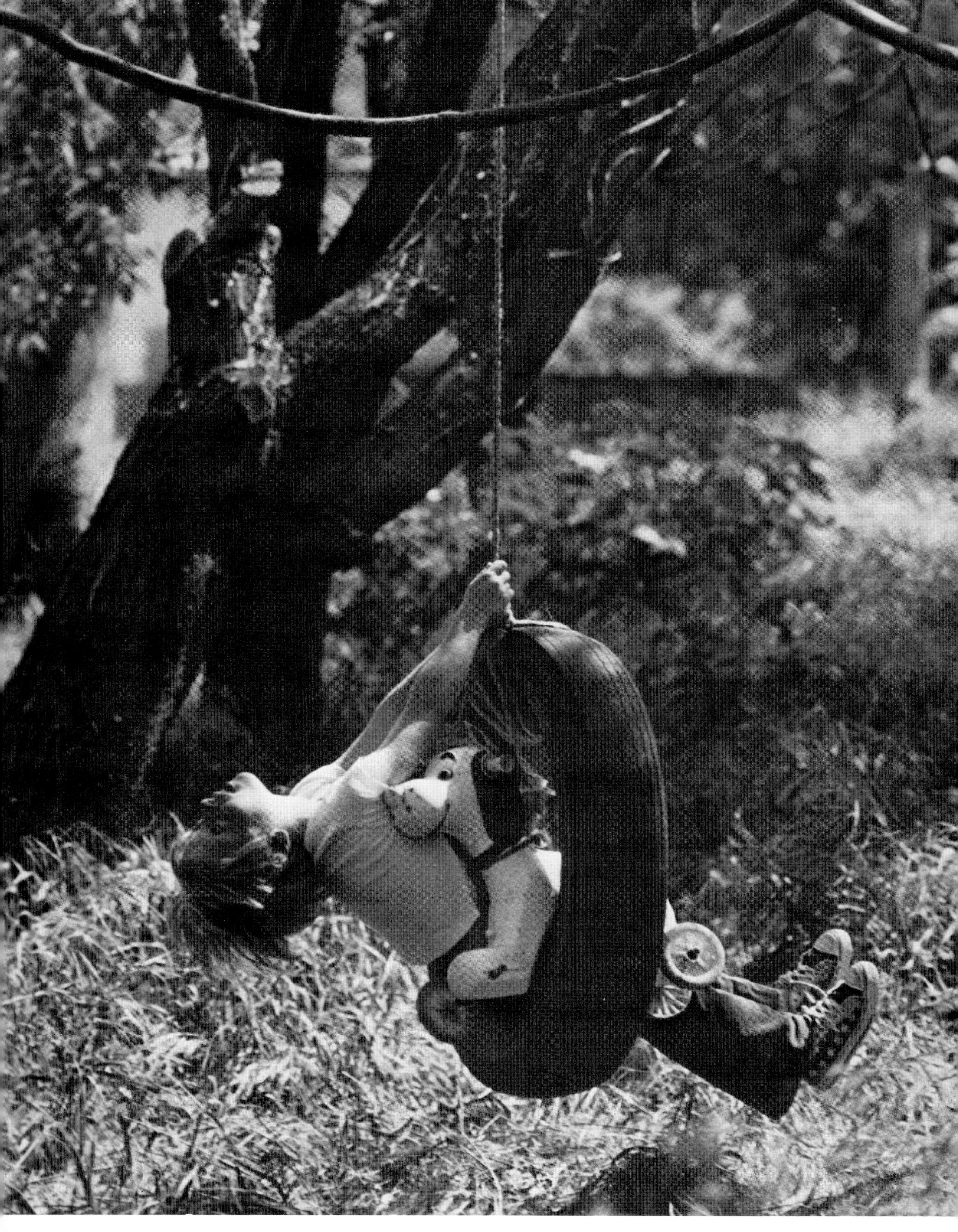

Chapter 7 gives you tips on vacation photos. Included is advice on equipment and the use of filters, which can increase the drama of your photos. With a minimal amount of preplanning and the use of story-telling techniques, you can produce a documentary the whole family will enjoy.

Pets and hobbies are also important parts of family life, and they should be included in your photographic collection. In Chapter 8 you will learn how to make your pet look its best and how to photograph family members enjoying hobbies. Also included is information on making a photographic inventory of your house and your possessions. Such a record can be valuable if you are the victim of a burglary or a natural disaster.

Finally, you will find many suggestions for displaying and using your photos. Many times, prints and slides are tucked away in a shoe box and forgotten. This last chapter will show you how to decorate your home with photos, how to use them for greeting cards, how to assemble them into a slide show, and how to organize your files so photos can be quickly found.

Too often cameras are brought out only on special occasions. In fact, some of you can probably recall when the Valentine, Halloween, and Christmas photos were on the same roll. But a good family photographer takes photos often. Avoid being one of those who frequently says, "Gee, I wish I had my camera."

In addition to the big, attention-getting times, look for the small, quiet moments. Even everyday events do not last forever. Avoid becoming bogged down in technicalities. With sensitivity and thoughtfulness you can become a communicator, historian, and artist whose photographs will preserve those special memories.

Everyday events do not happen every day forever. Use your camera to capture the little things as well as the big moments in your family's history. Photograph by Joseph A. Frisina, Jr.

CHAPTER TWO

CAMERAS AND FILM

Choosing and using

Among the most perplexing tasks in photography is the selection of a camera. The designs, features, and accessories are often confusing. Even professionals disagree on which types are best. And although many salespeople are quite knowledgeable about equipment, they often give conflicting advice.

Fortunately this confusion can be viewed as a positive indicator. There are, in fact, many cameras that perform quite well. Nevertheless, you may still want some advice on finding a good buy and on separating the features you really need from those rarely used.

110 POCKET CAMERAS

Perhaps the most convenient cameras for family photography are the 110 pocket cameras. These diminutive devices are easily loaded, conveniently carried, and quickly operated. The number 110 refers to the film size and cartridge type. The film is 16mm wide and is packed in a plastic cartridge that is dropped into the camera's film chamber.

Generally the lenses are either preset by the manufacturer for optimum focus or are designed for two-zone adjustment. The two zones include close-up and distant. Such lenses eliminate time-consuming focusing and are convenient for eyeglass wearers. They are also adequate for most family photos.

Complicated exposure controls are eliminated on most 110 cameras, either by fixed shutter and lens settings or by built-in devices that automatically set exposure. In addition to making photography relatively simple, the elimination or automation of controls keeps camera costs down. You can buy a 110 camera for about the same price as a dinner for two.

By the way, Pentax and Minolta make 110 cameras whose controls can be set by the photographer. Such cameras are good for those who want both sophistication and compactness. The advantages of being able to set your own controls and of having interchangeable lenses will become clear as you read on. Nevertheless, many fine photos can be made with simple equipment.

Even if you consider yourself an advanced photographer,

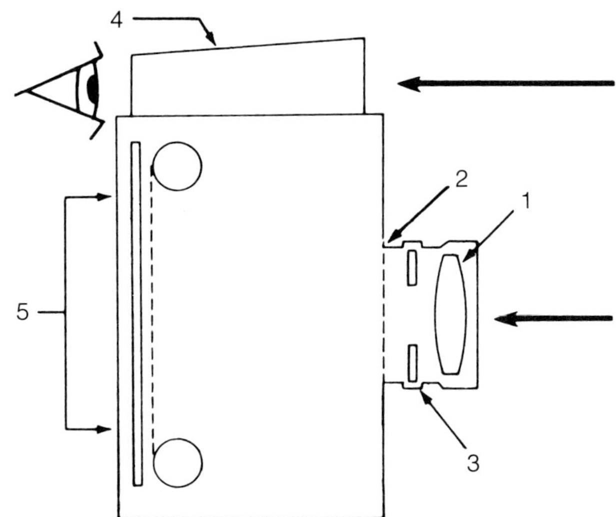

Every camera consists of the same basic elements: (1) a lens through which light rays pass, (2) a diaphragm that controls the amount of light admitted, (3) a shutter that opens to admit that light to the film plane, (4) a viewer that allows you to see what you are photographing, and (5) a film-advance system.

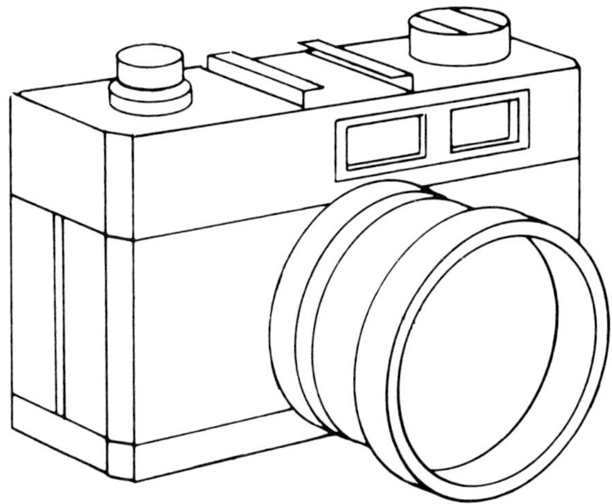

Because they can be highly automated, compact rangefinders are ideal for taking photographs quickly and inexpensively.

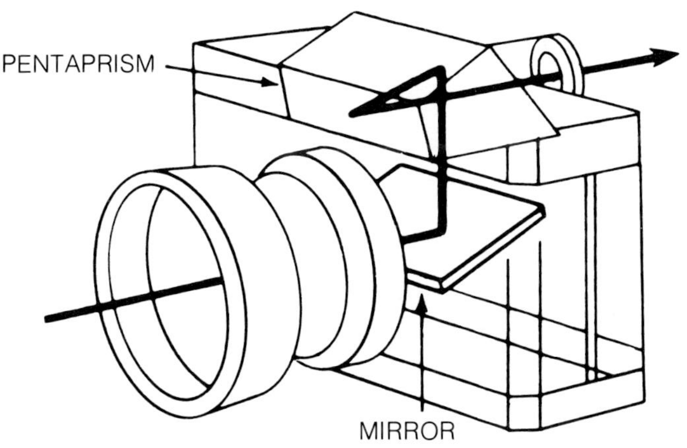

The single-lens reflex, with its interchangeable lenses, is popular with professionals as well as amateurs.

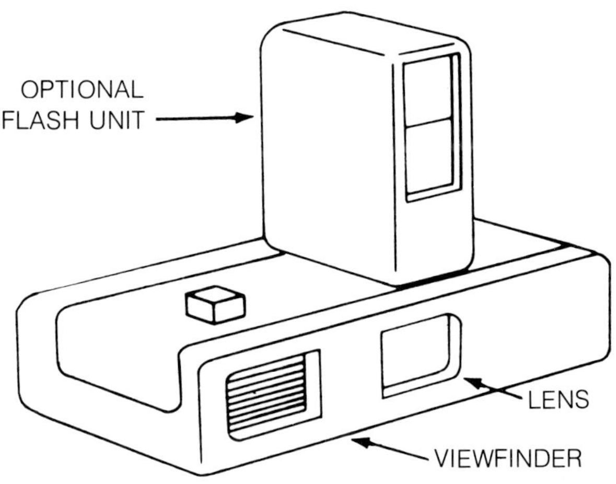

Conveniently carried, 110 pocket cameras are also easy to load and operate.

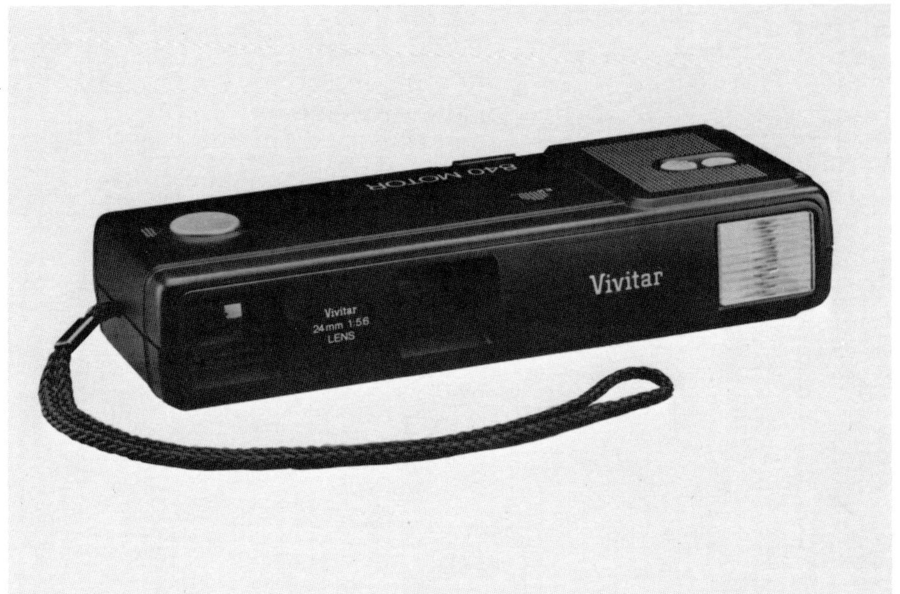

Simple 110 cameras like this one are great for those moments when you do not want to carry a heavier, more elaborate camera. The built-in flash facilitates making photos under weak light. Photograph courtesy of Vivitar Corp.

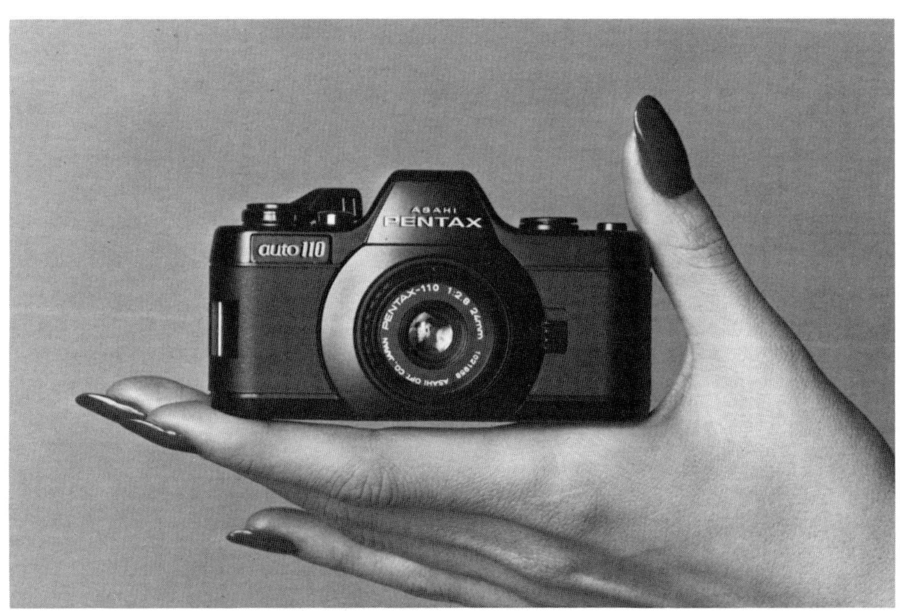

This tiny SLR uses 110 size film and is designed for the photographer who wants a small, yet sophisticated camera. The interchangeable normal, wide-angle, and telephoto lenses make this a useful tool for family photography. Photograph courtesy of Pentax Corp.

you may still want to have a simple camera among your more sophisticated equipment. They are especially handy when you need a camera that can be tucked into a pocket. They are also great for taking photographic notes. They can even challenge your creativity if you have been working with sophisticated equipment for a while.

35mm CAMERAS

For serious amateur photography 35mm cameras are the most popular. There are more brands of this camera and more accessories for it than for any other. And chances are you will ultimately find this camera the most versatile.

As with 110 cameras, 35mm refers to the width of the film.

Originally these cameras were designed for professional motion-picture film, which has been available in 35mm widths since the late 1800s. There are two main types of 35mm cameras: rangefinder and single-lens-reflex.

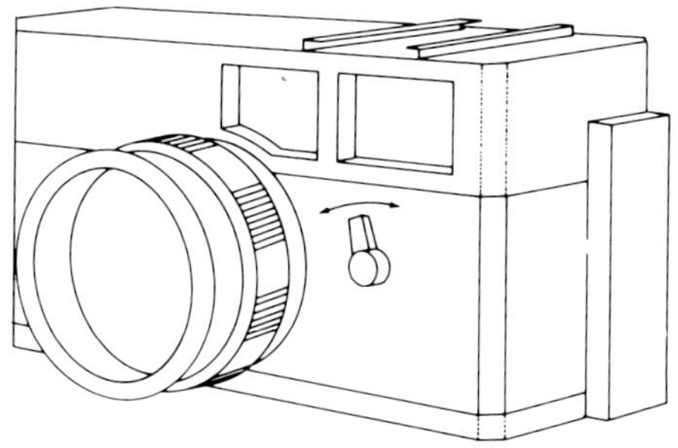

This is an example of a rangefinder camera. Rangefinder cameras are easily identifiable by its two windows and the lack of pentaprism housing on the top of the camera.

Rangefinder Cameras

Rangefinder (RF) cameras are generally less expensive than single-lens-reflex cameras, and they usually give a brighter image in the viewfinder. This is especially helpful in dimly lit areas.

You can recognize an RF camera by the two windows adjacent to the lens. (See the accompanying illustration.) A major drawback to all but the most expensive RF cameras is that the lenses are not interchangeable. With these cameras you won't be able to use wide-angle, telephoto, and zoom lenses.

Another disadvantage is that at close distances you don't see exactly what the lens sees. Known as parallax, this problem is due to the offset between the viewfinder and the lens. Although many RF cameras incorporate mechanical devices to correct this, they all have their limitations and extreme close-ups are difficult to take.

Some photographers prefer RF cameras despite these drawbacks because they are generally equipped with leaf shutters. This permits using an electronic flash at a number of shutter speeds. (See Chapter 5.)

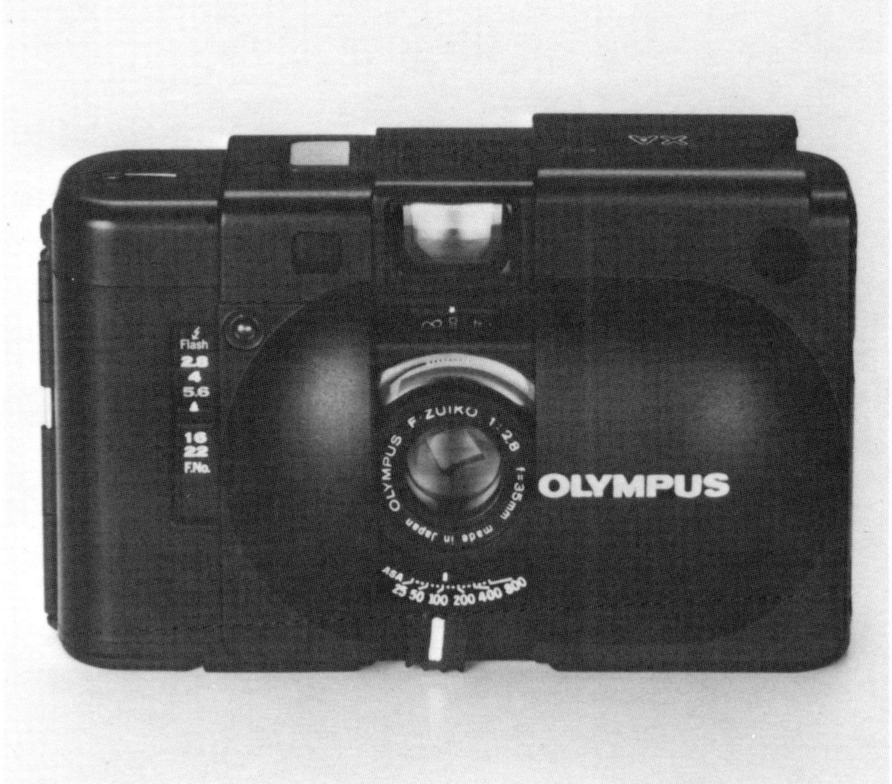

This extremely compact 35mm rangefinder camera is designed with a protective cover that closes over the lens. This would be a good choice for the traveling photographer who wants to use 35mm film but does not want a large or elaborate camera. Photograph courtesy of Olympus Camera Corp.

Single-lens-reflex Cameras (SLR)
The most popular type of 35mm camera is the single-lens reflex (SLR). It is called a "single-lens" camera because a single lens is used for both viewing and taking the photograph. It is called a "reflex" camera because a mirror reflects the viewed image onto the focusing screen.

Here's how a SLR works:

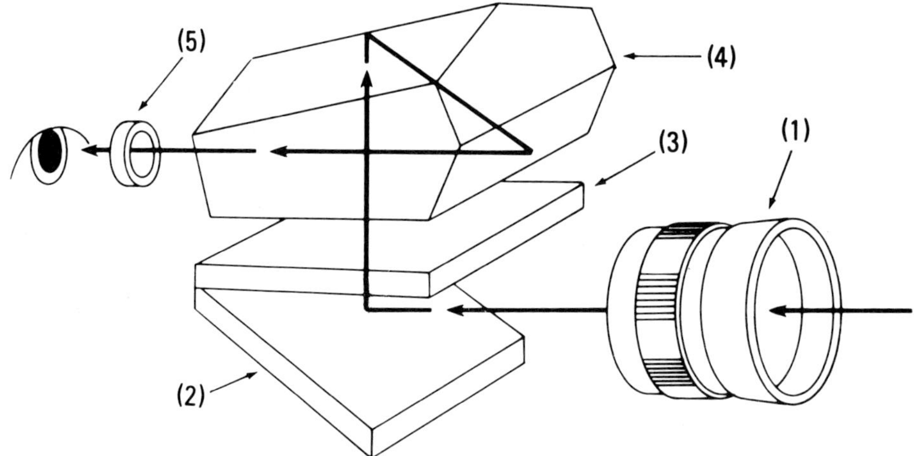

The image enters the camera (1). The mirror (2) then reflects it onto the focusing screen (3).

The glass prism (4) reflects the image from the focusing screen to your eye (5).

When you make an exposure, the mirror quickly folds up. The shutter opens to expose the film, and the mirror returns to its normal position.

As you can see, being able to look directly through the lens not only avoids the problem of parallax, but it also allows you to use different lenses without an auxiliary viewing system.

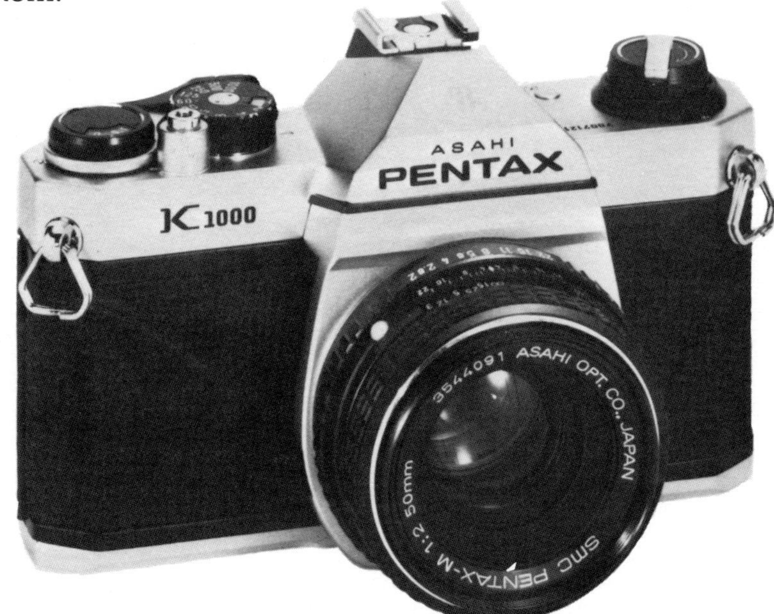

Single-lens-reflex cameras, such as this Pentax K1000, offer maximum versatility for the family photographer. Lenses and accessories are available to produce any photographic effect. Photograph courtesy of Pentax Corp.

EXPOSURE CONTROLS

Each type of film requires a different amount of light to record an image. Too much light results in overexposure and a light, washed-out print, or slide. Insufficient exposure produces a dark, muddy print, or slide.

There are two devices in a camera that control light. They are the shutter and the iris diaphragm. The shutter is simply a door that is normally closed to prevent light from reaching the film. It opens for a brief time, and the length of this time is controlled by the shutter-speed dial on the camera. (Some automatic exposure cameras do not have shutter-speed dials. More about this later.)

The iris diaphragm is like the iris of your eye. It opens and closes to control the amount of light that flows through the lens. When it is open, more light passes through than when it is closed. The hole in this iris diaphragm is called the aperture. The term *f*-stop refers to the size of this hole.

Before there were in-camera light meters, photographers had to find the appropriate aperture and shutter-speed settings by using a separate light meter. They had to aim the meter at the subject, align dials on the device, and then duplicate those settings on the camera. Many cameras still require this cumbersome technique, but usually their use is limited to advanced amateurs and professionals. Most modern 35mm cameras have automatic exposure control.

AUTOMATIC CAMERAS

The word *automatic* has recently been applied to almost every machine in our advanced society, including cameras. When applied to a camera, automatic can mean several things: including automatic exposure control and automatic film advance.

Automatic exposure

Automatic exposure means the camera contains a light meter. This meter can be mechanically or electronically connected to the shutter, the aperture, or both. As the meter senses the brightness of the scene, it sends commands to the shutter or the aperture or both. Proper exposure settings are then made automatically.

When buying an auto-exposure SLR, you will hear a lot about aperture-priority and shutter-priority cameras. These terms refer to how the exposure controls will be set. Aperture-priority means you set the aperture, but the meter automatically adjusts the shutter. Shutter priority is just the opposite. You set the shutter, but the camera's meter sets the aperture.

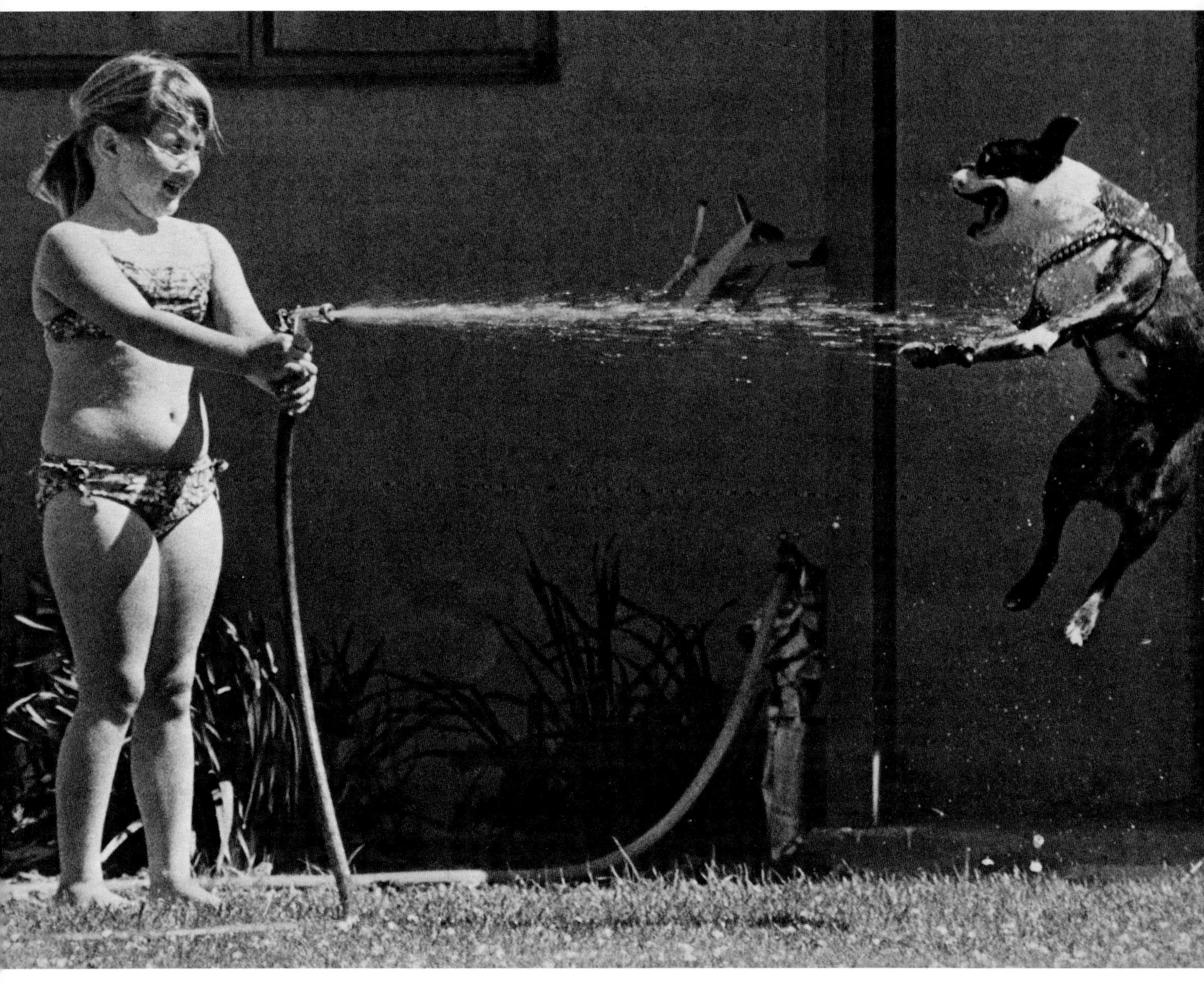

Above: *Photograph by Joseph A. Frisina, Jr.*

Right: *Instant cameras produce on-the-spot prints and enable you to immediately enjoy your photos. Photograph by Joseph A. Frisina, Jr.*

In use both systems work equally well, and you should not let the advocacy of a salesperson interfere with your decision. I prefer shutter-priority systems. This is because camera and subject movement are the main causes of bad photos, and having the ability to set the camera at a shutter speed high enough to stop such motion is important.

On the other hand, aperture-priority cameras may be slightly less expensive. Because you are setting the lens, the complex mechanisms of shutter-priority machines are eliminated. In addition, some aperture-priority cameras can take older (hence used and low-priced) lenses without losing exposure automation. Finally, by controlling the aperture, you can make an aperture-priority camera use different shutter speeds. You will see how this works as we go on.

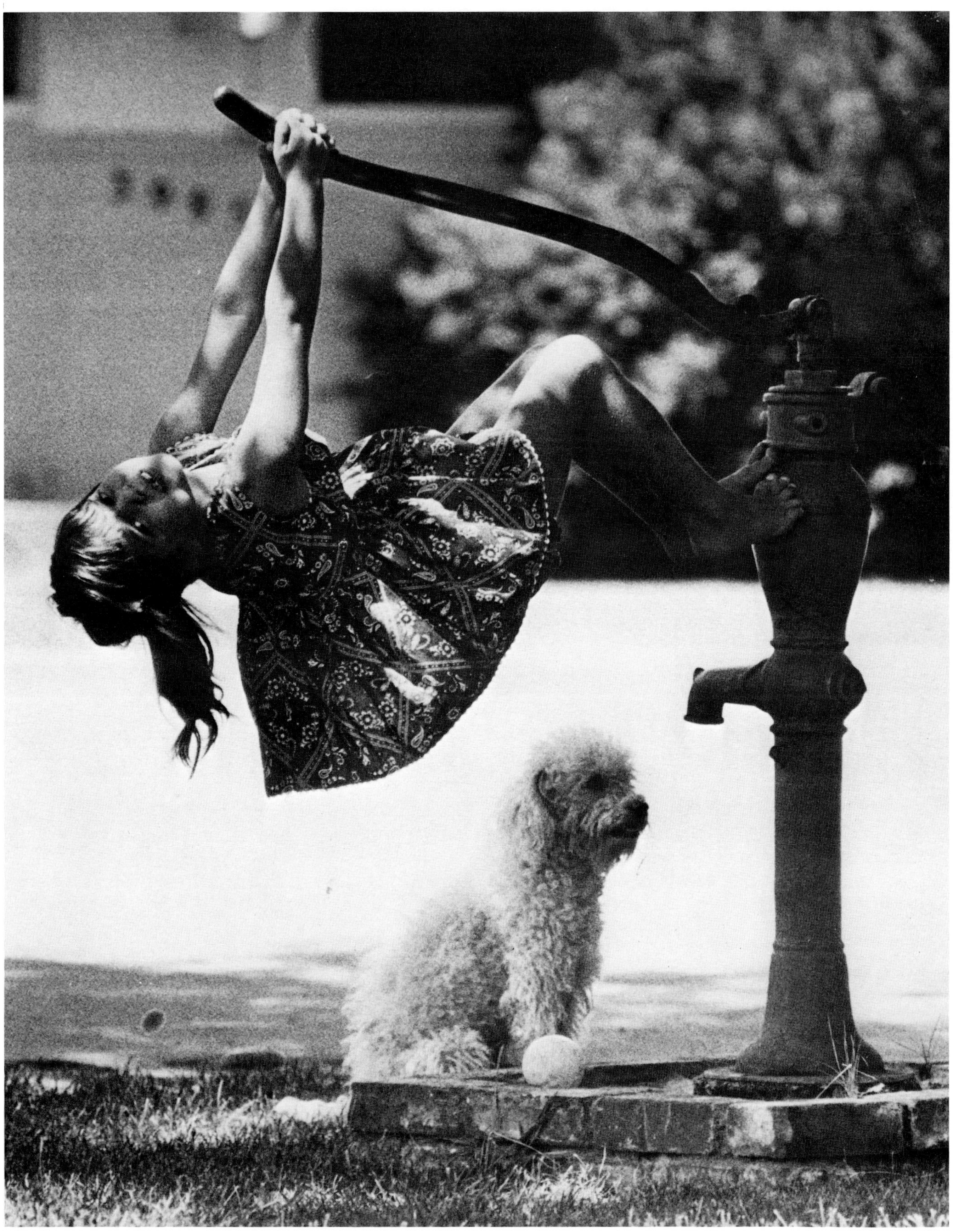

Manual override
When buying a camera with automatic exposure features, you should be sure you can disengage these features. Disengagement is necessary when the meter is likely to be fooled by extra-bright or extra-dark subjects. For example, it would be necessary if you were shooting directly into a sunset.

Also, the automatic exposure systems of many new cameras require healthy batteries to work. Therefore you should buy a camera that can operate (usually at one setting only) even without batteries, since batteries can suddenly die. Consider, too, the cost and ease of replacing batteries. One camera rumored to be in the design process requires a repair technician to replace a battery. Although that camera's battery is supposed to last five years, imagine the disappointment you'd feel if the battery failed on your vacation.

Autowinders
These accessories are attached to the bottom of a camera and relieve your thumb of operating the film-advance lever. Although they are useful for shooting sports or other action situations in which you must expose several frames in rapid succession, they are a luxury for simple, everyday photography. Instead, consider expanding your visual enjoyment. A better investment would be a lens in a focal length new to you.

INSTANT CAMERAS

Family photography can easily turn your whole clan into both photographers and subjects if you provide them with a Kodak or Polaroid instant camera. Children, because they are visually oriented, will be eager to experiment with a camera that produces prints on the spot. You, too, can benefit, since rapid results will allow you to make changes in the midst of a photography session.

LENSES

For family photography a normal lens is frequently sufficient. Taking in about the same perspective as your eye, it can be used for portraits as well as for gatherings around a table.

You will quickly find, however, that there are times when the normal lens just won't give you the results you want. You will find it hard, for example, to peek out the kitchen window and take candid photos of the kids playing in the yard. You won't be able to get close enough. You might also find that without a wide-angle lens, you won't be able to fit everyone into a group photo at Christmas.

A telephoto lens and a 1/1000 sec. shutter speed were used to stop this joyful action.

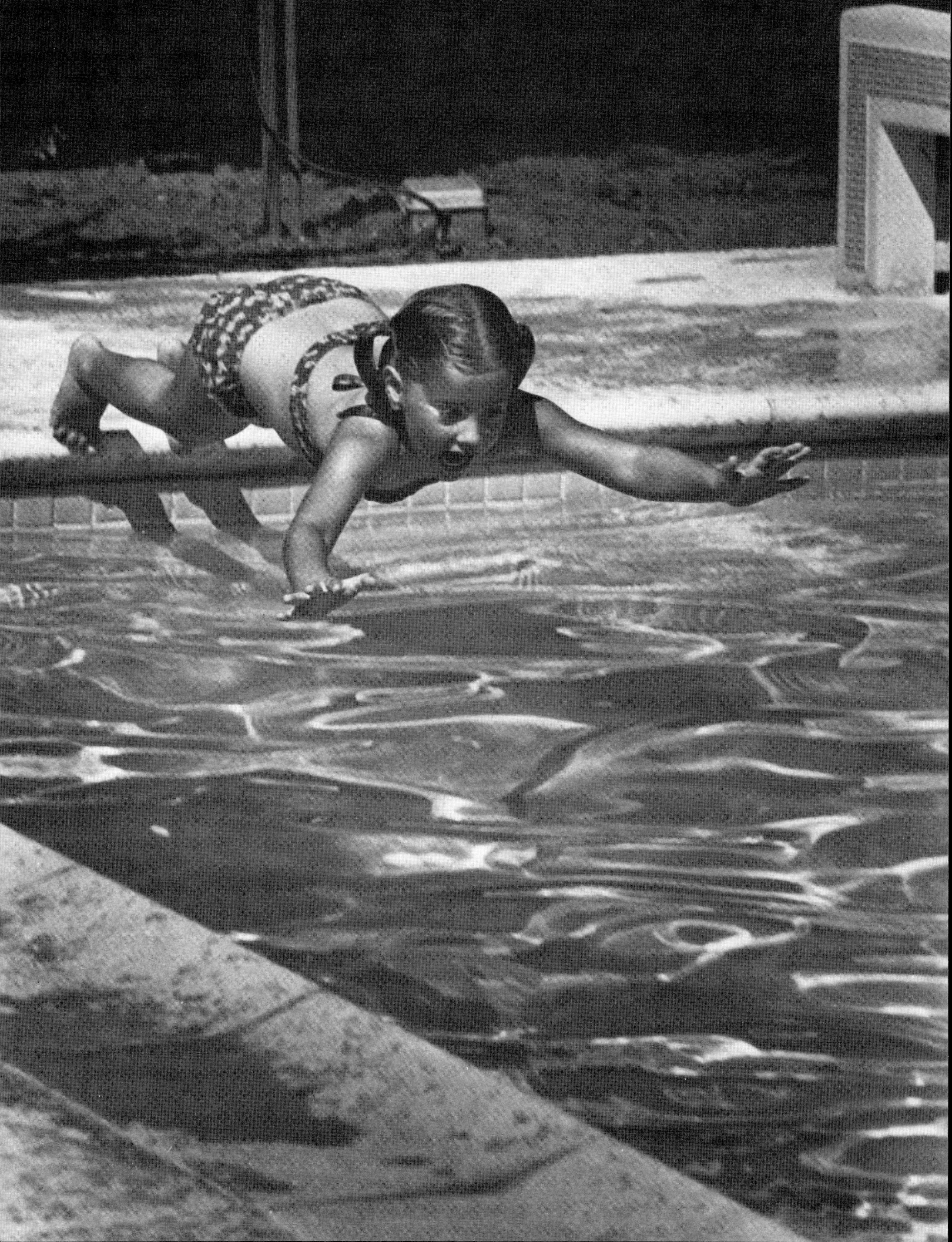

Wide-angle Lenses

The focal length of a normal lens on a 35mm camera is about 50mm. Any lens whose focal length is less than that is a wide-angle lens. Common wide-angle focal lengths are 35mm, 28mm, and 24mm. For family photos I prefer a lens with a focal length of 35mm. Such a lens is wide enough for full-length portraits and average-size group photos. Furthermore it will produce less distortion than most of the wider lenses. It is also a useful focal length for photos of vacation locales.

When used at a small aperture, the depth-of-field (see Chapter 3) of wide-angle lenses makes focusing less critical, an advantage when working quickly at close range.

Telephoto Lenses

Telephoto lenses allow you to move closer to your subject visually without moving closer physically. Such lenses, for example, can be used for those candid shots out the kitchen window. They will prevent the kids from being so small in the picture that they appear to be specks in the distance.

Common telephoto lenses range in focal length from about 85mm to 200mm. About the longest practical focal length for anyone but the most sophisticated pro is 500mm.

For general use a 105 or 135mm lens is good. This focal length is ideal for taking portraits or candid shots from a distance. Longer lenses are difficult to use for portraits because they put you too far from your subject. And the shorter lenses don't give the image magnification needed for candid work.

Zoom lenses

One of the best solutions to the problem of lens selection is to buy a zoom lens. Modern zooms cover both telephoto and wide-angle ranges, and they frequently provide close-up capabilities. Zooms in the telephoto range usually cover focal lengths from about 70mm to 200mm. Portraits can be made at the 70mm end of the range, while sports, nature, and candid shots can be captured at the maximum focal length.

Midrange and wide-angle zooms cover a range from about 28mm to 70mm. And they are excellent for many of the family photos you are likely to take. Since some of these lenses also come with close-up capabilities, you might want to consider buying one of these first.

If you are thinking of buying a zoom lens, remember that they are often heavier than a fixed focal-length lens, and because their maximum apertures are smaller, they are less versatile in low-light situations. Still, they are among the most popular lenses, and these drawbacks shouldn't detract much from their versatility.

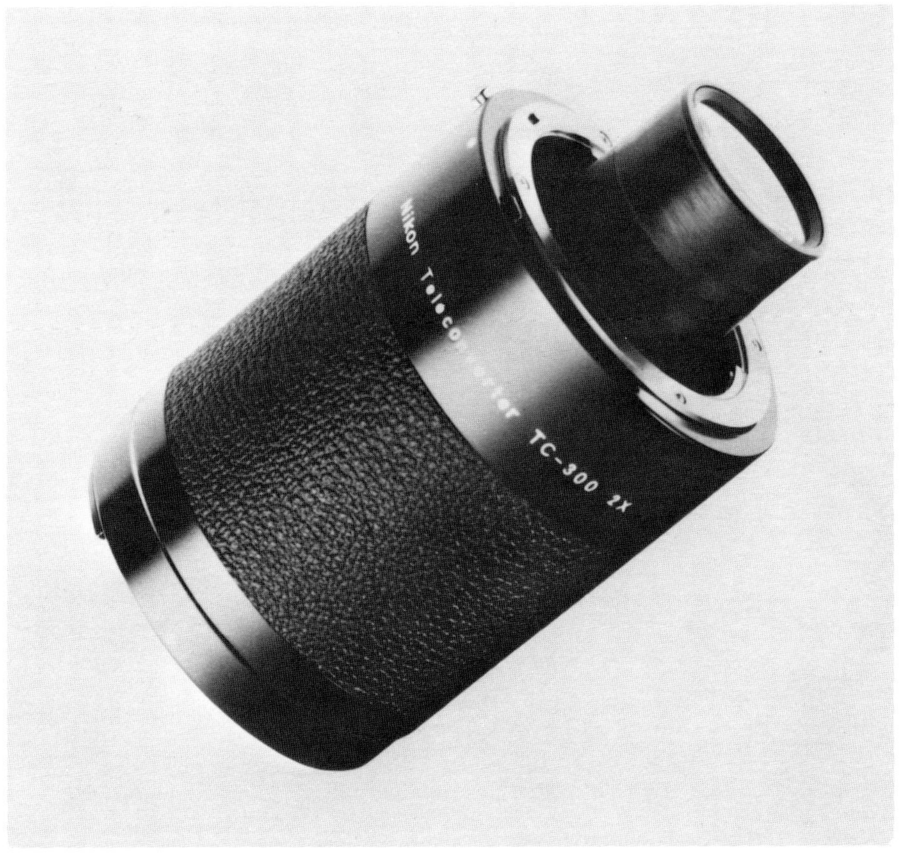

When this lens extender is placed between your lens and the camera body it effectively doubles the focal length of the lens. Teleconverters are a convenient way to increase your range of focal lengths without buying more lenses. Photograph courtesy of Nikon, Inc.

Lens extenders

Lens extenders increase the focal length of the lenses you already have. You simply attach the extender to the camera body, then fit the lens onto the extender. A 2× extender will double the focal length of your lens; a 3× extender will triple it. Extenders also work with zoom lenses. For example, a 70–210mm zoom becomes a 140–420mm zoom when a 2× converter is attached.

Although these devices absorb some light, the light meter in your camera can compensate for this loss. The instruction manuals of your camera and extender should explain any adjustments you may need to make.

HOW TO CHOOSE A LENS

Many first-time lens buyers feel intimidated by the recommendations of lens manufacturers and salesmen. Some of this apprehension can be dispelled by disposing of two myths. The first is that you must buy lenses made by your camera's manufacturer. Many professionals opt for camera-brand lenses because they are designed for heavy use. However, many independent firms also make lenses that are perfectly acceptable. And they usually cost less than the brand-name gear.

The second myth concerns lens tests. Some people, because they are looking for the perfect lens, continually test and compare lenses. But ask yourself if you really need the level of mechanical and optical quality those people are seeking. When commuting to work, for example, you don't need the precision of an Indianapolis-500 race car. For family photography, the extra dollars spent on a premium lens could be better spent on an additional accessory or on the film and processing.

When deciding what focal lengths would be most useful, check local camera stores for lens rentals. This is a great way to discover what you like. One suggestion is that you buy a camera body without the customary normal focal length lens, then add a 35–70mm zoom lens, and a 70–210mm macrozoom or a lens extender. With all three optical pieces, your needs would be well met for years to come.

FLASH

The second most important piece of equipment for family photography is probably a flash. This is because many of the photos you will want to take will need to be taken indoors where light levels are low.

Flashbulbs

Flashbulbs are most frequently used with 110 cameras, although this format can use electronic flash (EF) just as well. (In fact, there are 110 cameras with EF's built into their bodies.)

Bulbs are available in both cubes or strips. Some advantages of bulbs include:

They are initially very inexpensive.

Some types do not need batteries.

The battery-fired types can be set off with weak batteries.

Strips or cubes can be fired in faster sequence than an electronic flash, which is particularly helpful if you are taking action photos.

Bulbs often give off more light than an inexpensive electronic flash.

Flashbulbs do, however, have disadvantages. For example, they are good for only one shot, requiring you to keep a continual supply on hand. A major drawback is that they won't work with all automatic exposure systems.

Electronic flash

Electronic flash (EF) units are both convenient and popular. Sometimes they require little more space than a pack

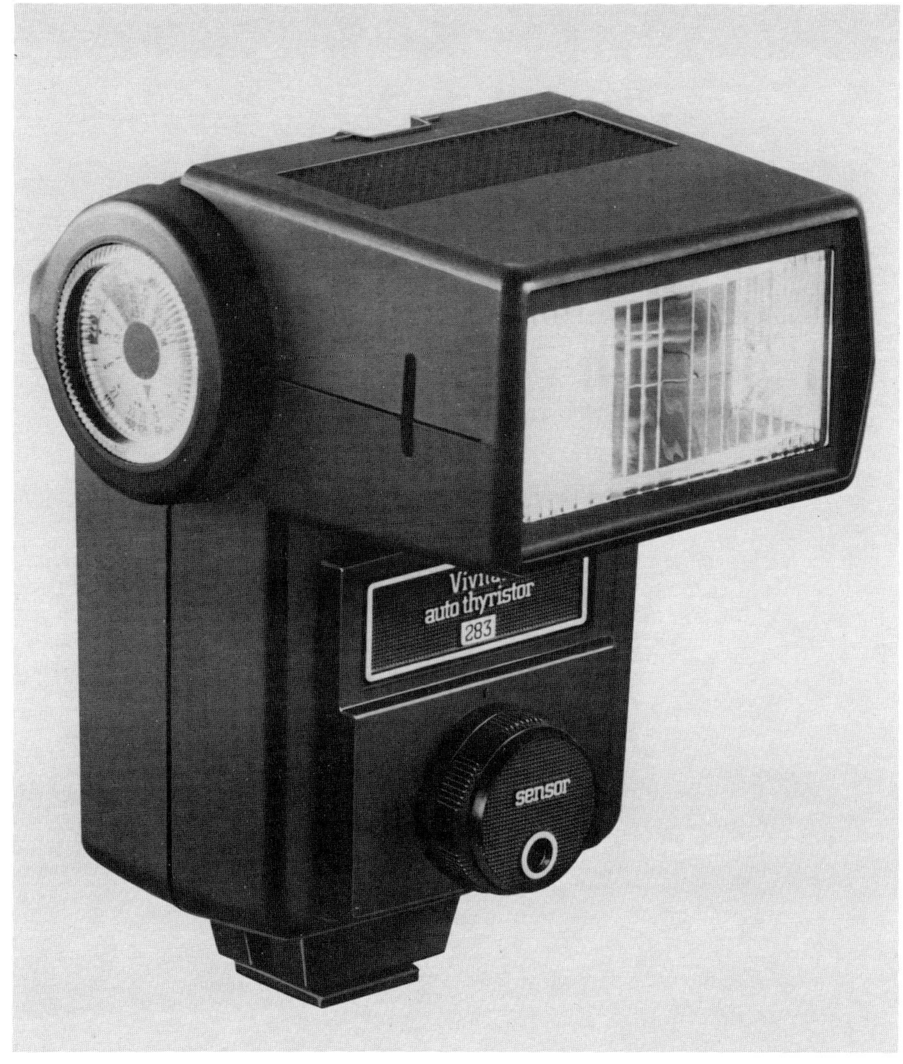

An electronic flash unit is a useful accessory and should be high on your list of "must own" equipment. Photograph courtesy of Vivitar Corp.

of flashcubes. Some of the advantages of EF units include:

They almost never wear out.

Their short bursts of light are easy on a subject's eyes.

Their automatic capabilities eliminate complicated exposure calculations.

The supply and disposal problems of bulbs is eliminated.

Few things are perfect, however. And one of the drawbacks of electronic flash units is that they require strong batteries for recharging. In fact, if your flash needs are infrequent, you may find expensive batteries sitting in your closet losing power. Secondly, as mentioned in the previous section, many inexpensive EF units give off low light. Although such small units are fine for distances of 8 feet or so, serious family photography often requires more light.

EF power
When buying an EF unit, your primary consideration should be its light output. Although there are several ways to determine the output of a flash, guide numbers are the most common.

Guide numbers match the light output of the flash to film speed. For active family photographers a flash with a minimum guide number of 60 when used with ASA 25 film or a guide number of 120 with ASA 100 film is recommended.

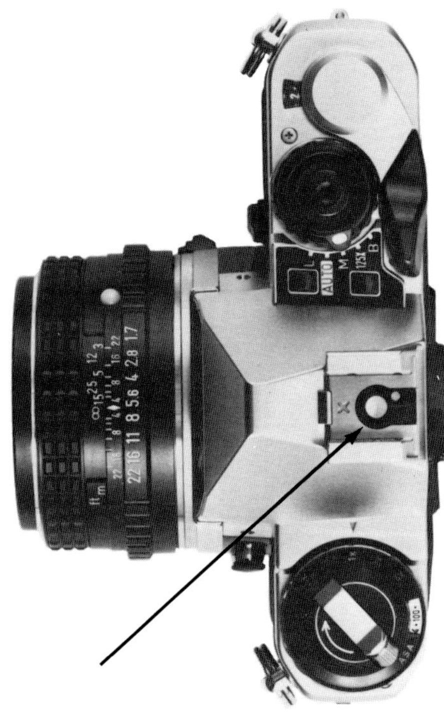

This top view of the Pentax ME shows the "hot-shoe" contacts for dedicated flash units. This type of system solves many flash exposure problems. Photograph courtesy of Pentax Corp.

Automatic flashes
Exposure calculations for electronic flashes are somewhat more complex than those for natural-light exposures, and manufacturers have quickly adapted microelectronics to this task.

When using a flash, exposure is determined by the intensity of the light and by the distance from the light to the subject. To understand this, go into a dark room and hold a flashlight about 4 inches from a wall. Watch what happens to the intensity of that light as you move it farther from the wall—the brightness of the spot decreases. With electronic flash units the same thing happens. Thus as the light-to-subject distance increases, either the intensity of the light must be increased or the camera must admit more available light.

Auto-flash units do this by measuring the light as it is reflected back from the subject. When enough light has been received by the tiny meter inside the flash unit, the meter shuts off the EF's burst of light.

For the most advanced SLR cameras, you can now get dedicated flash systems. When the proper flash and camera are mated, the system is automatically set for flash exposures. All you need to do is tell the system, by setting a dial, the speed of film you are using. Techniques for putting your flash to work will be discussed later.

ACCESSORIES

One accessory that quickly becomes necessary is a camera bag. You will need one large enough to hold your camera, lenses, flash, spare film, and a few filters. Over-the-shoulder types are the most convenient because your gear can then be kept at your side while photographing. Attaché-type cases are impressive, but they are practical only for long-distance shipping. Padded bags will also help to protect equipment to some extent. When shopping for a bag, examine the construction carefully. You wouldn't want your equipment falling to the floor because of a poorly attached shoulder strap. Also, don't buy one of those pouches that wraps your camera tightly in vinyl or leather. Besides getting in your way, the front half is just another item to lose. And by the time you get the case unzipped, the expression you wanted to capture will have disappeared.

Tripods

For portraiture and extreme low-light photography and times when you want steady camera support, you may need a tripod. Buy the biggest and heaviest one you can afford. And be sure the head will tilt enough for both vertical and horizontal compositions. Open the device and test its rigidity by placing your hand on its head and giving it a wiggle. Also, see if it will extend high enough to meet your needs. Some devices won't provide an eye-level point of view to anyone more than 4 feet tall.

Cable release

To keep your camera steady when it is on a tripod, you will probably also want to use a cable release. A cable release is a flexible cord made out of cloth or metal that screws into a threaded socket on the shutter or camera body. When released, it will trip the shutter without moving the camera. Choose one long enough and flexible enough that vibrations won't be transmitted from your hand to the camera.

Filters

As you will learn in Chapter 7, filters change the way film reproduces an image. A basic camera outfit should probably include an orange and a red filter for black-and-white photos, a polarizing filter for black and white and for color, and possibly an FLD and an 80B for color. The FLD will produce acceptable colors when you're shooting outdoor film under fluorescent light, and the 80B should be used for taking pictures in an area lighted by regular light bulbs.

FILM

Today there are a variety of films available. So let's consider some of the things that should influence your buying decision.

Perhaps the most important consideration should be speed. You can tell a film's speed by its ASA, ISO, exposure index, or DIN rating. This rating will tell you how quickly the film responds to light. Fast films generally have ASA's in the 400 range, medium-speed films are those in the 125 range, and slow-speed films have ratings of 64 and below.

These ratings are important because you will need a sensitive ASA-400 film in low-light situations, while a slow ASA-25 film will give good results in bright sunlight. Although the high-speed emulsions also work well in bright light, the

SOME COMMON 35mm FILMS

ASA	B&W	Color Negative (Prints)	Color Transparency (Slides)
400	Tri-X Pan Ilford HP 5 Agfapan 400	Kodacolor 400 Fujicolor F-II 400	Ektachrome 400 Fujicolor 400-RH
125	Plus-X Pan Ilford FP 4 Agfapan 100 (ASA 100)	Kodacolor II (ASA 100) Fujicolor F-II CN (ASA 100)	Fujichrome 100-RD (ASA 100) Agfachrome 100 (ASA 100)
64	Ilford Pan-F (ASA 50)	Agfacolor (ASA 80)	Kodachrome 64 Ektachrome 64 Agfachrome 64
25	Panatomic-X (ASA 32) Agfapan 25		Kodachrome 25

These are some of the many types of film available today.
Choosing a film is a matter of personal preference; try several and then decide.

slower films need tripod-steadied cameras and long exposure times in low-light situations.

This discussion might lead you to believe that you should use high-speed films for all photographs; however there is another characteristic of film to consider—grain. Grain is a speckled effect caused by the minute clumps of light-sensitive particles in the film. Faster films have larger, more noticeable clumps. In the slowest films these clumps are barely visible. Although grain is an artistic tool and its use a matter of taste, many photographers prefer to use finer-grained films.

A third factor in your choice of color film should be color rendition. Some films produce cooler results; this means the print has a bluish-green cast. Other films have higher saturation; this means the colors look stronger, richer.

Because many family photographers use only color, they don't realize that black and white can also produce exciting results. Because the element of color does not enter into the composition, a different way of seeing is required. Do not judge the potential of black and white by the photos you get back from commercial processing. Visit an exhibit of black-and-white work, noting the results experts get. You can get similar results if you do your own processing or if you take your film to a custom lab.

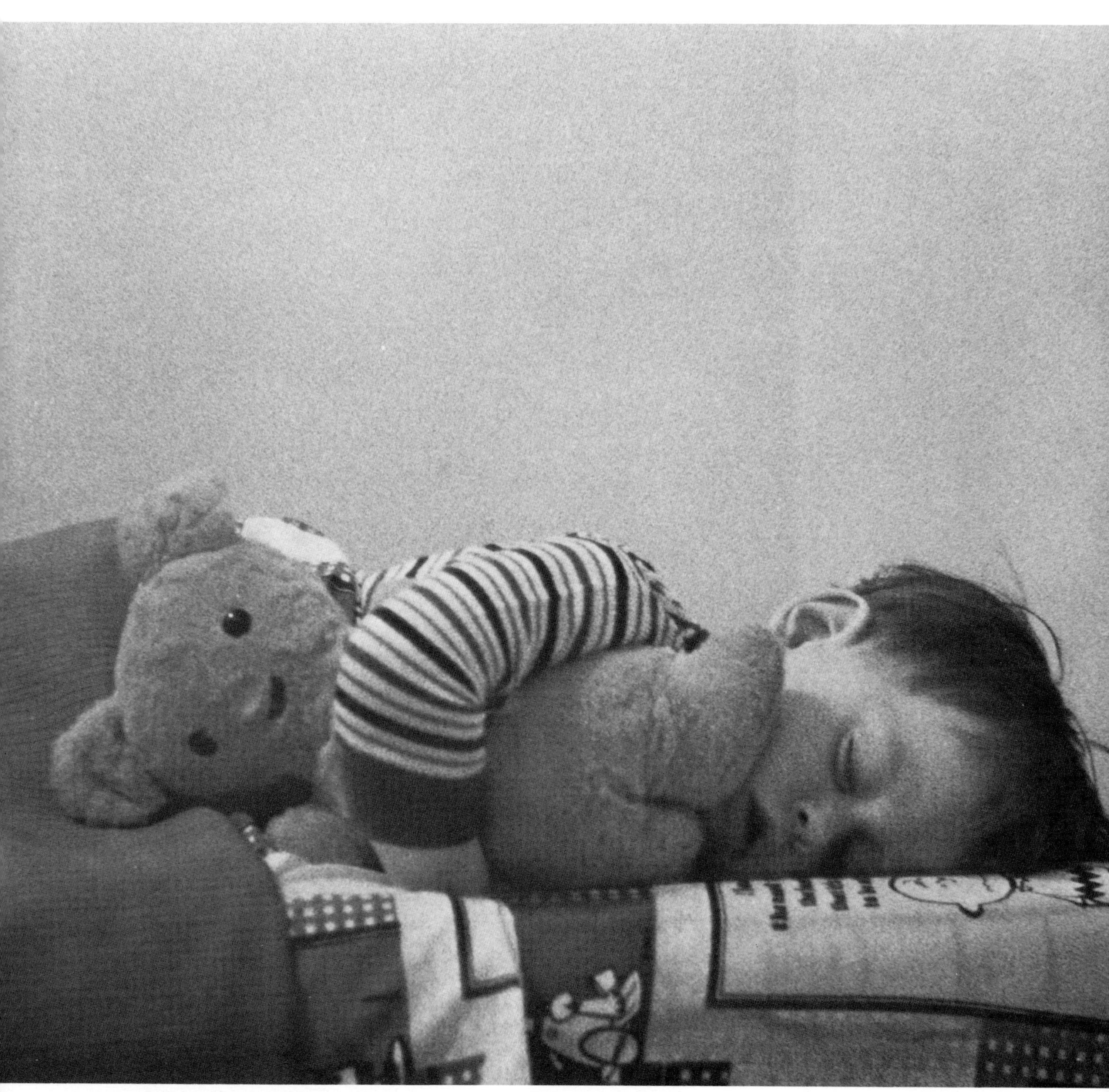

By using a high-speed film (ASA 400), you do not have to use a flash which might disturb the sleeping child.

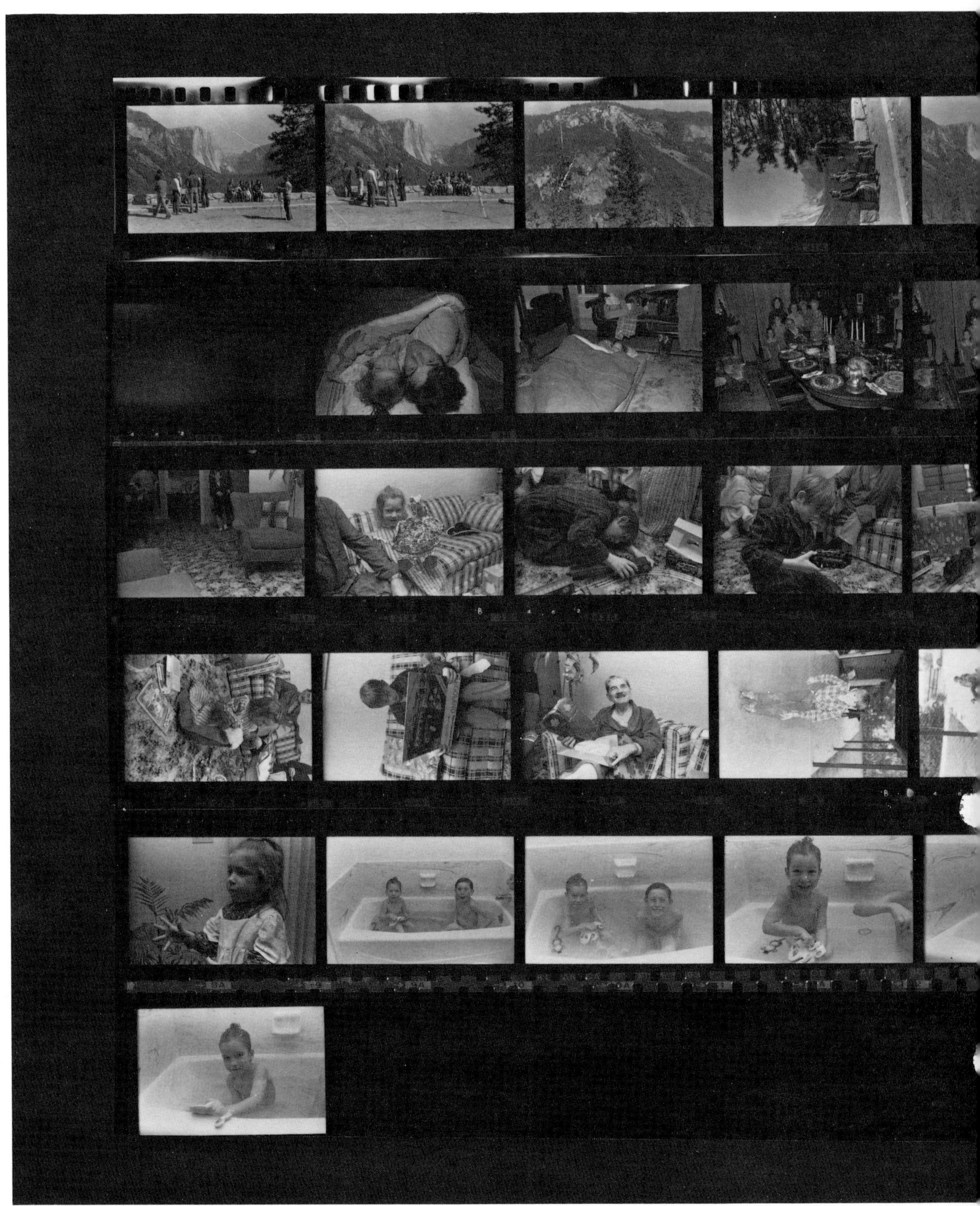

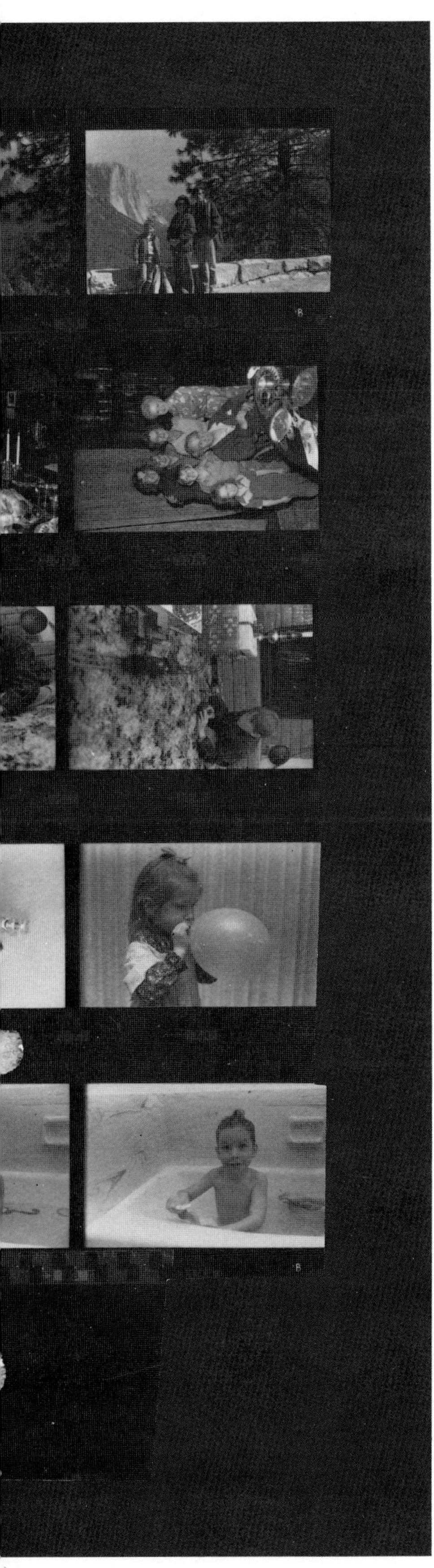

Types of film

Color films produce prints or slides. Although you can have slides made from print film and vice-versa, it is best to use the appropriate film in the beginning.

Generally those names with the suffix *chrome* produce slides, and those with the suffix *color* produce prints. See accompanying chart for examples.

The decision of which film to use is a personal one. Try a few types, examine the results, and then use those you like best. By the way, manufacturers spend a lot of money on those instruction sheets that come with each roll of film. They will give you exposure information, flash information, and processing details.

How to reduce processing costs

One disadvantage of using commercial processing is that you often end up paying for prints you don't want. Expressions may not be quite right or the picture may be technically faulty.

You can save on such costs by sending your film to a custom lab and by giving them these instructions: "process and contact sheet." The lab will then develop the film and make a contact sheet from the negatives. You can then examine the sheet and decide which frames you want enlarged. The illustration shows a portion of a contact sheet.

You can save money on processing by having a custom lab make a contact sheet of your negatives and then selecting the ones you want enlarged.

CHAPTER THREE

FAMILY AND FRIENDS

Helping them look their best

You have probably heard people say "I never look good in photos" and perhaps you secretly feel this way about yourself. Usually, though, the problem is not the subject but the pictures. Cameras are aimed carelessly at people, and little concern is given to the differences between how a camera sees and how people see.

With a little practice you can learn a few basic techniques that will make people eager to have their pictures taken.

CAMERA VISION *vs.* HUMAN VISION

Fundamental to your skill as a photographer of people is an understanding of the differences between camera vision and human vision. The most important difference between the two is in their interpretive abilities. When people look at a scene, they automatically separate important elements from visual waste. For example, when a father sees his child smiling at him, he blocks out most of the other objects in his view; this is known as subjective viewing.

In contrast, the camera sees everything equally; this is known as objective viewing. Thus all the background and peripheral details will be visible in the print unless the photographer controls the camera's vision.

This subjective-objective viewing problem goes far beyond the physical items in a scene. There are many ways in which your eye can be fooled by the interpretative powers of your brain into believing something is evident when it is not. For example, you may look through your viewfinder of your camera, see your child racing across the field during a soccer game, and want to capture the energy and excitement of what you see. But what you may not realize is that the camera cannot pick up those details at that distance.

Furthermore, outside stimuli affect your visual perception of an event. At that soccer game, you were involved in the emotions of the moment. You were cheering for your team,

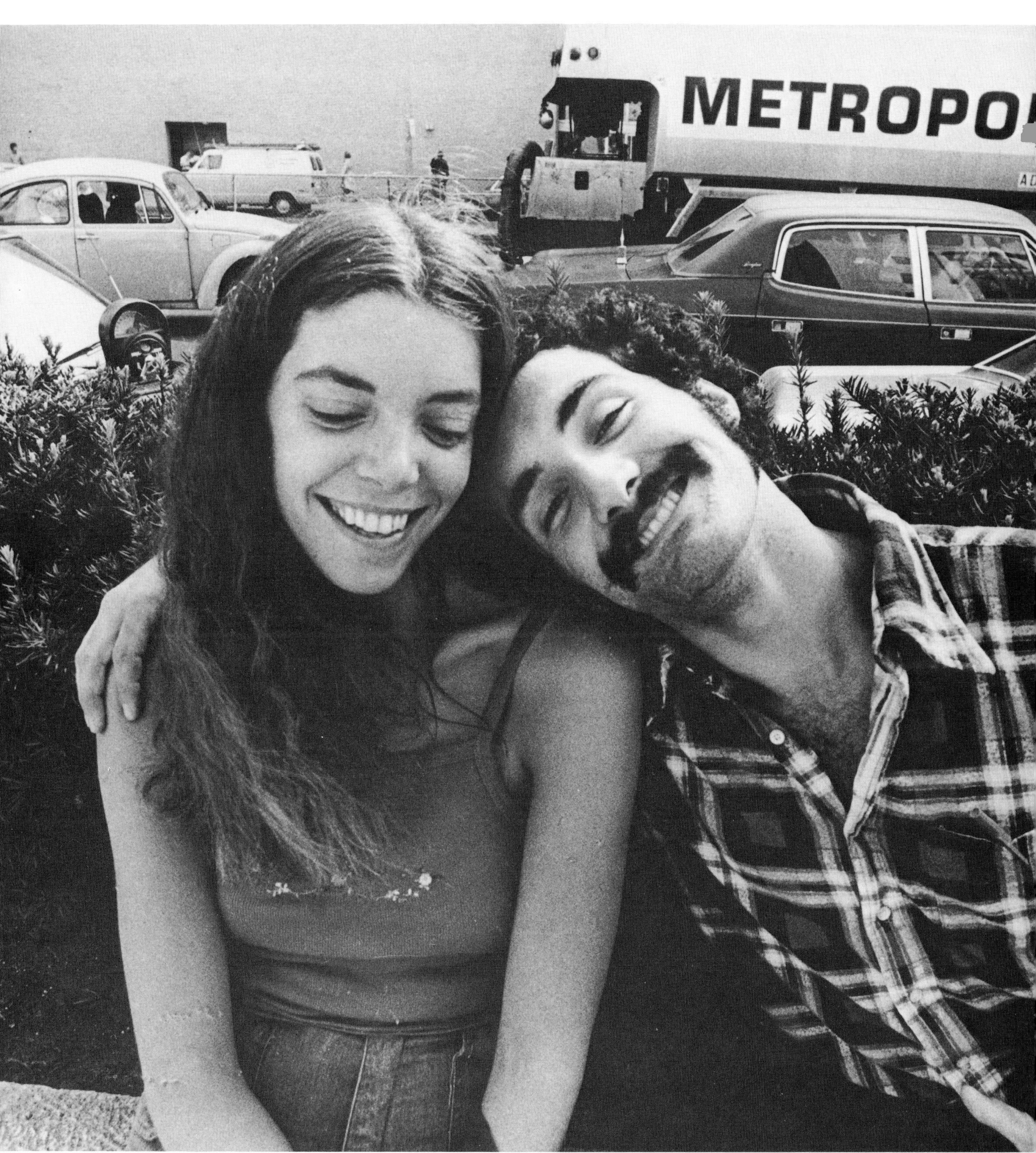

By learning a few basic techniques, you will make your family and friends eager to be in front of your lens. Photograph by Michael O'Connor.

SOME DIFFERENCES BETWEEN CAMERA AND EYE

Eye	Camera
Subjective	Objective
3-dimensional	2-dimensional
Sees in context of time and other stimuli	Sees out of context
Wide field of view	Narrow field of view with most lenses
Central vision sharp, edges blurred	Sharp across plane of focus
Extreme color accuracy	Color subject to film characteristics
Mind controls attention of viewer	Sees all in its view

and you were hearing the others cheering around you. You were feeling the wind across your face and smelling crisp, clean air. All these factors influence your perception of the event, but the camera recorded only one factor. It is up to you, the photographer, to compensate for the missing stimuli. You had to either add or subtract elements to get the image you wanted.

A third factor is the time. For example, a facial expression, such as a smile, is a flowing thing. It builds to a peak, then moves to its next phase. You experience it as an uninterrupted whole, while the camera picks up only an instant out of context. In a successful photo that instant represents the peak of the expression and accurately sums up the whole experience. But in an unsuccessful photo—one taken just before or after that peak moment—the expression doesn't represent the whole.

The key to this factor is timing, learning to anticipate when those peak moments will occur and being able to press the shutter at just the right moment.

Memory fault

Another factor that can affect the result of a photo is memory fault. This occurs when a photo means more to its photographer than it does to other people. Although such photos are perfectly acceptable if limited to the photographer's notebook, they do not communicate anything to others.

Memory fault occurs when a photograph triggers a photographer's memory, making him see things in the image

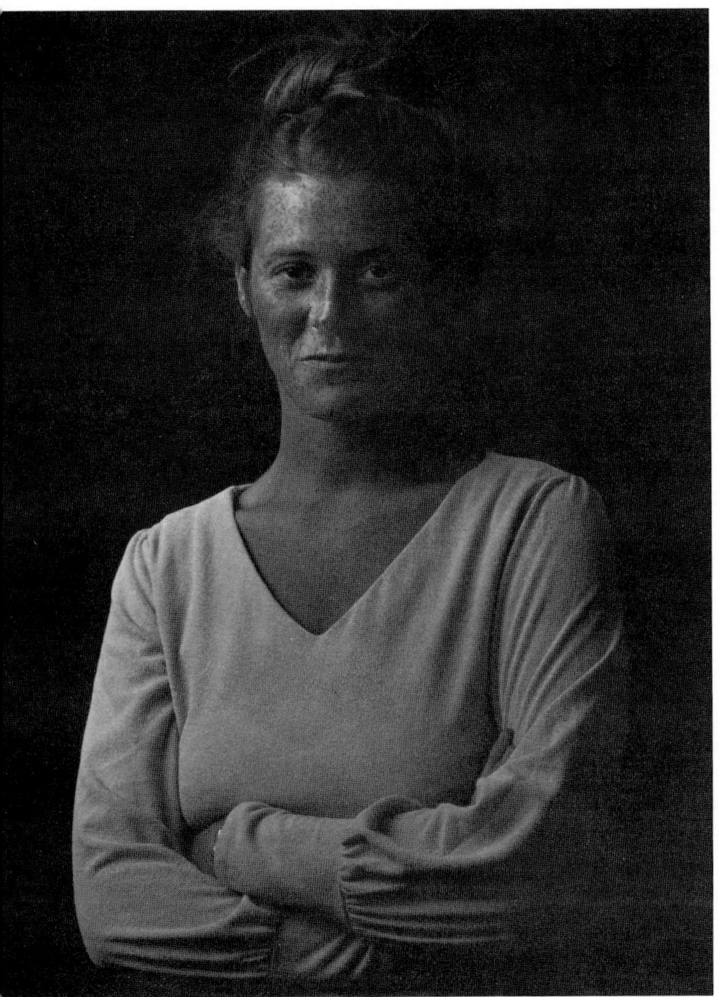

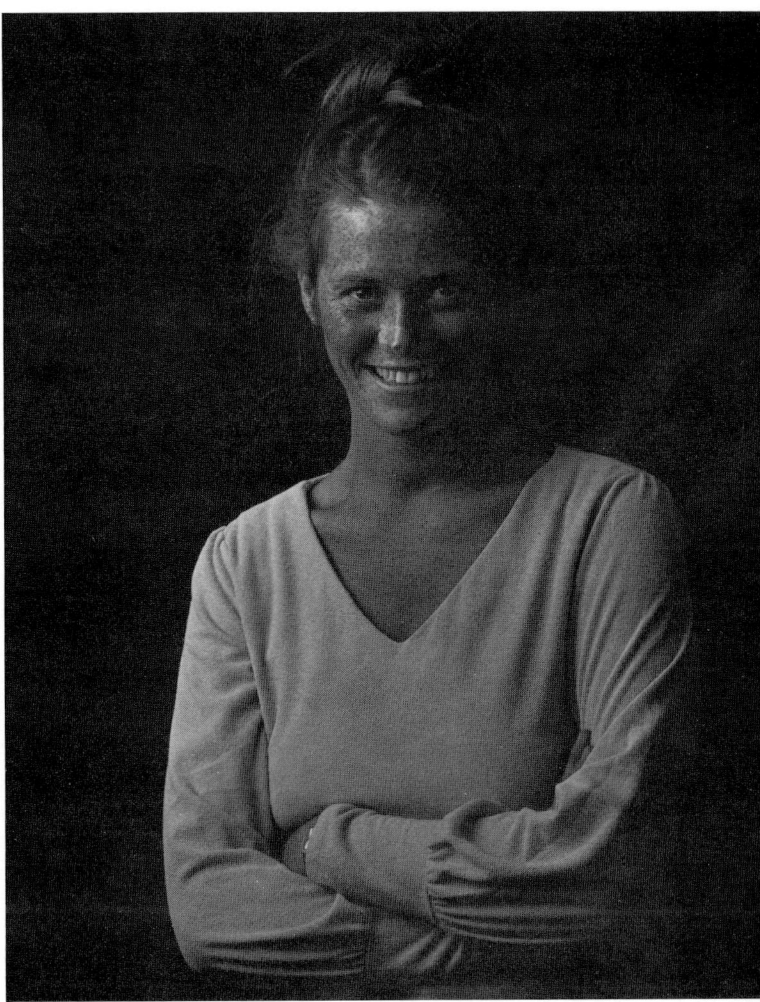

The photo at the left was made during a transitional moment, while the photo on the right was made at the peak of the expression.

that aren't there. Being personally involved, he reads into the photograph his private thoughts and attitudes and remembers the stimuli being received when the image was made. Thus he falsely increases the value of the image.

An example of memory fault is when a friend shows you his boring vacation photos. He is reliving his vacation while you are fighting to stay awake.

Physical differences

In addition to the psychological differences between camera vision and human vision, there are some important physical differences. Most people see in three dimensions, but the camera sees in only two. This affects our photos because the object we are focusing on stands out to us, while the camera tends to place it and the background on the same plane.

Another difference is field of view. Your eye takes in a much wider area than most camera lenses, yet your sharpest vision occurs in the center of that area. The camera, on the other hand, generally takes in a narrower area, but within that area things look equally sharp.

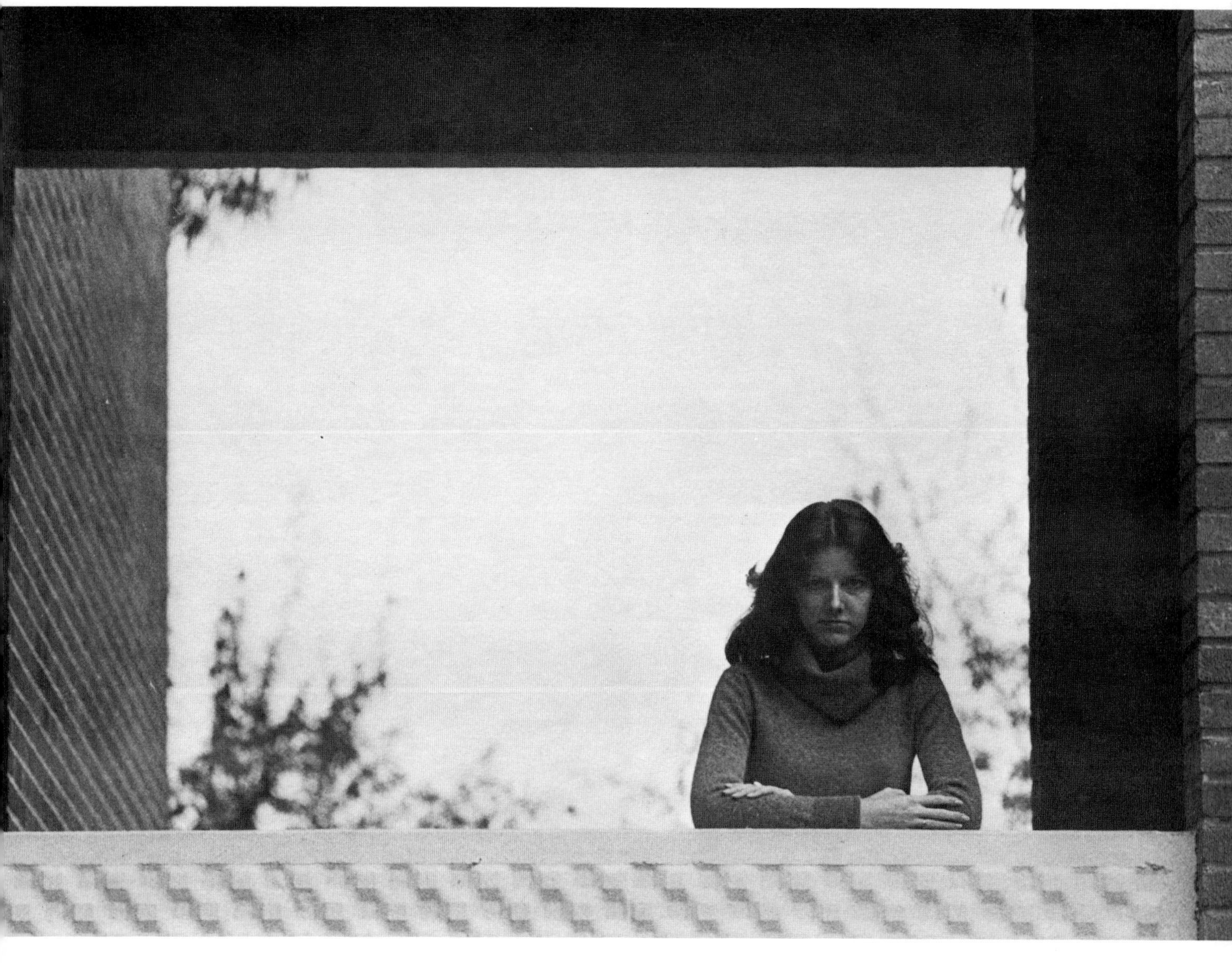

TECHNIQUES FOR IMPROVING YOUR PHOTO VISION

As we discuss ways to improve your photo vision, remember that we are dealing with a visual language, one that has a vocabulary and a syntax all its own. Some concepts are hard to translate into words, so the best way to continue your visual development is by studying photos you like, looking for the factors that make them successful.

Photo design and composition is like arranging furniture in a room. There are no set rules, but it would certainly be awkward to place a couch across the front door. In photography there are techniques that work most of the time, but there are also times when successful photos contradict those generalities.

All 35mm cameras produce horizontally framed images, when held normally; however, you will see that many of the photos in this book are in a vertical format. Remember to try vertical framing when the subject is also a vertical design. When you can not decide, shoot both ways. Which one of these do you like?

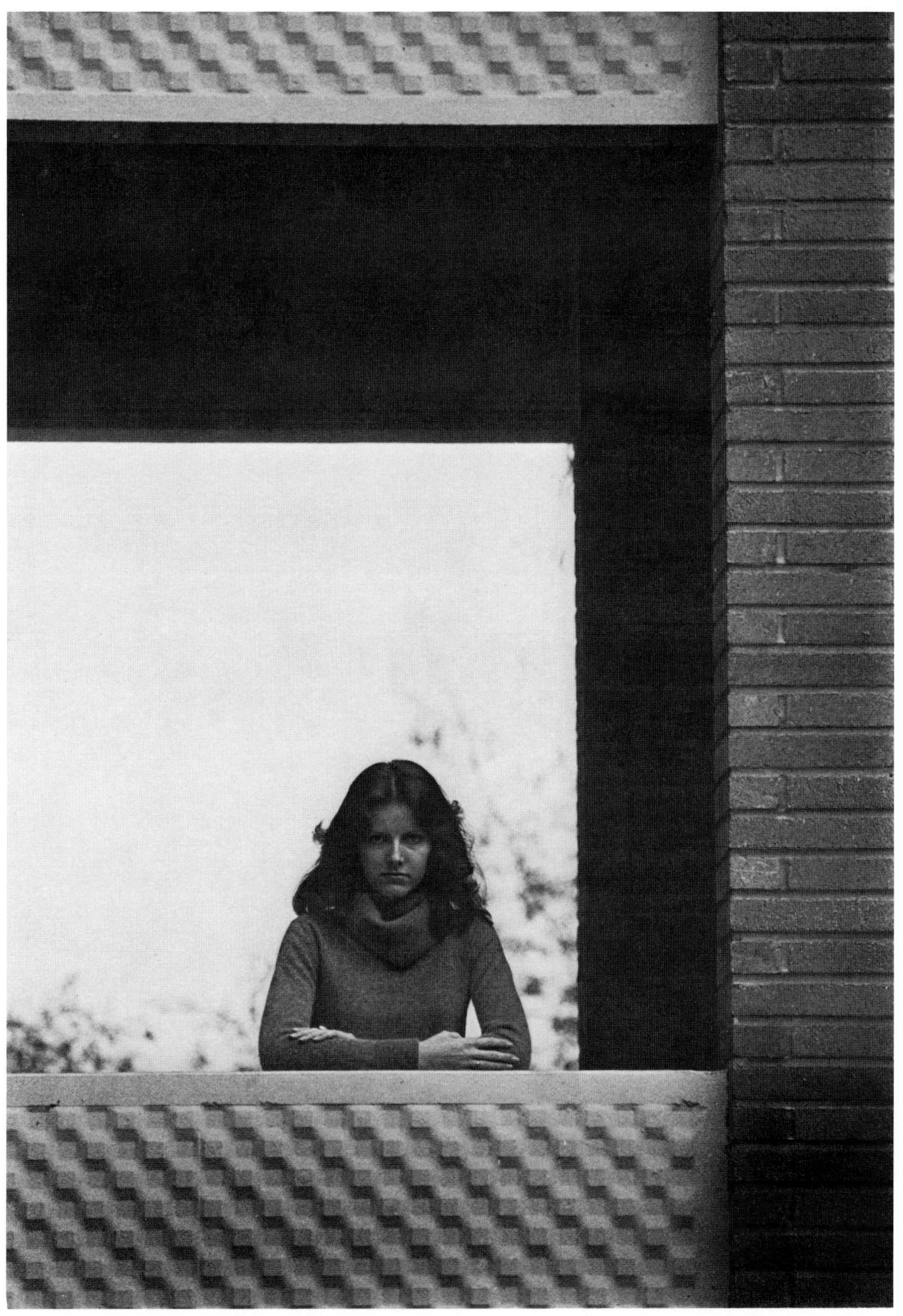

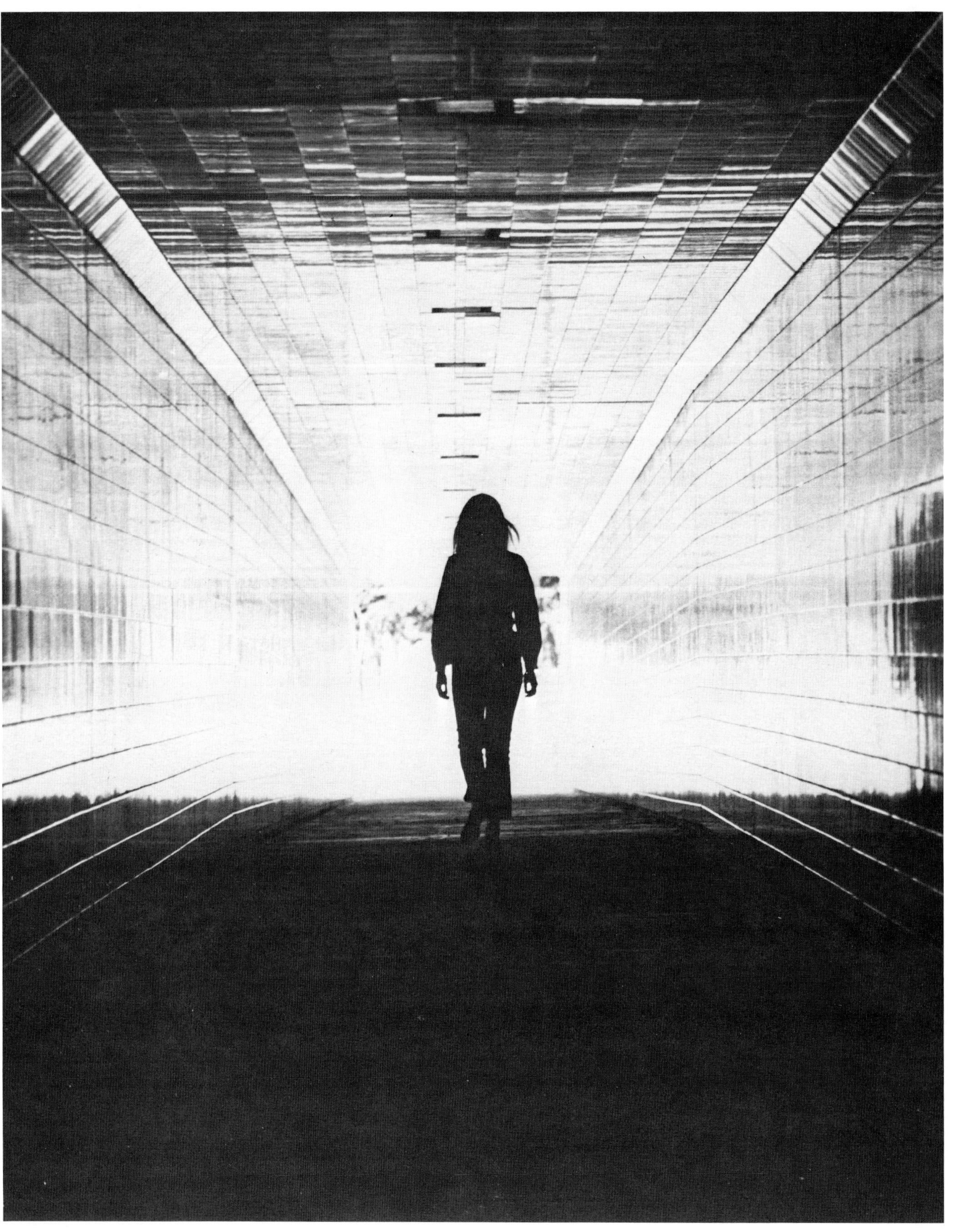

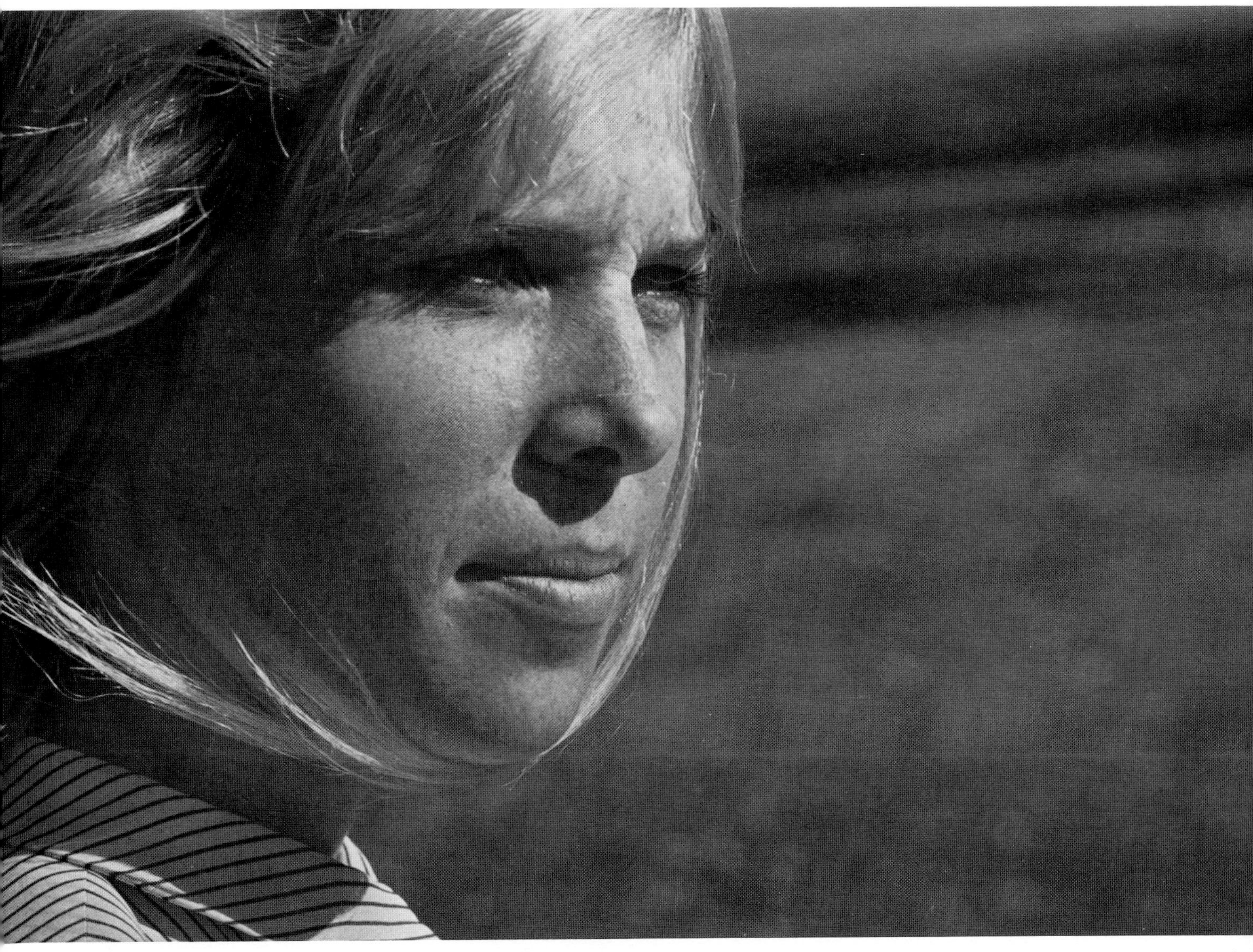

Above: *Curved lines are the dominant compositional element in this photo.*

Left: *Leading lines are useful devices to direct the viewer's eye to the subject. The tiles on the walls of this pedestrian tunnel create lines which converge on the center of the image.*

Lines and shapes

In photography three-dimensional reality is represented on two-dimensional paper by lines and shapes, the most basic elements of photography.

Lines have many meanings, and these meanings add to the value of your photo. Vertical lines, for example, signify strength, power, and dignity. Think of the symbols for the Supreme Court, the tall columns that are an architectural feature of the building. Vertical lines also suggest height and lightness. A less obvious suggestion by a vertical line is depth. On a flat piece of paper, when something is receding into the distance, a line actually goes up as the distance increases.

Broad, curving lines are symbols of beauty, grace, love, and nature. Strong horizontal lines signify peace, calmness, weight, breadth, and finality. Short, multidirectional lines

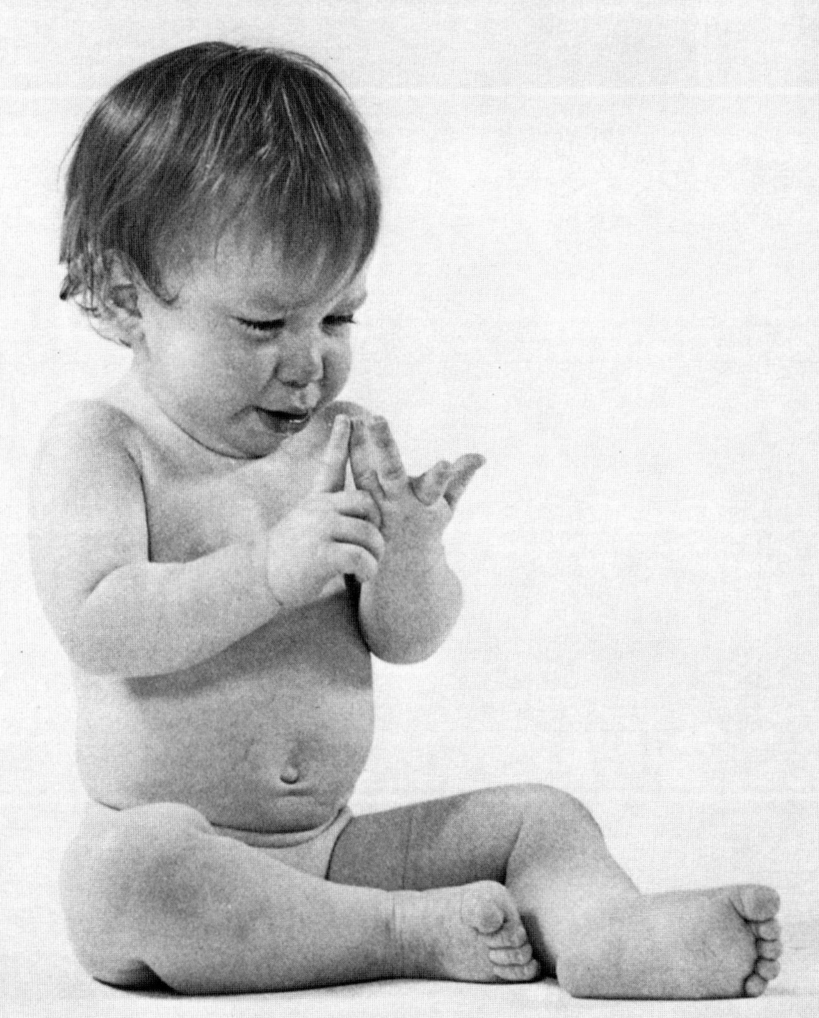

indicate confusion and tension. Angled lines can symbolize action, awkwardness, or passivity, depending on the subject. Examine the illustrations throughout this book for examples.

Shapes are combinations of lines with the addition of mass. Thus the meaning of a shape goes beyond the meaning of each individual line. There are, for example, clean geometric shapes that people automatically associate with the design concepts we call modern. Other shapes are associated with the Victorian period. In a more subtle sense, we associate sweeping curves, rounds, and ovals more with the concept of love than we do sharply angled shapes.

Texture

Texture is an important element because it tells us about the surfaces in the photo. Our inspection of the subject is limited by what the photographer shows us. Many textures are visible only at close distances, others are apparent only when we step away.

How we interpret a texture depends on our previous experiences. For example, since we have seen and felt hard things before, we interpret similar textures in photos as being hard.

Tone and Color

General attributes can be assigned to tones of grey and to colors. For example, white can symbolize goodness, cleanliness, and warmth, while black can symbolize evil, dirt, mystery, and coldness. Reds and yellows are usually colors that move forward, while greens and blues usually recede. There are many exceptions to these broad generalizations, however, and the context in which a color or tone resides is important.

Generally the use of a few strong colors in a neutral overall scene will be more dramatic than a collection of bright colors. Therefore, when planning special photo sessions for your family, tell the family members to wear subtle colors rather than bright ones. Too many bright colors will detract from people's features.

A black background will give a stronger, moodier feeling to your photos than a white one. A portrait of your brother with his cello, for example, would be quite dramatic against black, while a new baby and his mother would look warmer and softer against white.

This high-key photograph was made by placing the baby on a piece of white background paper. The paper was tacked to a wall and unrolled down onto the floor toward the photographer. Many camera stores carry seamless paper in colors, as well black, white, and gray.

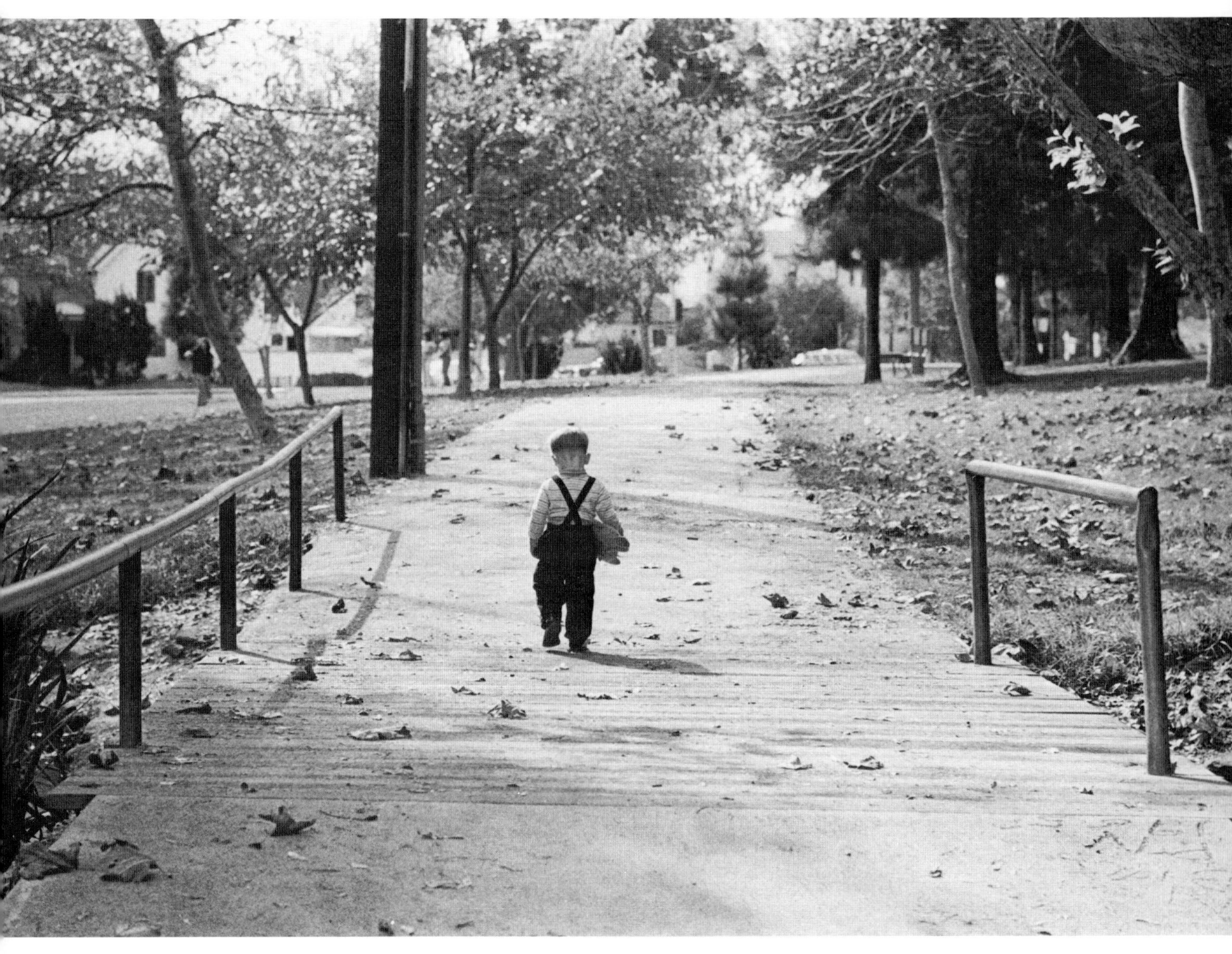

This photo has a strong focal point. The compositional elements of light and shade, the railings, and the walkway lead your eye to the subject.

FOCAL POINT AND BALANCE

A frequent problem with family photographs is a weak focal point. The focal point is the area of prime interest. It is the largest, most colorful, most active, or most interesting feature of the photo. All successful photographs have strong focal points.

Balance

Some photos have more than one focal point, although one is usually dominant. In an exciting photo, the focal points are in balance with the other parts. If you placed the parts of the photo on a set of scales, the focal points would weigh the same as the other elements combined. (You can see how this happens by examining the illustrations here.)

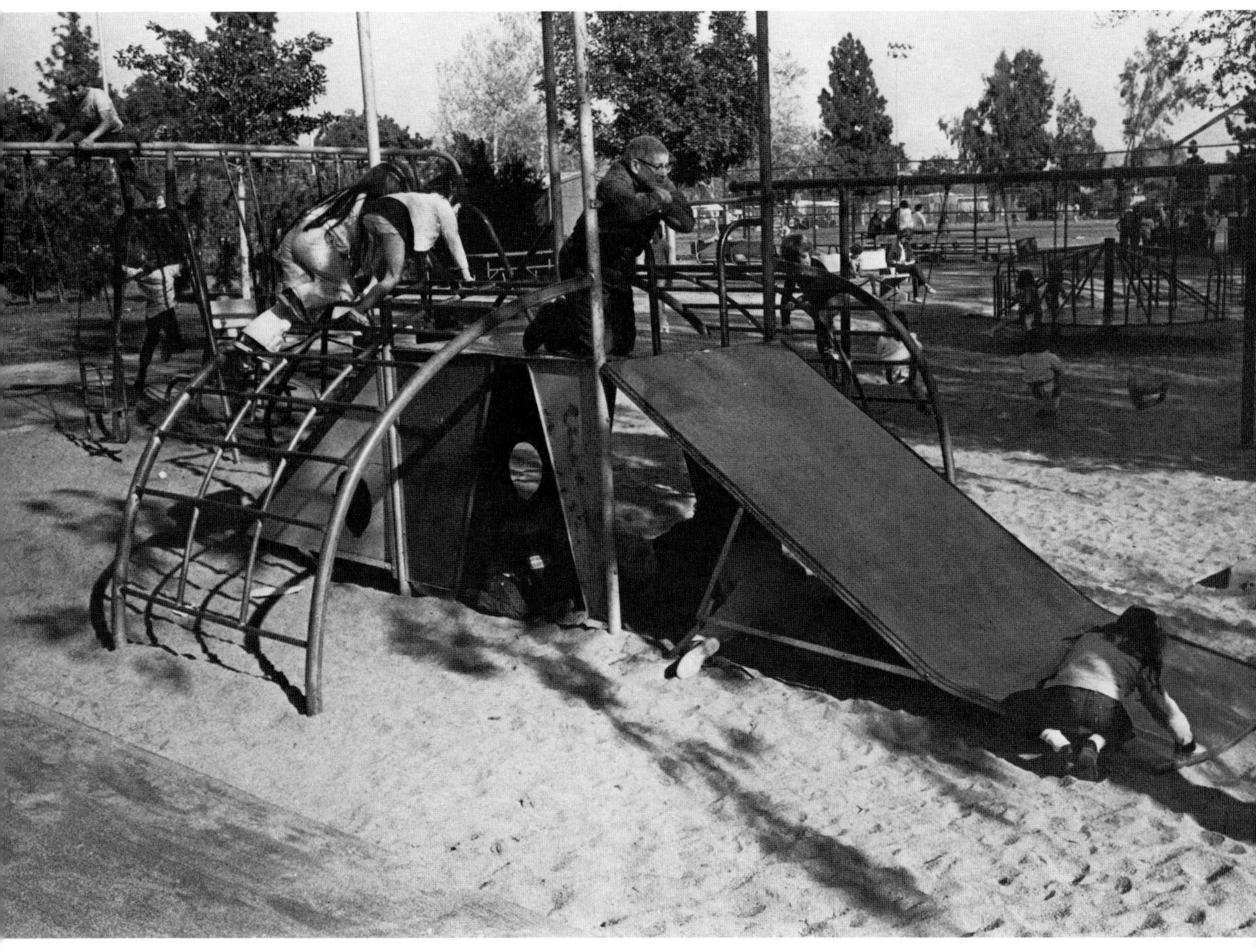

This photograph has no focal point. The photographer should have decided what the subject was and moved in to emphasize it.

COMMON VISUAL MISTAKES

One way to improve your photos is to learn what not to do. Don't take photos that don't contain a strong focal point. Be sure that a focal point will be evident to the viewers.

Confusing backgrounds

A second common problem involves the background of a photo. Although some people develop an unconscious awareness of these problems, others have to consciously examine their backgrounds before snapping an exposure. For example, check for distractions, such as a tree that looks like it's growing out of someone's head. Also check that the background won't creep forward and hide your subject. This problem can occur when there isn't enough contrast be-

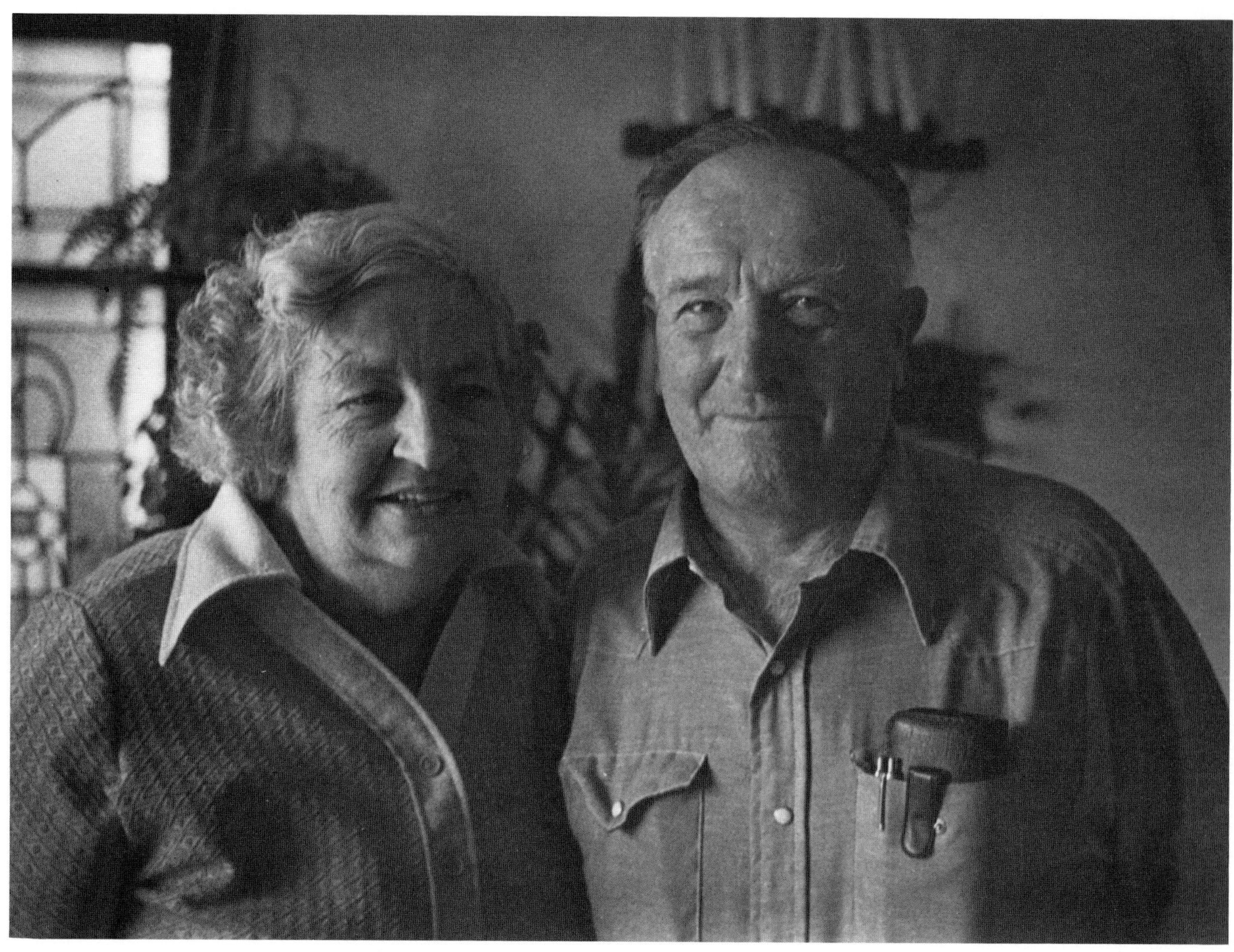

When concentrating on your subject, do not forget to check the background. The effectiveness of this portrait is diminished by the candles seeming to form a crown on the man's head.

tween the color of your subject and that of your background.

Listed below are some ways to correct a bad background:

Move to a better location.

Use a high camera angle.

Use a low camera angle.

Use a minimum depth-of-field, which will put the background out of focus.

Controlling backgrounds with depth-of-field

Depth-of-field refers to a camera's range of sharpness. The illustrations that follow show extreme uses of depth-of-field.

With auto-exposure SLR's you can easily control a background by controlling the depth-of-field. Although the aperture works with the shutter to regulate exposure, it also determines the depth-of-field. When the aperture is set for a small opening, such as f/16, you will get maximum depth-of-

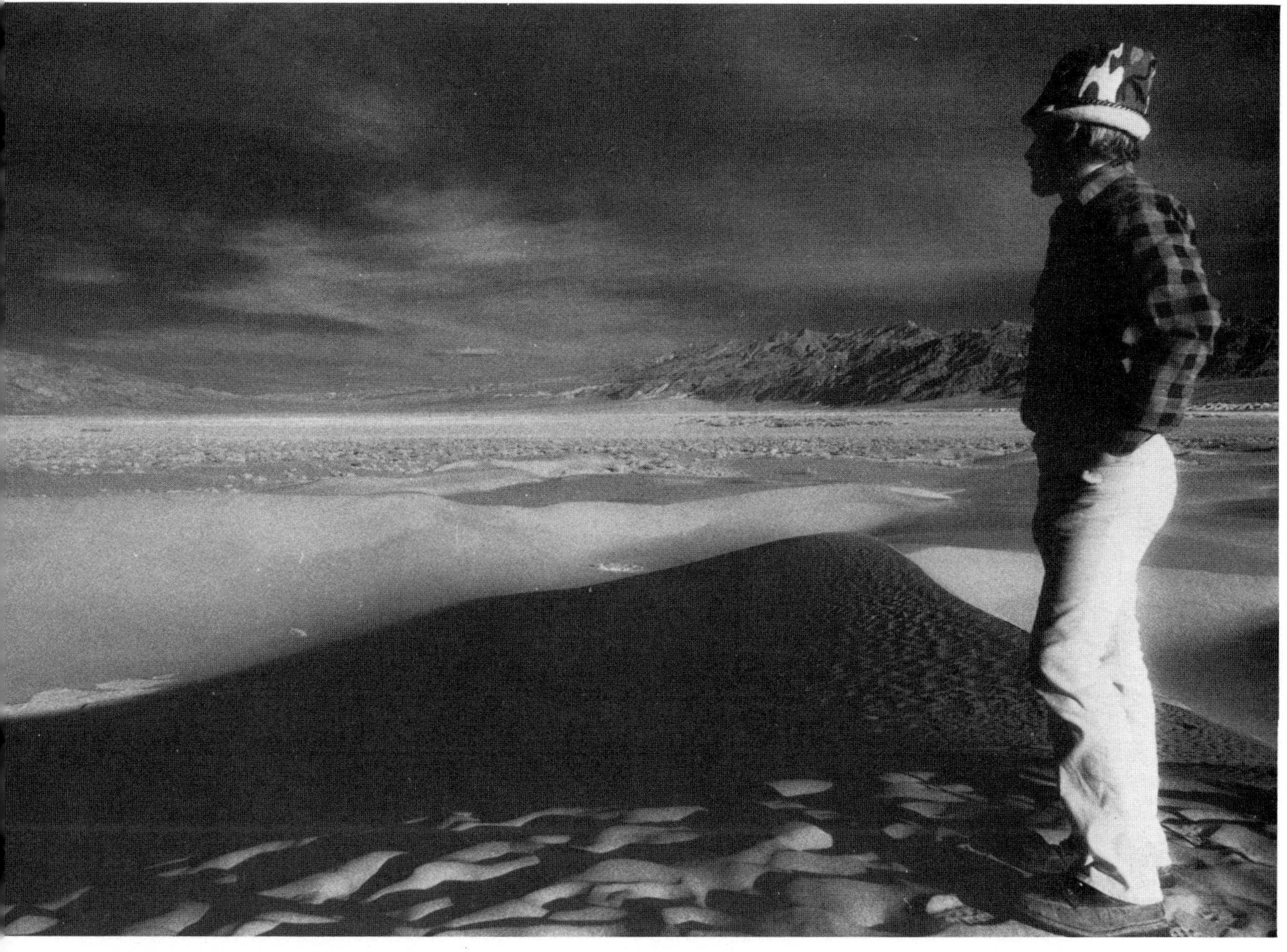

This is an example of maximum depth-of-field. The text explains how to set your camera so both foreground and background are sharp.

field. This would be important if you wanted the background to play a major role in your photo. Such as a scenic view with someone in the foreground.

When the aperture is set for a wide opening, such as f/2, the photo will have minimal depth-of-field. Generally a wide aperture is used to place the background out of focus.

If you have an aperture-preferred camera, it is simple to set the aperture on the widest or narrowest setting. Watch the exposure indicator in the viewfinder. As you change the aperture ring on your lens, be sure you don't change the aperture so much that an incorrect exposure results.

If you have a shutter-preferred camera, you can still control the aperture and hence the depth-of-field. Simply reset the shutter speed—higher for decreased depth, lower for increased depth. Again, watch the exposure indicators in your viewfinder for the limits of this adjustment.

These methods work because the correct exposure is a combination of aperture and shutter-speed settings. If one of these settings is changed, the other automatically changes.

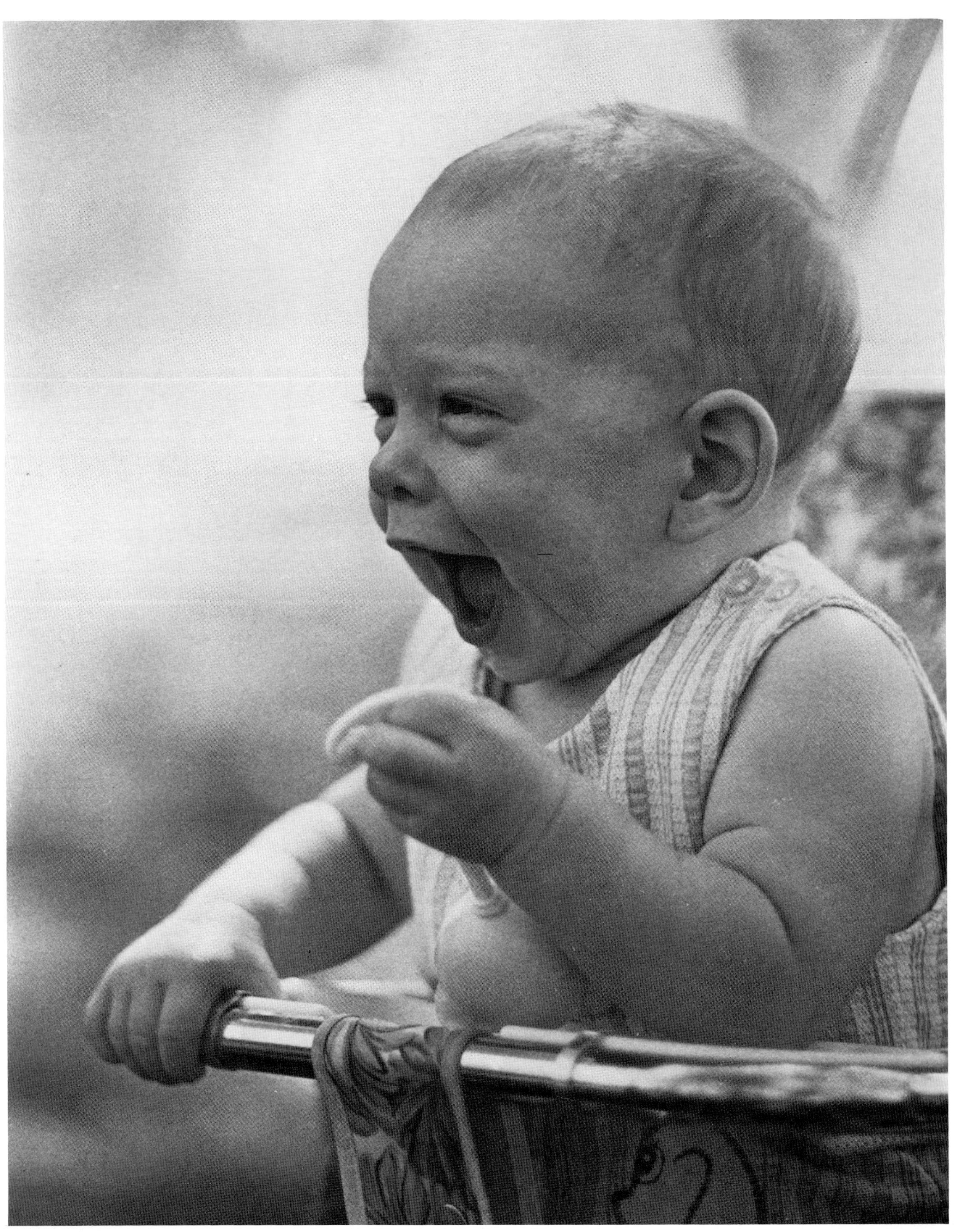

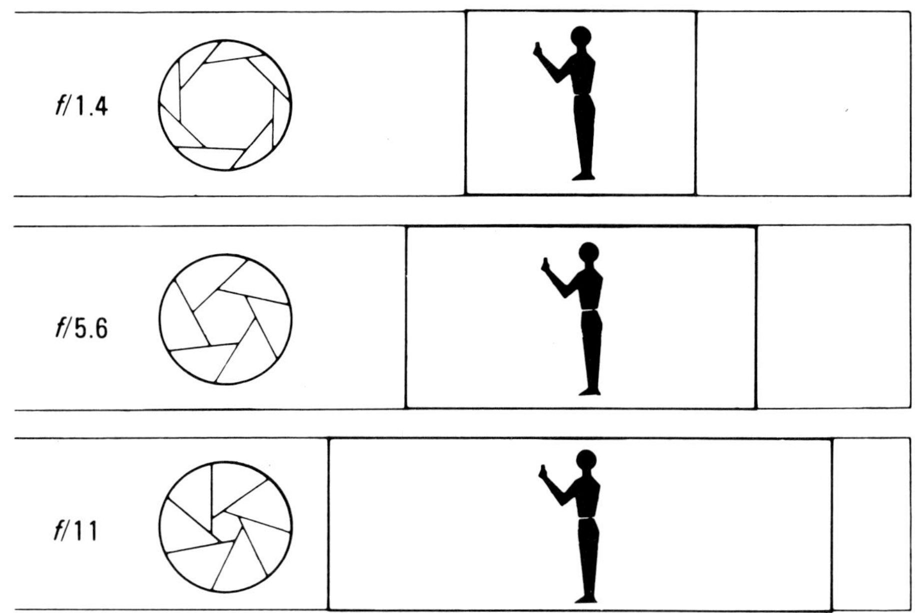

For the greatest depth of field, close the aperture down all the way. For limited depth of field, open the lens aperture. The vertical lines in this illustration show the range of area in focus in front of, and in back of, the subject.

Tilted horizons

An easily corrected problem is horizons that run downhill in a photo. Although you may not notice this in photos taken in the mountains, we all know that lakes and oceans don't slope to the left or right. Hold your camera level and double-check before you shoot.

Too far away

Another frequent problem in family photos is that people's features are so small you can barely see them. Remember, the face is the primary human communicator. If you want to capture a person's personality, concentrate on the face. To do this, you need to move in close.

Next time you are photographing a person, check your distance by trying this test. Just before pressing the shutter release, put the person's image along one edge of the frame. You can easily see the size of your subject in comparison to the rest of the frame this way.

Furthermore, you will find that by moving closer you can eliminate visual clutter, which often competes for attention.

This is an example of minimum depth-of-field. By using the widest aperture setting possible, you can place the background out of focus and draw attention to your subject.

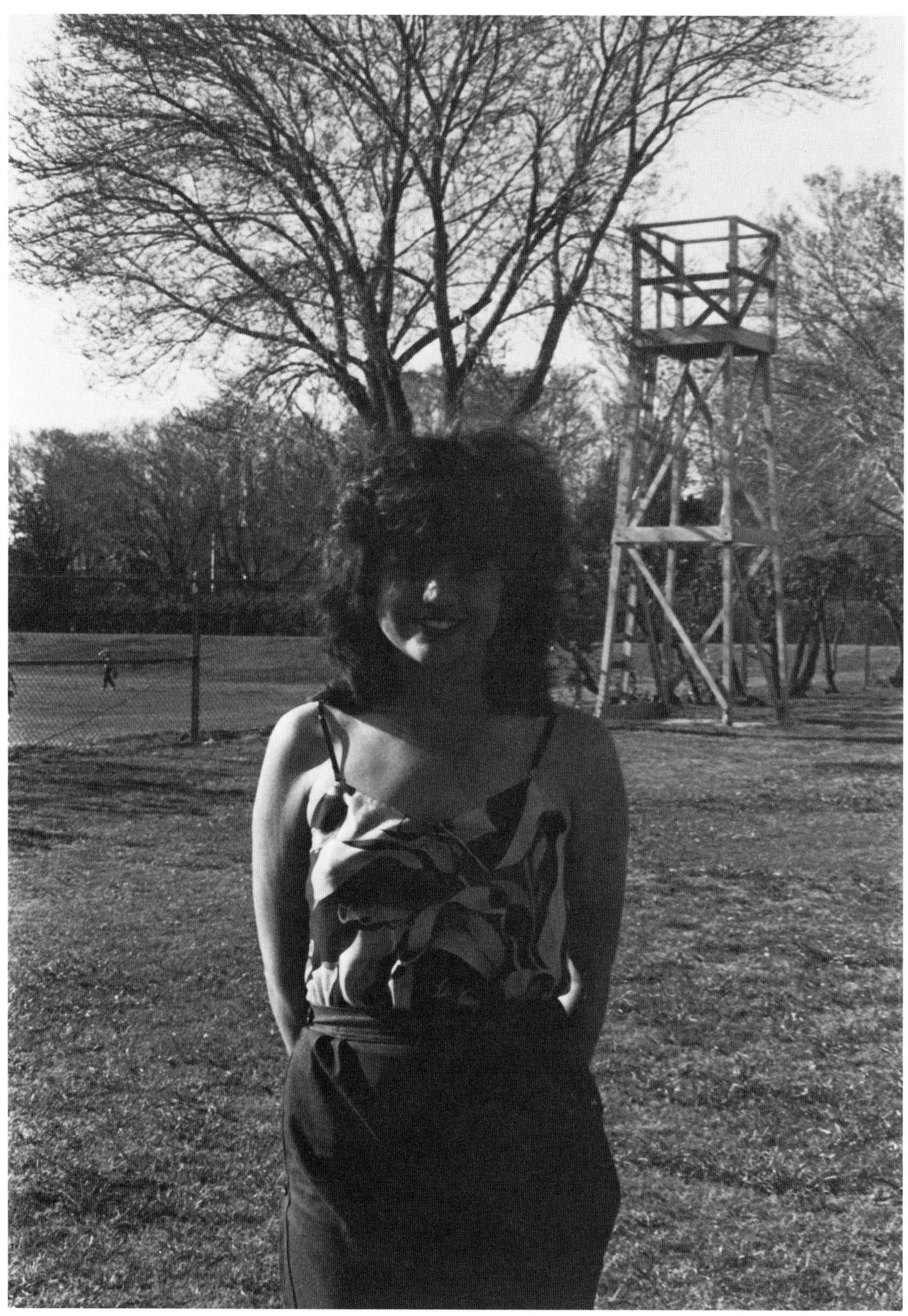

This photo is an example of several common errors. First, the background is terribly distracting, and the tree appears to be growing out of the woman's head. Secondly, her face is placed in the center of the frame, a static place in the composition. Thirdly, if this is to be a portrait, the photographer is too far away; there is too much extraneous material in the scene around her. Finally, her face is in such deep shadow that we can not see her expression clearly. Photograph by Mark Zahner.

Bull's-eye vision
The center of the frame is a static, dull, and formal place. Yet many photographers place their subjects there. This bull's-eye vision is probably caused by a combination of camera design and lack of attention. For one thing the critical focusing aid in the camera's viewfinder is in the center of the focusing screen. As you can see in the illustration, it is easy to focus on a person's face. But it makes for a more exciting photo if the face is placed elsewhere.

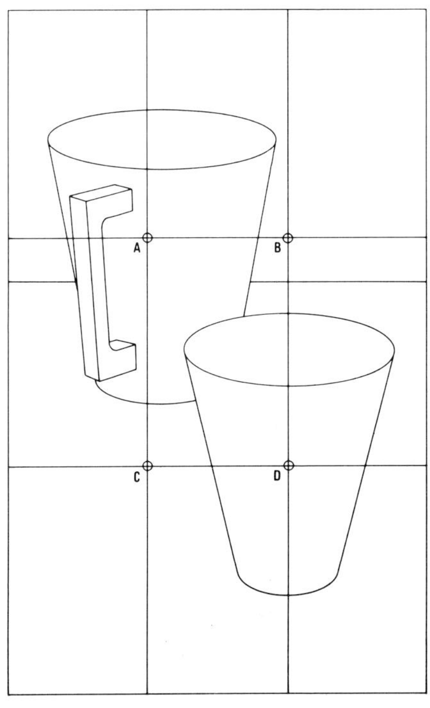

Above: *This drawing shows the imaginary lines of the rule of thirds. Any subject appearing at points where lines intersect (A,B,C, or D) will be the major point of interest.*

The rule of thirds
One way to attack the bull's-eye vision syndrome is with the rule of thirds. By making imaginary lines on your focusing screen, divide the screen into three equal parts, as shown in the sketch. The intersections of these lines are good places to put your focal points. The lines will also help you with the placement of other elements.

Tips for stronger compositions
Listed below are tips that will help you improve your compositions:

Make the image in the viewfinder match what you expect to see in the final photo.

Eliminate the visual clutter; have a strong focal point.

Try the rule of thirds.

Check the edges of the frame and the background for distractions.

Move in close when you want to emphasize faces, emotions, and personalities.

The viewing frame
By using this homemade device, you can practice composing without taking photos. You can also concentrate on the content of your photos rather than on camera mechanics.

Find a piece of lightweight cardboard about 8 × 10 inches square and cut a rectangular hole in the center about $3\frac{1}{2} \times 5$ inches. To simulate the field of vision of a normal lens, hold this viewing frame about 7 inches from your eye. Practice making dynamic compositions by using the techniques just discussed. The differences between strong and weak photos will be easier to discern when the camera is not interfering between your eye and your subject.

OTHER PROBLEM PICTURES

There are other problems that arise frequently in family photos. In the following photographs, several of these problems are illustrated.

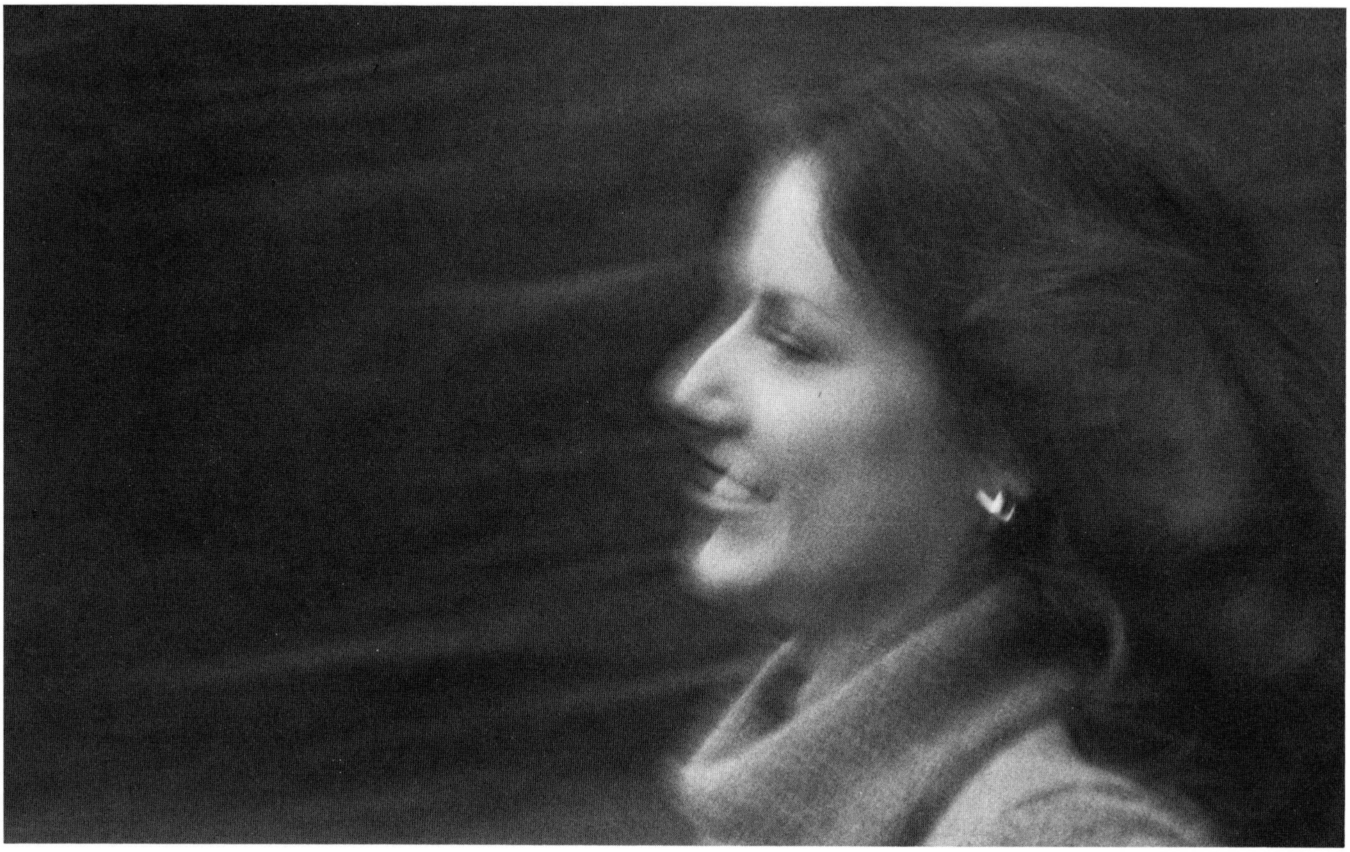

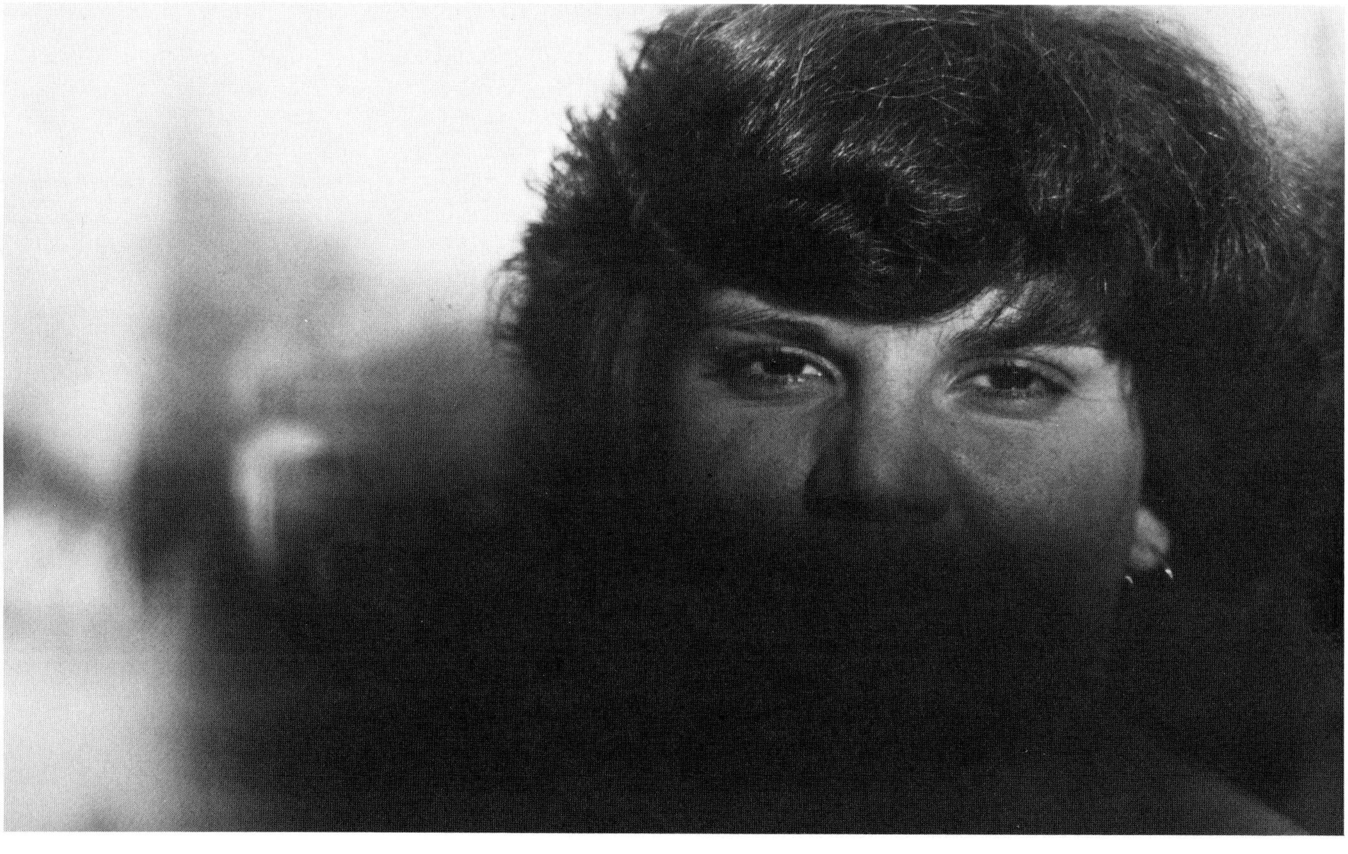

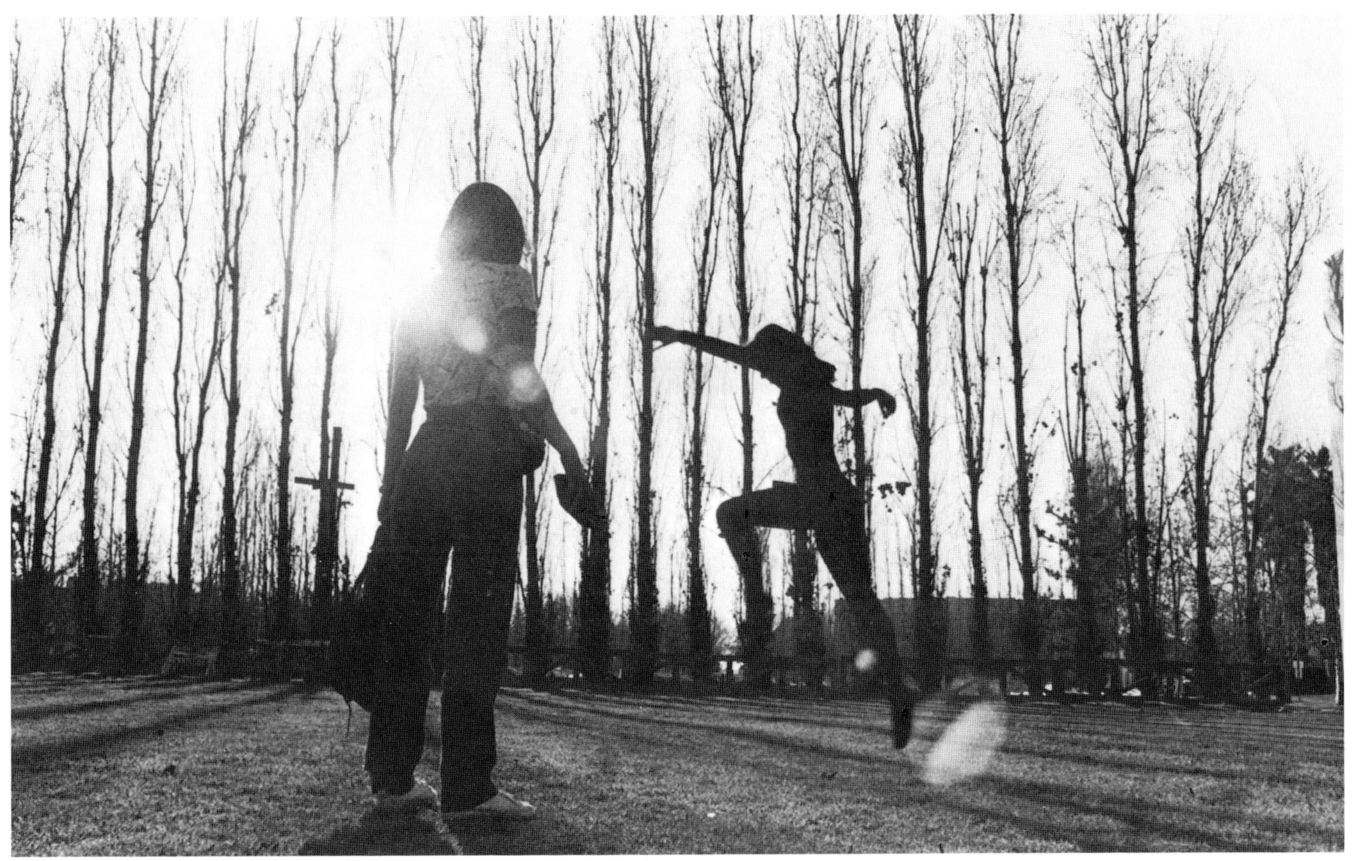

Above left: *Camera and subject movement are major causes of technically unsatisfactory photos. In this example, you can see a double image along the front edge of the woman's profile. This is your clue to a movement problem. A photo that was merely out of focus would not have this double image effect.*

Left: *The strange dark area in the lower center of this photo is the result of the camera's case blocking the lens. Photograph by Mark Zahner.*

Above: *Although rather pleasing in this interpretative shot, lens flare from the sun can spoil portraits and other photos in which you want to see detail. We would not have been able to see the girls's faces if they had been facing the camera. To prevent this, use a lens hood and avoid aiming the camera into the sun. Photograph by Mark Zahner.*

CHAPTER FOUR

CAMERAS AND CHILDREN

Photographing your offspring

Children are exciting, and if there are some in your family, you will certainly want to aim your camera in their direction. Children are also quite clever and uninhibited about their feelings. Capturing all these traits on film is one of the best ways of preserving those all-too-short years.

If you are a parent, you probably know that children can sometimes control a situation more than you'd like. For example, if they are upset or feeling uncooperative, they can sometimes spoil your photos. Therefore, you must learn to accommodate for some of their needs.

When photographing children, remember:

Sitting quietly is hard for children. Five minutes can seem like 500.

Being neat doesn't feel right to them.

Taking directions isn't fun for anyone, especially children.

Respect your child's feelings and limits. Consider how you'd feel if you were hot, tired, or hungry. Remember that these feelings are often stronger in children. Work when they are at their peak—rested, fed, comfortable, and secure.

Also, they know when you are trying to fool them, so be honest. Explain why something is being done, and do not underestimate their capacity for understanding. For example, if you must move for better light or ask them to hold a pose, let them know the reasons. Ask them for ideas. If you let them share in the creativity, they'll feel more like a part of the project than like a victim. Above all do not embarrass them. Be sensitive to the child's self-consciousness, a trait particularly accentuated in adolescents.

If you are discovered while taking candid photos, don't try to hide what you are doing. This will only lead to suspicion. Satisfy the child's immediate curiosity and continue your project.

Control the urge to give directions like an Army drill in-

Although this photo was made with a 35mm wide-angle lens, the photographer moved in close to the subject to eliminate background distractions.

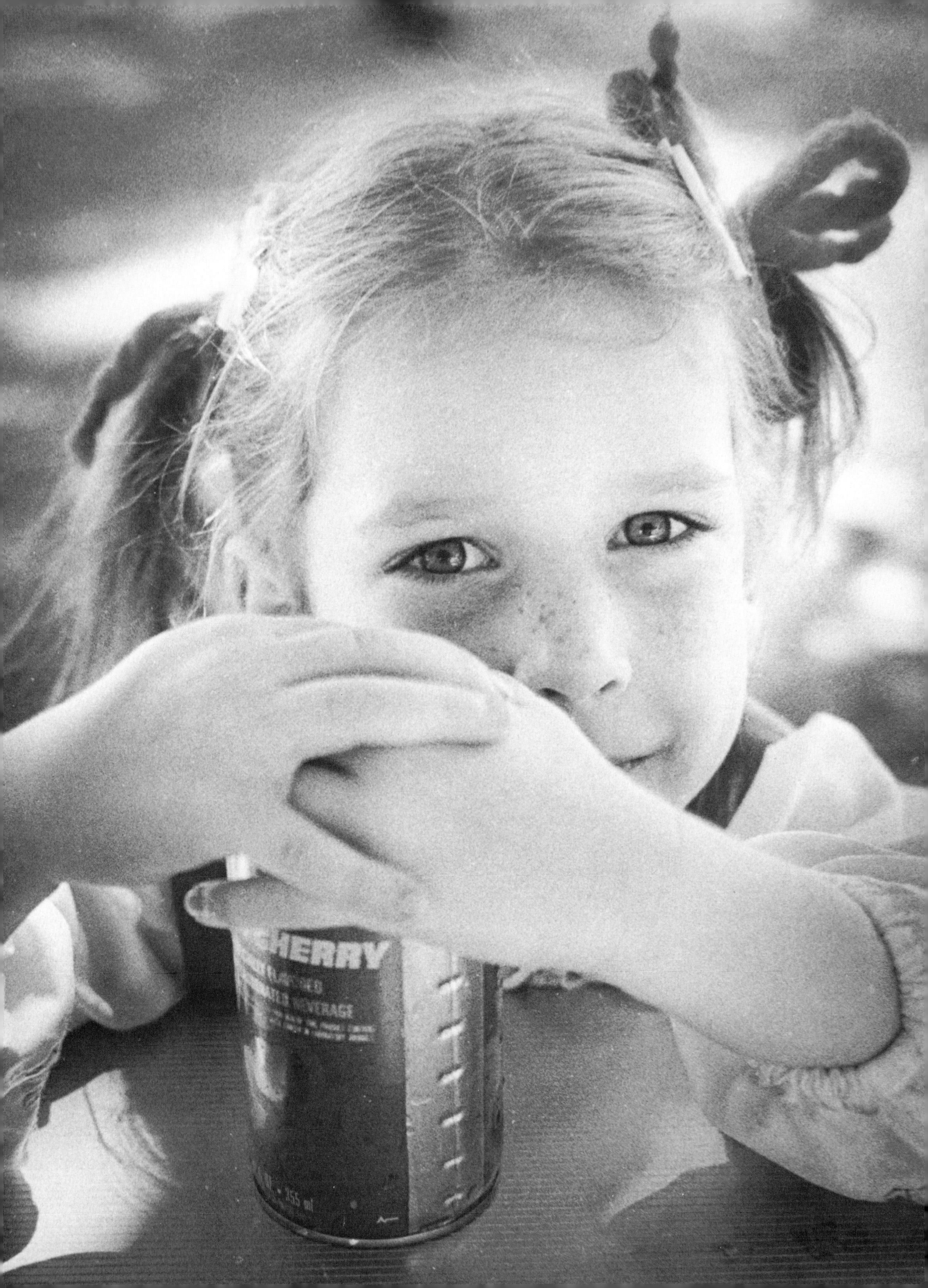

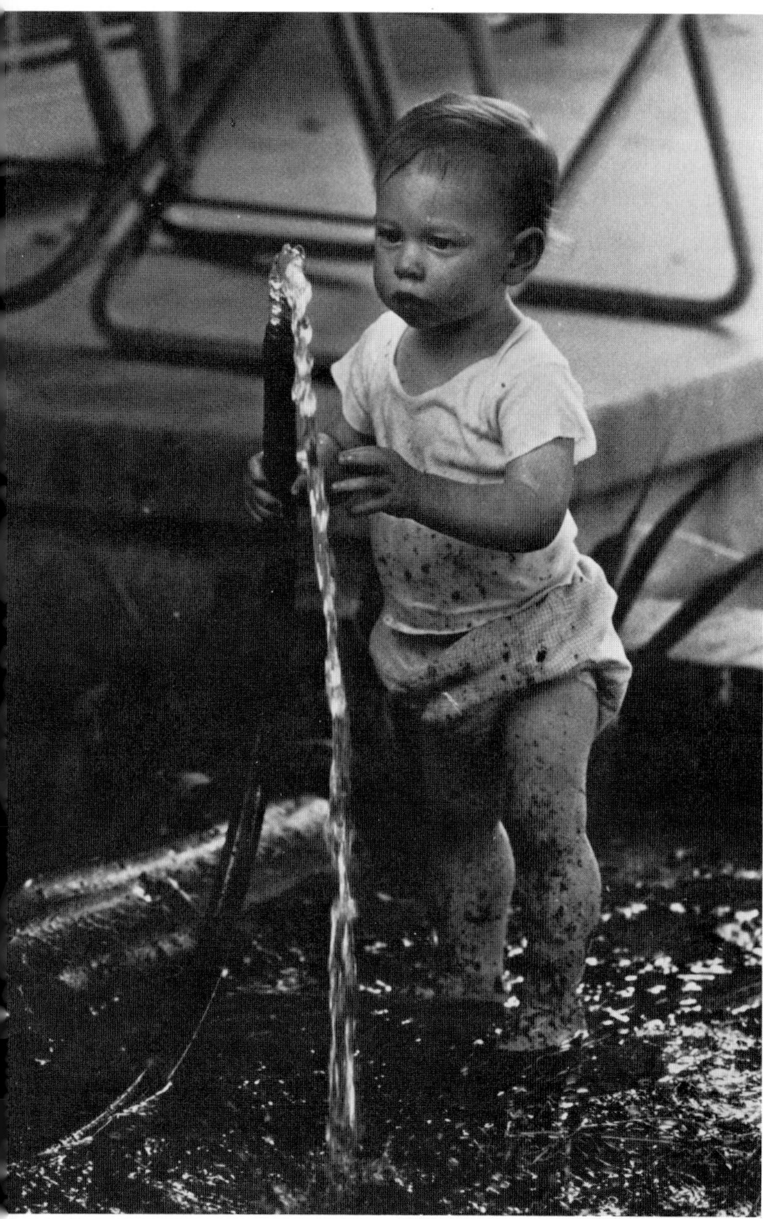

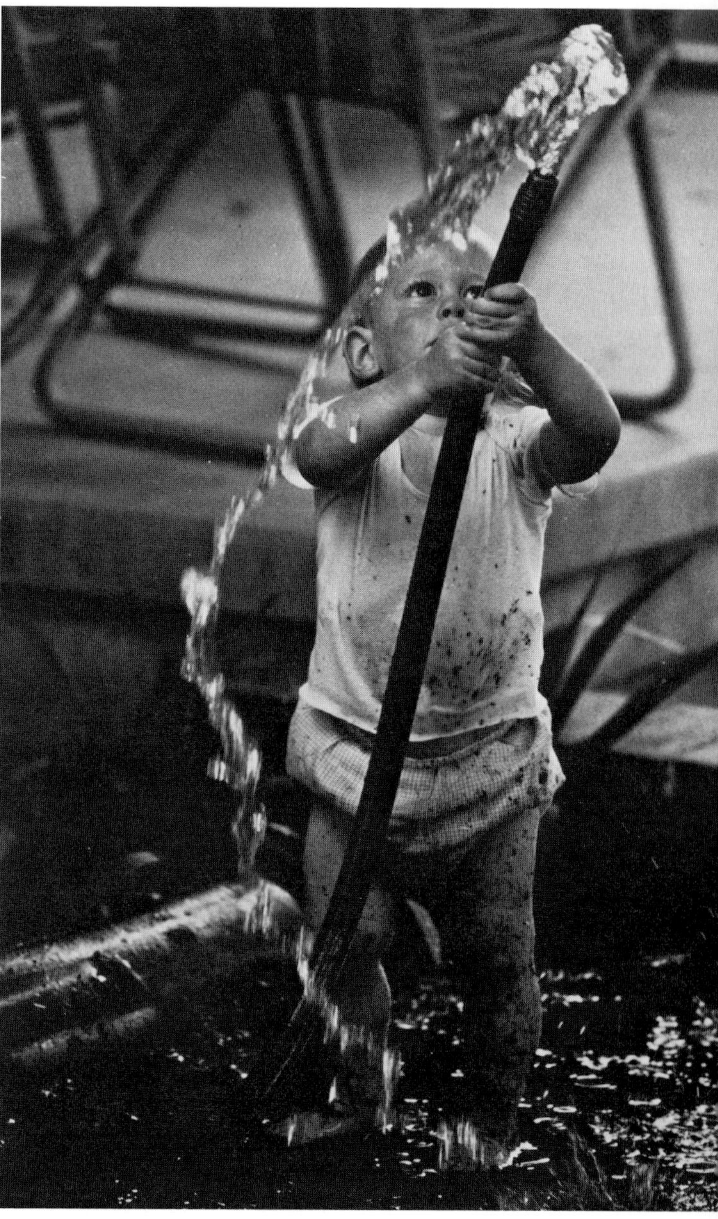

This little fellow's lesson in hydraulics is told more effectively with a series of photos rather than in one shot.

structor. And don't expect the children to be squeaky clean and wrinkle free for every photo session.

How to avoid missed shots

To be sure of catching those fleeting moments, *always* have your camera loaded and your flash ready. Also, make sure you have fresh batteries in the camera and that the camera is set for average conditions. I must admit that I have lost a few good photos because my camera wasn't ready at the right moment.

Practice your technique so time isn't wasted fiddling with equipment. If the children are waiting, they will soon lose patience. If it is a candid situation, it is likely to disappear quickly.

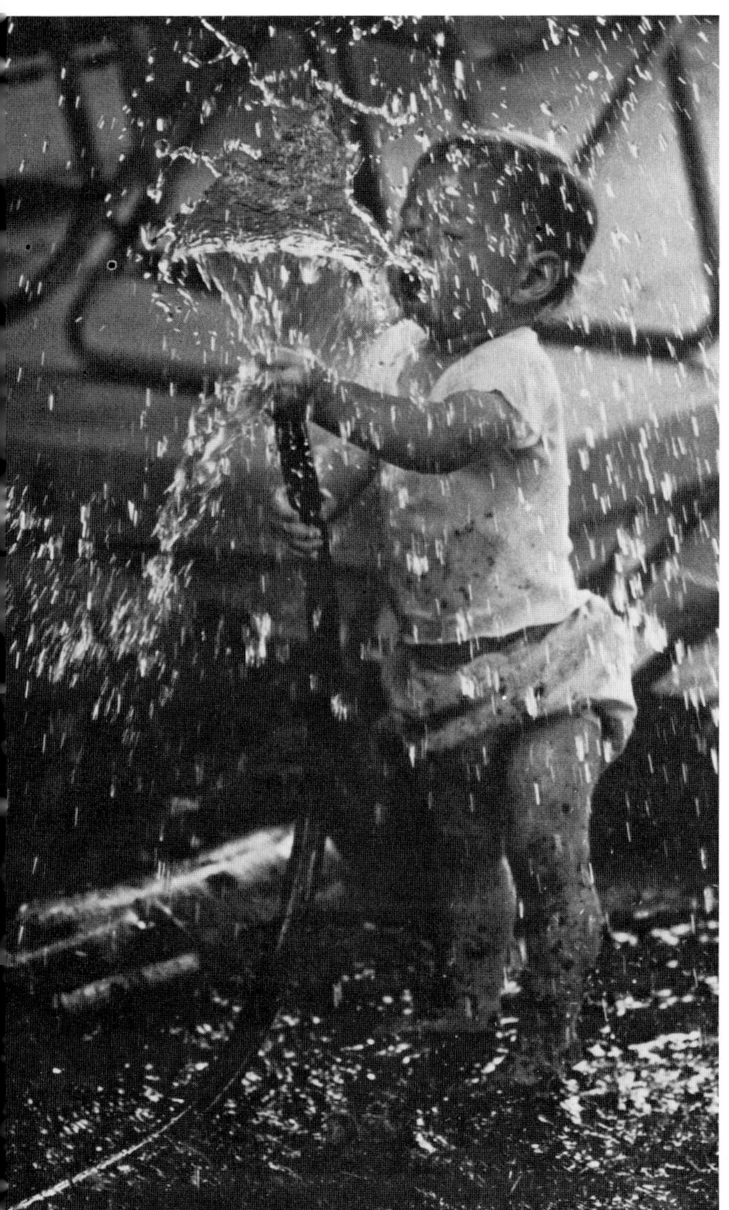

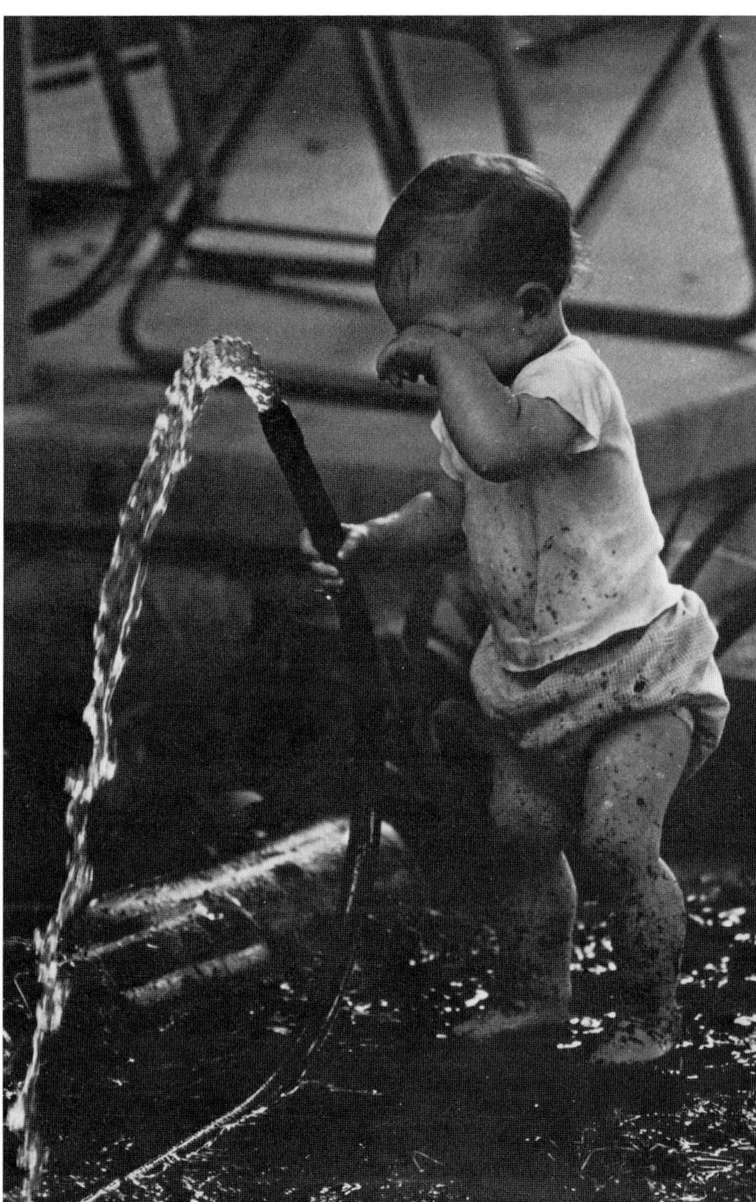

Expect, too, a high shooting ratio. This is a motion picture term for the amount of film shot in proportion to the amount finally used. Don't expect every photo to be a success. Some top professionals only expect one outstanding shot from each roll. And even if you only bring back one satisfactory shot for every ten frames, you will have done quite well.

THE DIRECT APPROACH

There are two ways to photograph your children. One is direct, where the two of you work together to make photos. The other is indirect, where you are an observer catching glimpses of them as they play and work.

The direct approach is the one you would use to shoot a

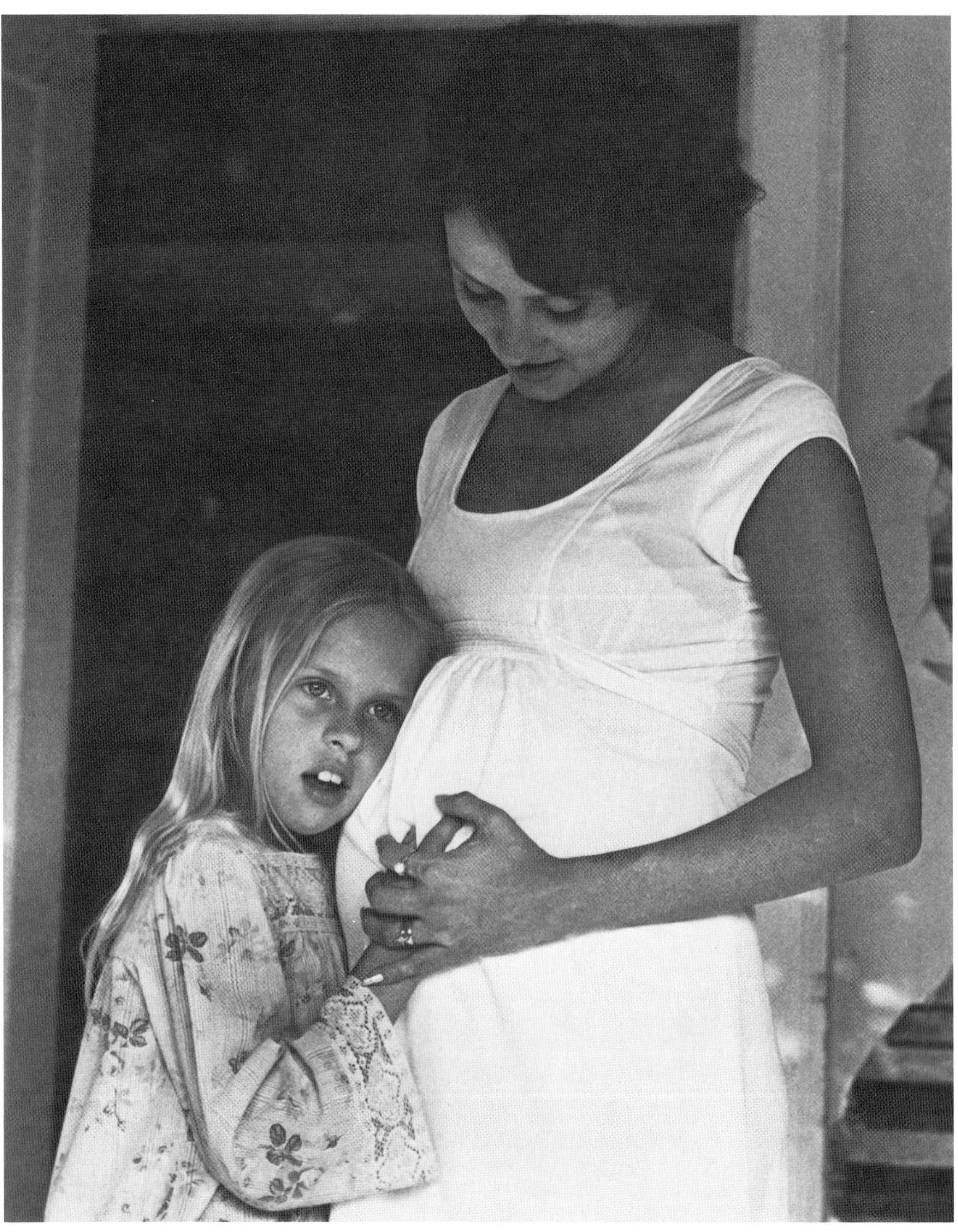

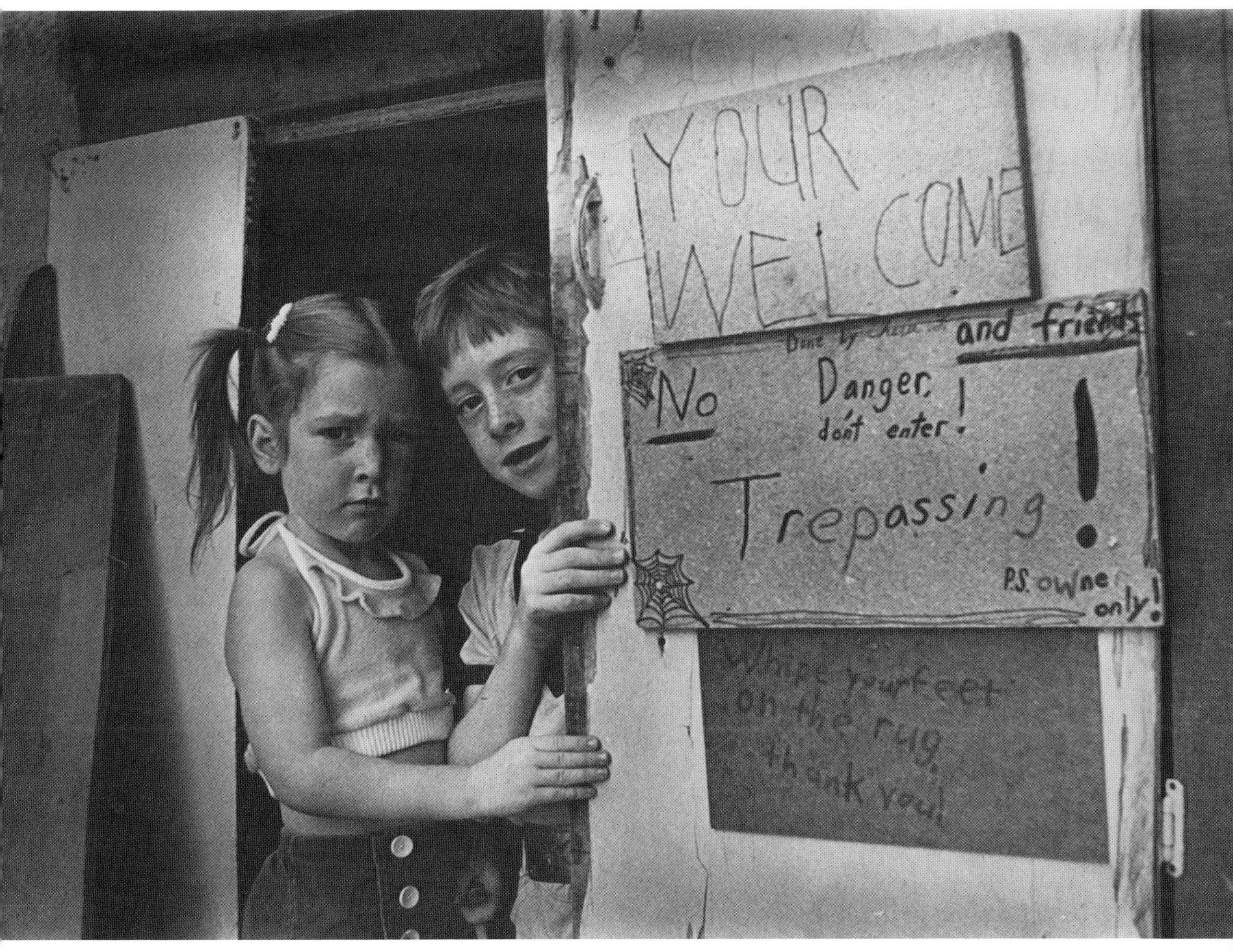

Above: *This photo was made with a direct approach. The children were asked to stand in the doorway to their clubhouse; however, they were not asked to smile because this frequently results in contrived expressions.*

Left: *To be sure of catching sensitive moments like this, always have your camera loaded and your flash ready. Photograph by Edward H. Pace, a winner in the Kodak International Newspaper Snapshot Awards (KINSA).*

portrait, for example. The child would be in a controlled setting in which lights, props, and background would be arranged. Listed below are some techniques for using this method successfully:

Have the children help you. Photography is always more fun for the subjects if they are a part of the process. Ask for their ideas. Also ask what kinds of pictures they would like to have taken. Then be sure to take them.

Avoid bribes. These payoffs can backfire when the time for cooperation arrives and the reward doesn't. Also, at this time the payee sometimes decides to increase his price.

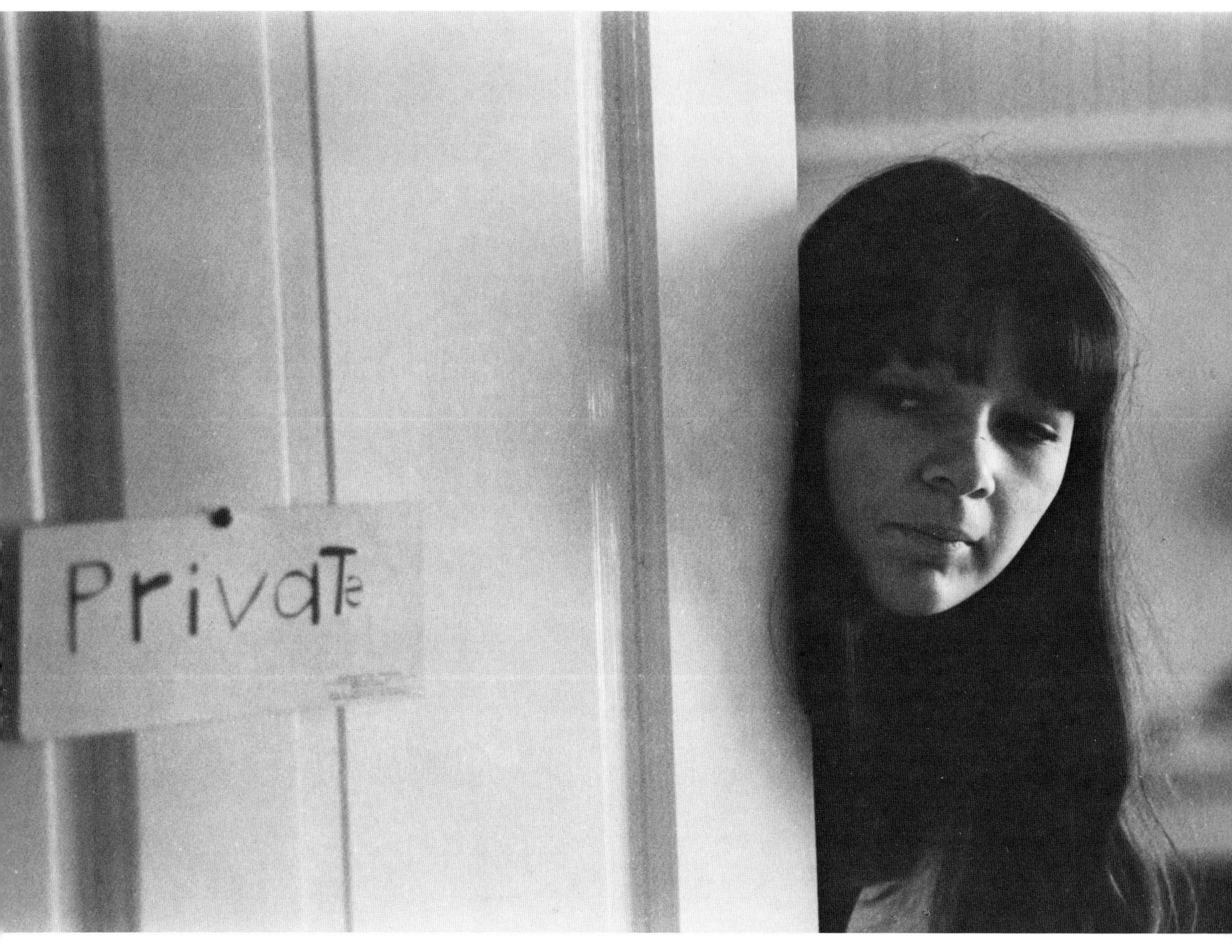

In some of your photos, try to include visual symbols which tell about the person. This sign was on the door of this girl's bedroom.

Work in a children's environment. Because they will be most comfortable there, you will get more natural responses. In fact, ask them where they think the best place would be.

Use fantasy and imagination. Simply asking a child to sit and smile usually results in a camera smile. Instead, ask him if he can see the elephant sitting on your head. Or simply say, "Make believe you are a ________ ."

To photograph older kids, ask them to do an everyday activity and photograph them doing it. This might mean working on a model or simply thinking about something that interests them.

Use props—their proud possessions. You might even ask them to set up a display of their favorite toys or creations for a photo.

Solve technical details in advance. Kids will not like waiting while you fiddle with lights and exposure settings. When you are ready to shoot, work quickly. Elyse Lewin, a nationally known photographer who began her career by photographing children, has said that even professional child-models are at their best for only the first ten minutes. The good photos are usually taken at the beginning of the session.

Don't insist on perfection. Even if something is not quite right, take the photo. Continual changes make the child think he's not pleasing you.

Give positive strokes. Let the child know when you have something exciting in the viewfinder. They enjoy success, too. And they shouldn't have to wait for praise until the photos are processed.

Respond to individual needs for attention in a group. Be sure to let each person know that his contribution is important.

Watch for tolerance levels. End the session before exhaustion or boredom have reached the crisis point. Fun-filled sessions are the best way to breed positive attitudes toward other sessions. Remember, too, there are some days when people don't feel like being photographed. Respect a child's feelings if he isn't in the mood and reschedule the session.

How to deal with stubborn children

If you have a child who just doesn't want to be photographed, try finding out the reason. It may even be necessary for another family member to ask the questions when you're not around. If the answer remains "I just don't want to," then ask the child to help you photograph something else, such as a favorite toy.

If the problem is a contest of wills, you might expose your own feelings to the child. Instead of saying "You are really troublesome today," you might say, "You know that grandma's birthday is on Monday. She would love to have a picture of you. And it makes me very sad that you don't want to help make one for her." Then put your camera down and walk away.

Don't expect an immediate change. The child will want to allow enough time to pass to make the change look like it came from him. Be prepared, too, for a second round: "I know you don't feel like being photographed today, but sometimes we all have to do things we don't want to. If we don't make the photo today, it won't be ready in time for grandma's birthday."

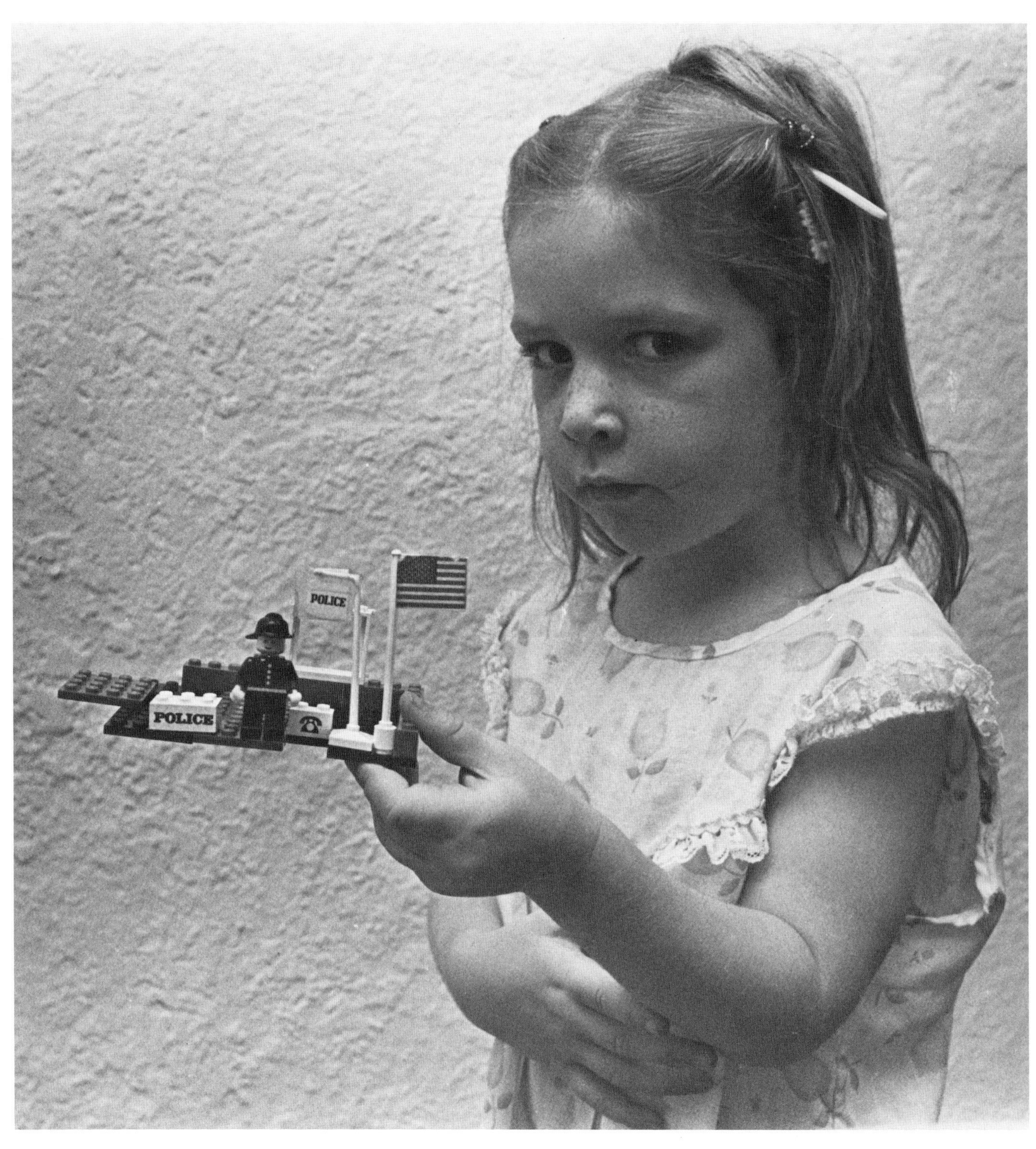

Although Lizzie did not want to be photographed, she decided to share her toy with the photographer.

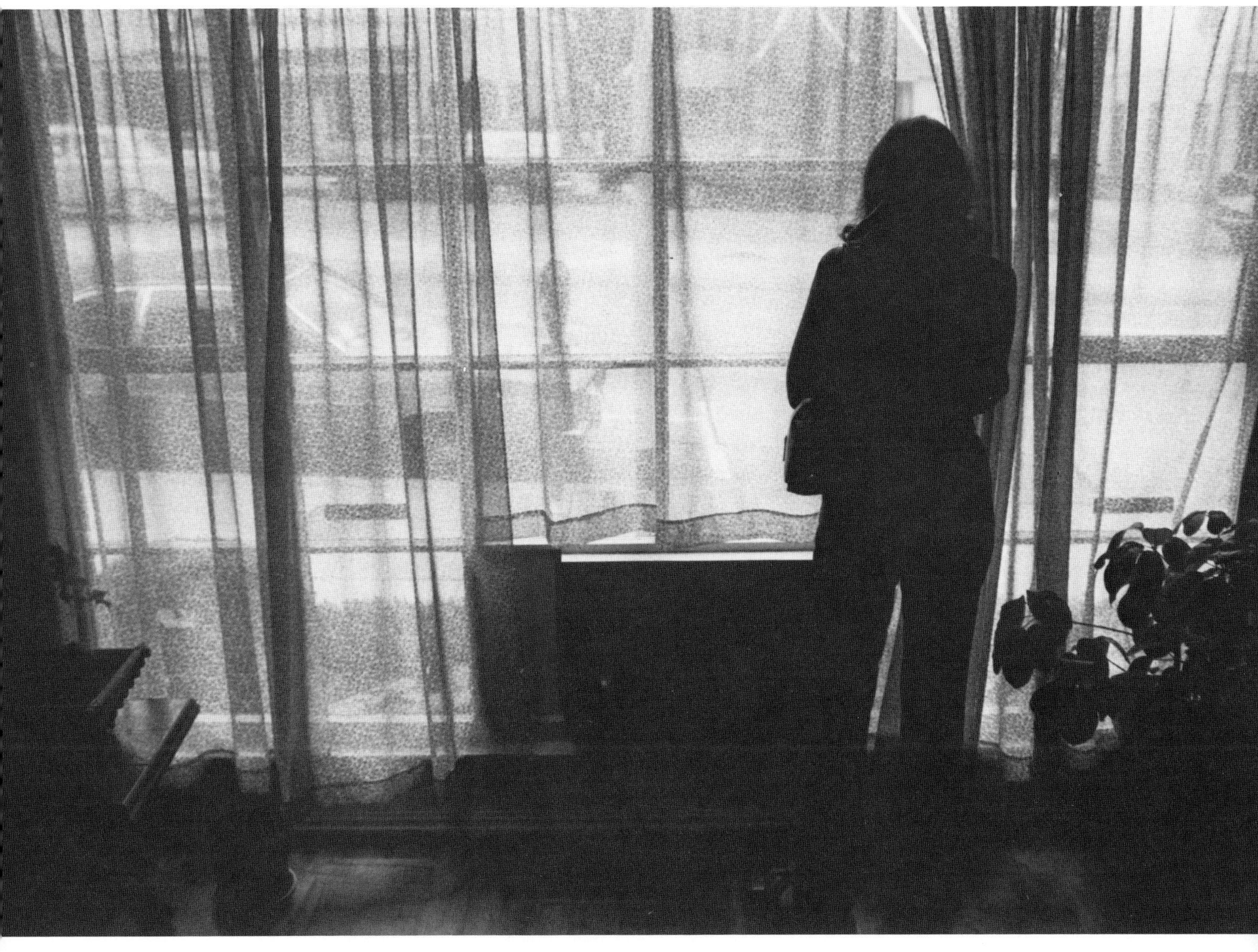

You can make photos of quiet, thoughtful moments without intruding upon your subject.

THE INDIRECT APPROACH

This is the candid method. This is the way you take natural photos of your children as they are playing or working. Good photographers who use this method are always on duty, and their cameras are never far from reach. An exciting picture possibility may appear at any moment, and you must be ready instantly.

Listed below are tips for using this method successfully:

Take lots of photos. As your family becomes used to your camera, they will become less self-conscious. This will increase your candid success rate. Also, expect your ratio of bad to good photos to be slightly higher than with the direct approach.

Tell your subjects to pretend you are invisible. Do this especially in classrooms and other situations in which you are likely to be a distraction. Once the kids know who you are and what you are doing, they will work very hard to ignore you—particularly if you say, "If you look at my camera, I won't be able to take your picture." Be sure to back up this threat if someone tests you. This approach works at all age levels.

Don't wait for a better shot. It may not happen. Shoot quickly, then be ready for an improvement if one should come.

Watch for the unpredictable. Suppose your daughter falls off her tricycle and your son goes to comfort her. Your first reaction might be to join the rescue team. But first snap a photo of this sibling affection.

Watch for the predictable. If you give a toddler a bowl of chocolate pudding, you should know what will happen. Similarly, you should be able to predict certain reactions in older children, and your family record should show some of these.

Be omnivorous with your camera. Be sure to include photos of tears as well as smiles, but don't embarrass the child or ignore the needs the tears are expressing. Photograph both the messes and the quiet moments (while respecting privacy). Look for scenes of parent-child interaction, such as when your daughter's hand wraps around her father's thumb as they leave for a walk. Also look for moments of spontaneous joy, such as when your son runs across the lawn just because he's feeling good.

Catching fast-moving kids

As you know, children can move quite fast. In fact, they can often move faster than your shutter's ability to stop them, resulting in blurred photos. One advantage of an auto-exposure camera is that you can control how motion is captured. You can either freeze an action or allow it to blur for dramatic effect.

Obviously a shutter that opens and closes in 1/1000 of a second will stop most action, and a shutter that opens for 1/30 of a second or longer will blur action.

You can control the shutter speed of your camera by using the method discussed in Chapter 3. To increase the camera's shutter speed on an aperture-priority camera, adjust the aperture for a wide setting. To decrease the shutter speed, close down the aperture. The viewfinders of many

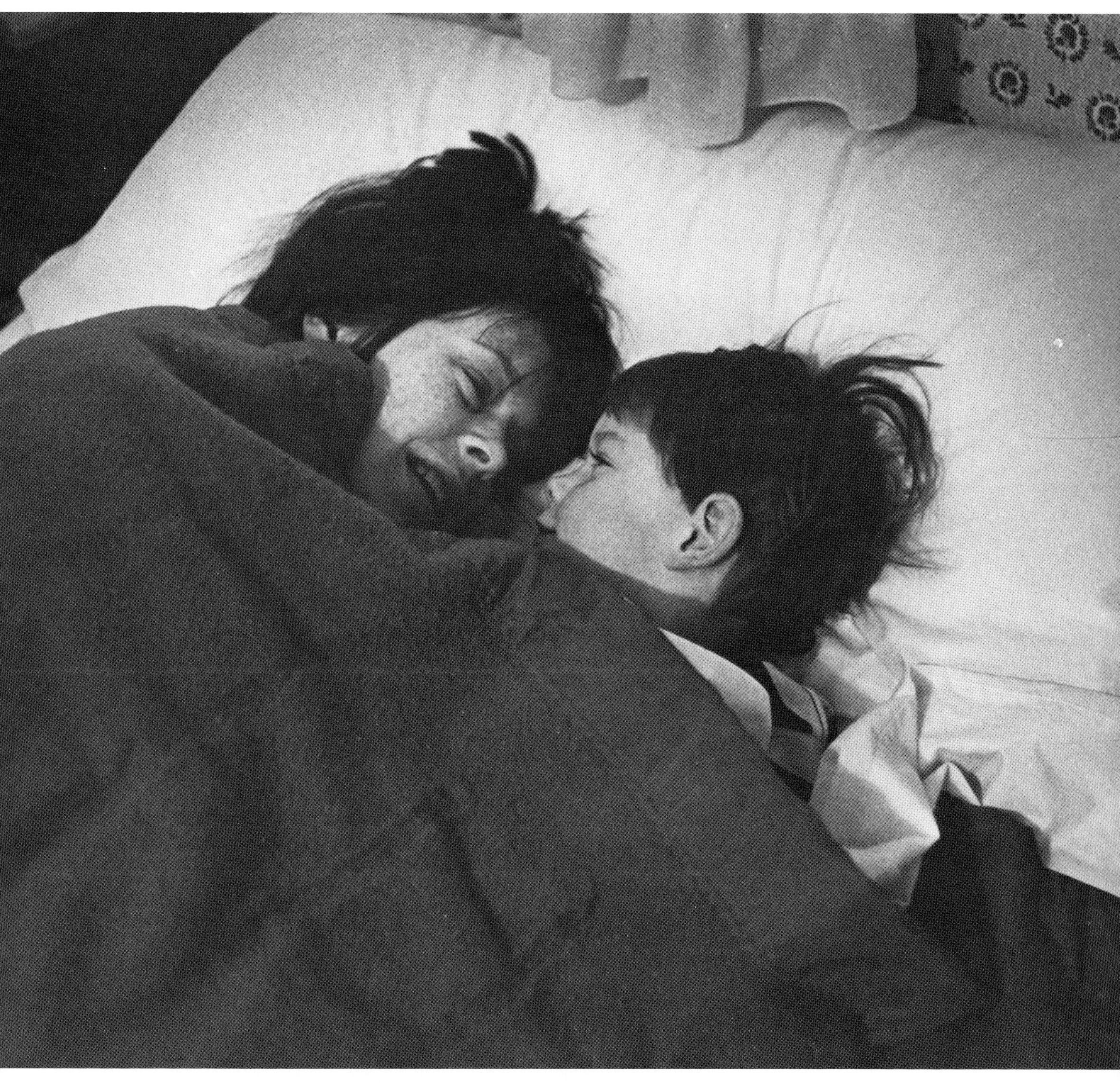

A sensitive, but dimly lit moment was captured with high-speed (ASA 400) film.

cameras include indicators which show what shutter speed has been selected by the exposure system.

If your camera is a shutter-priority type, simply set the desired shutter speed and allow the camera's electronics to set the appropriate aperture. Again, in either case, watch the exposure indicators to be sure you have not gone beyond the limits of correct exposure.

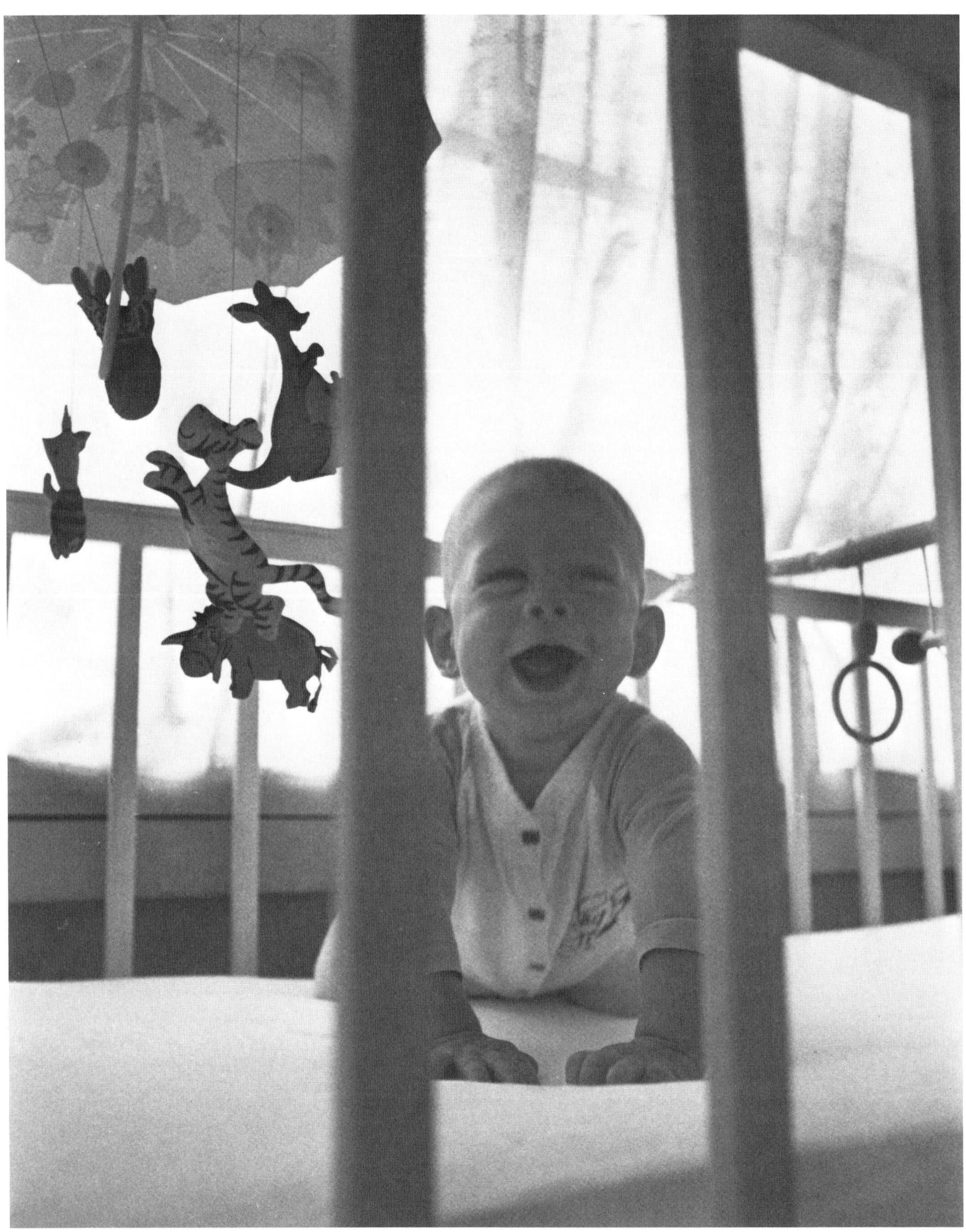

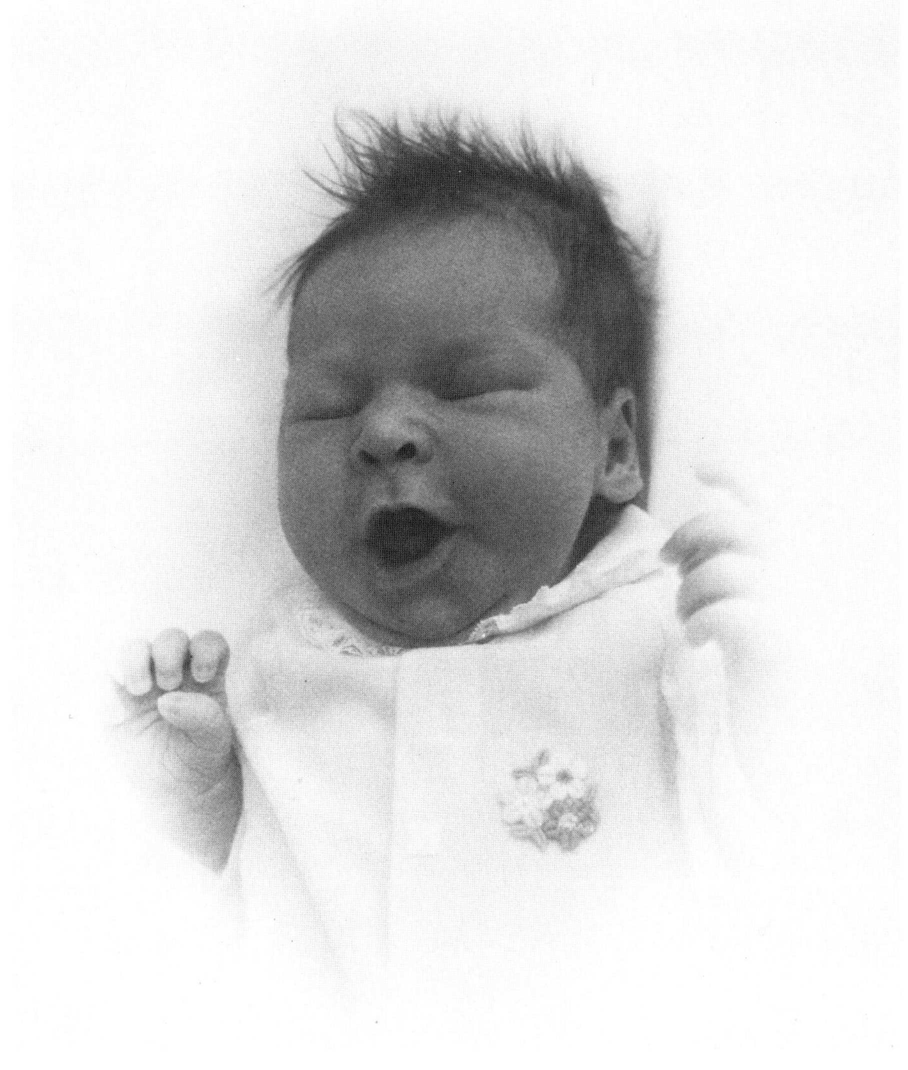

This baby was photographed while lying in her crib. It was printed as a vignette to make the image fade away at the edges. Custom labs should be able to make vignetted prints for you.

BABIES

Almost any photograph you take of a baby will be fun to look at, and taking good photos of babies is not difficult. Perhaps the most important technique to remember when working with babies is patience. If you have ever had a baby of your own, you know that they are the ones in control.

Listed below are some tips for taking baby photos:

Happy, attentive reactions usually occur after meals and naps.

A helper is sometimes necessary to elicit reactions or to hold babies too young to sit up for more formal photos.

Attention-getting tricks only work for a limited time, so shoot quickly.

Photos should be taken from the child's level. Stand-up viewpoints make the baby appear more like an object than the important person he or she is.

Opposite page: *When photographing babies, be sure to get down to their level. Modern high-speed film made it possible to take this photo using only the ambient light in the room.*

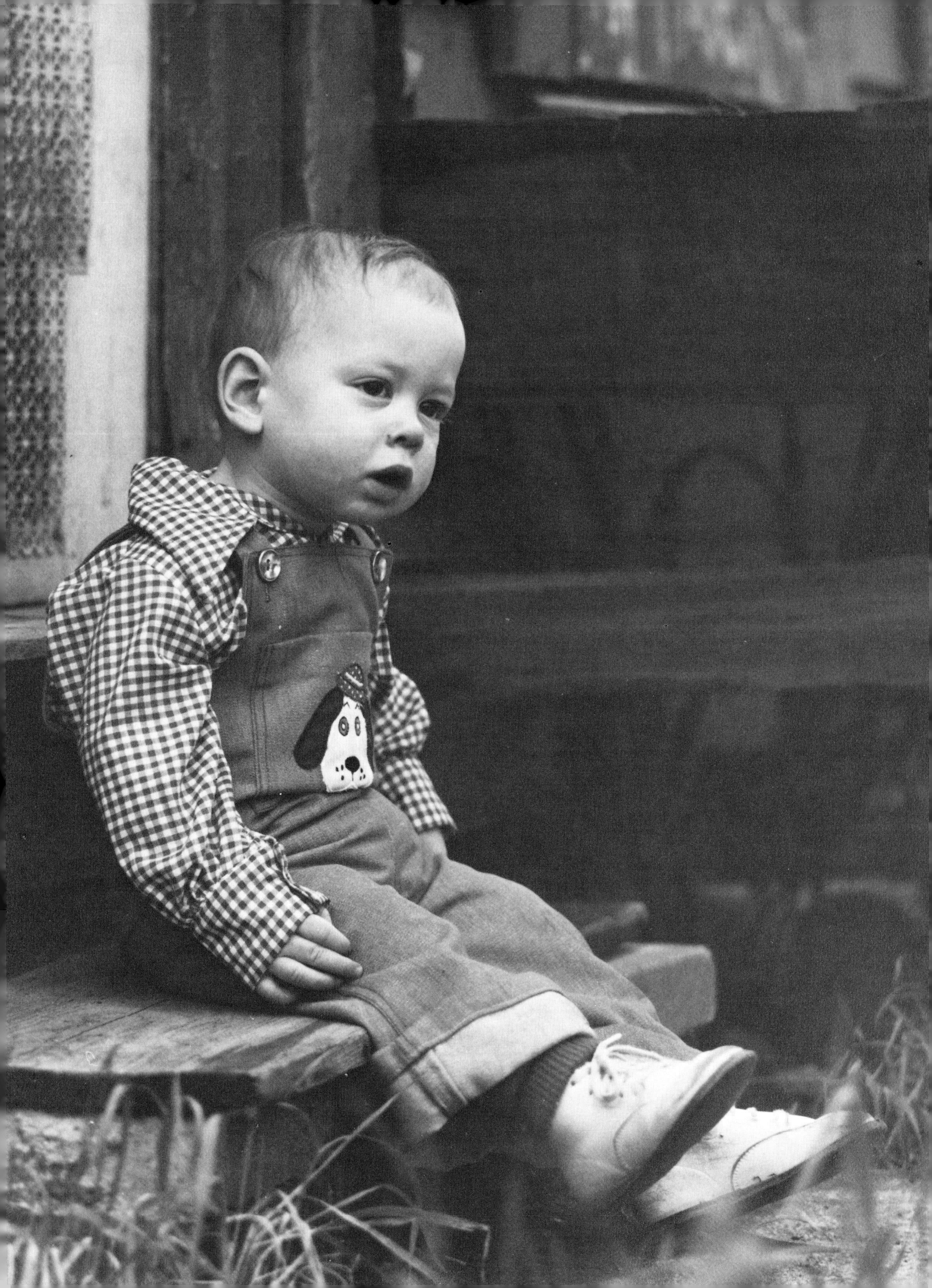

Soft light techniques, as discussed in Chapter 5, compliment the baby's soft features.

Babies grow fast, so shoot weekly.

Infants who have become mobile require a shutter speed of at least 1/125 and as small an aperture as possible for sharp photos.

In summary, there is no ultimately right or wrong way to photograph children. Many people only photograph on holidays or special occasions, but children change so quickly it is important to take photos every week. Be sure to date your images as your collection grows.

One interesting idea is to make a photographic growth record. Many years ago *Life* magazine found a family that had photographed a girl and her father at each of the girl's birthdays, from the first one until she was over twenty-years-old. The pose was always the same: full length, standing outdoors in the sun in bathing suits. To see the changes over the years was fascinating. The little girl grew into a woman as her father's hair turned grey. What a marvelous record of the growth and change of a family!

Look for tonal differences between your subject and the background. In this photo, the dark background helps make the subject stand out.

CHAPTER FIVE

LIGHT AND FAMILY PORTRAITS

The word *photography* means "writing with light," and to produce better photos, you need an understanding of the section of the electromagnetic spectrum known as light.

Light—photography's most important element

CHARACTERISTICS OF LIGHT

There are three characteristics of light that concern photographers: intensity, quality, and direction. Intensity is the brightness of the light, which must be high enough to record an exposure on the film. In addition, with high intensities you can use higher shutter speeds or smaller apertures to stop motion or to increase depth-of-field. Low intensities, of course, require wider apertures or slower shutter speeds, which decrease depth-of-field or blur action.

Light quality ranges from hard to soft. Hard light comes from such point sources as the sun, a photoflood bulb, or an electronic flash. Soft light comes from broad sources, such as the sky, light reflected from the ceiling of a room, or a northern window. The quality of light affects the feeling of a photo. Hard light is strong, intense, and sharply defined; soft light is calm, gentle, and quiet.

Shape and texture are revealed differently, depending on the direction of the light. When discussing light directions, direction refers to the position of the light in relation to the camera. Front light strikes the side of a subject facing the lens. Side light hits the subject at a 90° angle from the camera position. Back light comes from the far side of the subject.

PORTRAITS WITH CONTROLLED LIGHT

Taking portraits with controlled light is fun. You can adjust the light to create the effect you want. For light sources you can use photofloods or a flash. Household bulbs are not usually bright enough, but they can be used if you place them close to your subject and use a high-speed film.

The intense feeling of this portrait is aided by the contrast of the shadows and the hard light from the sun. Photograph by Karen Hapgood.

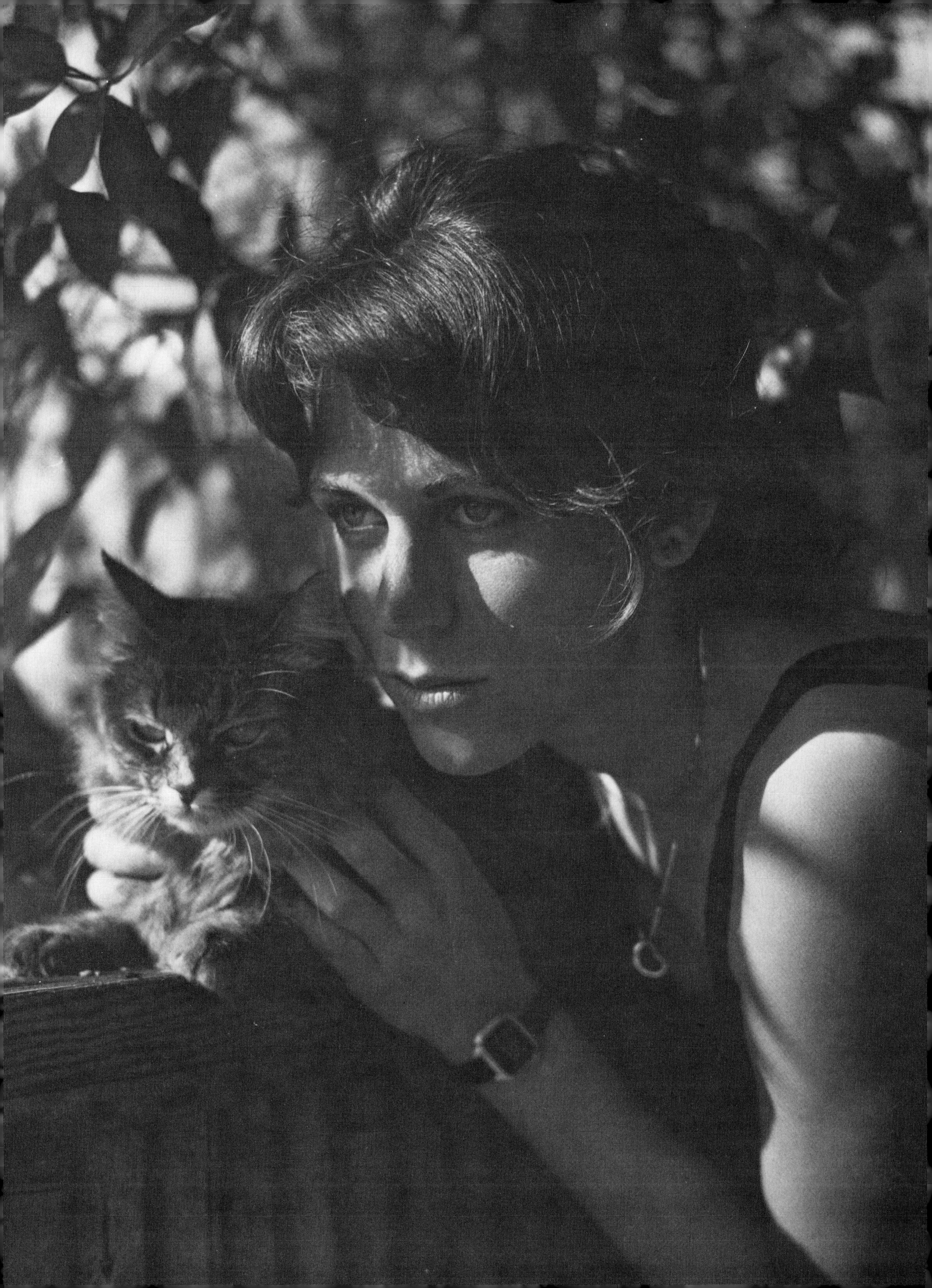

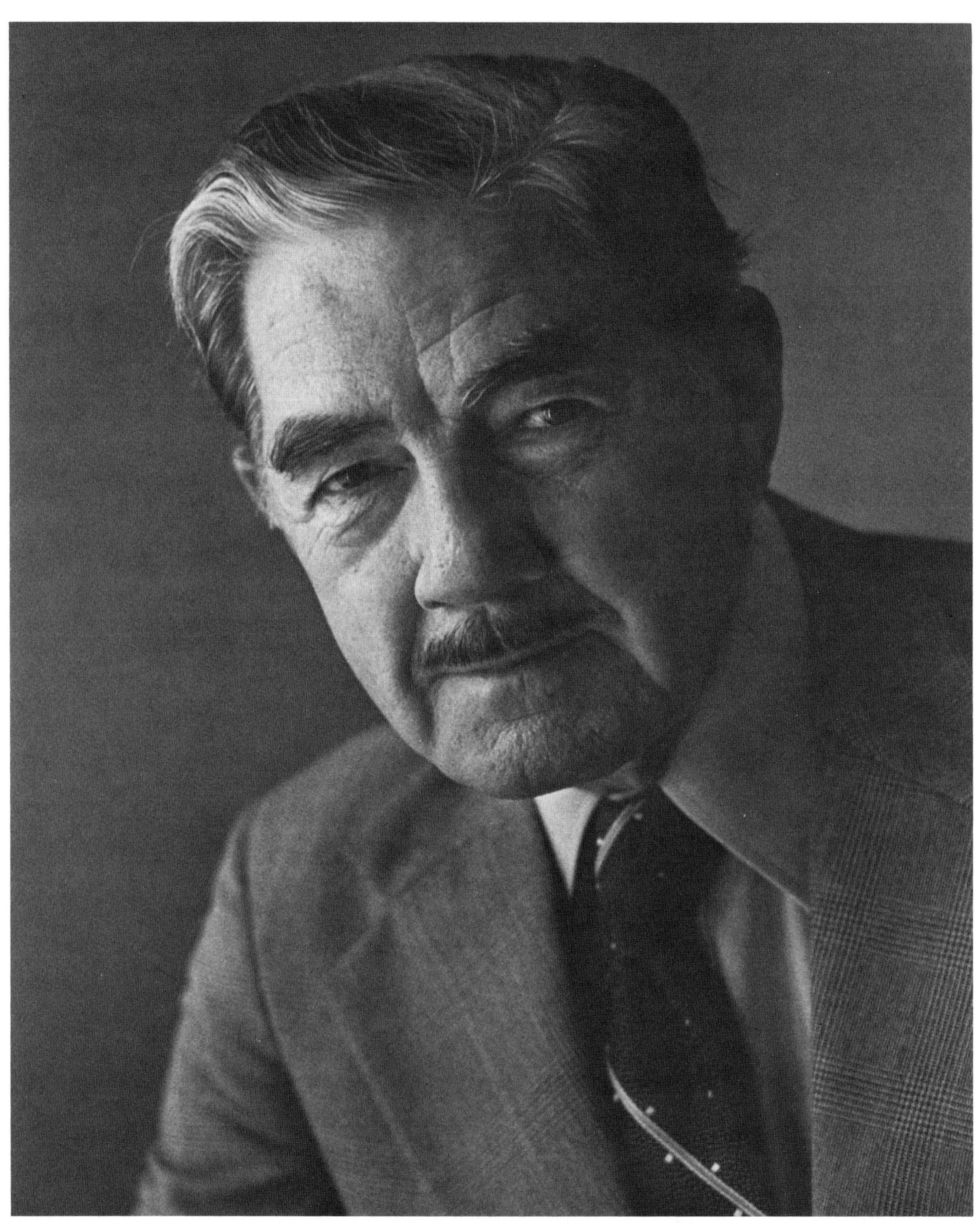

A window on the left provided the soft light for this portrait. The walls of the room reflected enough fill light into the dark side of the face to prevent it from being totally dark.

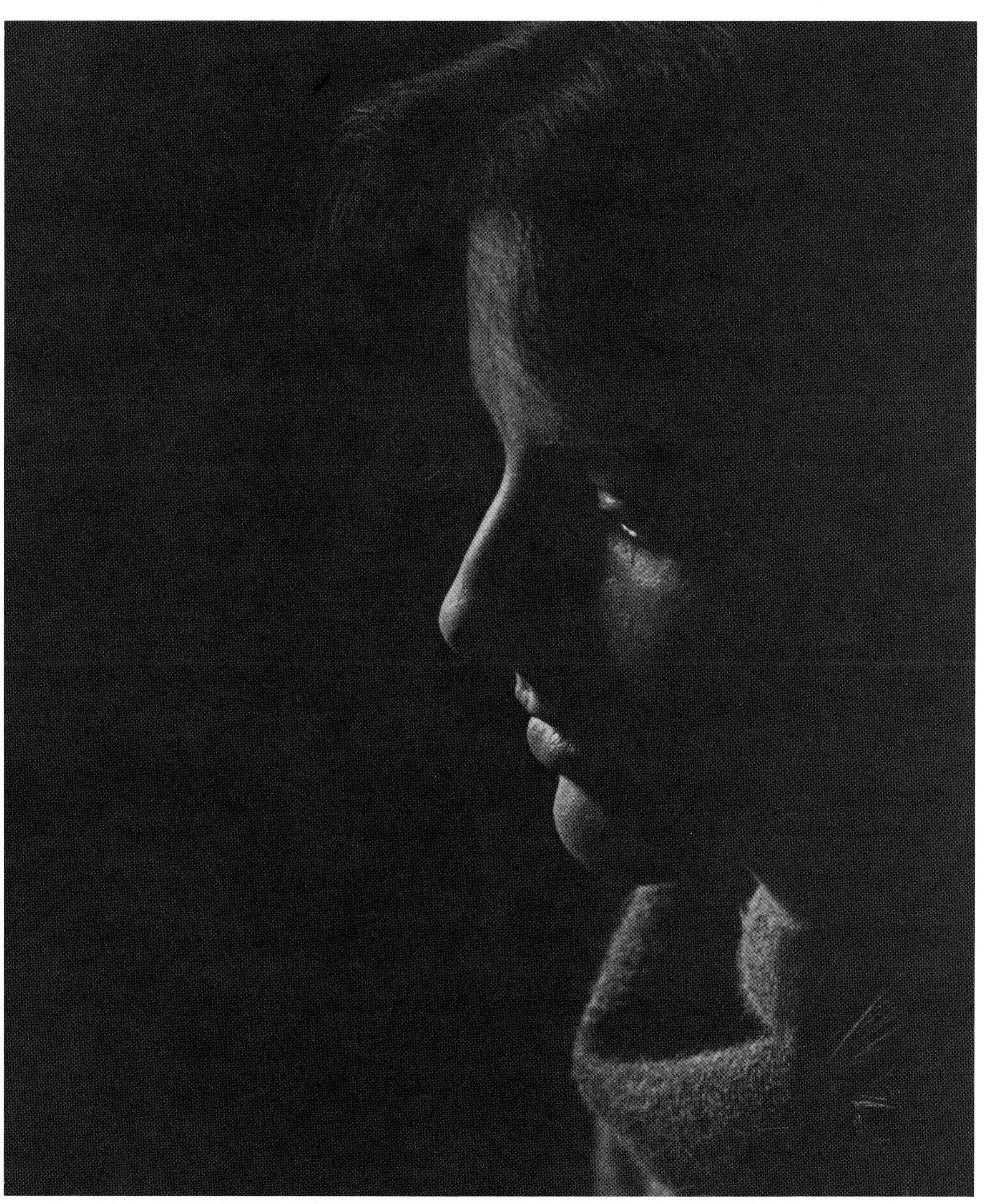

Sidelight that is slightly behind the subject is sometimes called Rembrandt lighting. *The photo was made against a black background with no fill light used.*

Floods vs. flash

There are two main advantages to photofloods. First, they are inexpensive. You can get a set of bulbs and reflectors for the price of one electronic flash unit. Second, you can see the effects of your lighting as you work. Photofloods do, however, create heat, which can make your subject uncomfortable.

Although flashbulbs are inexpensive, they must be replaced after each exposure, and this procedure often becomes tiresome. Electronic flash is bright, compact, and cool, but unless you devise a set of homemade modeling lights or use instant print films, you won't see the results of your lighting until you've developed the photos. Experience is one solution to this problem, and many photographers build skill by visualizing the effects.

Lighting the portrait

There are basically three types of lights used for portraits: main, fill, and accent lights. The main light is the one that appears to be doing the lighting. Outdoors on a sunny day, the sun would be the main light. On a cloudy day the main light would come from the sky. Indoors by a window the main light would come from the window.

The fill light is the one that illuminates shadows. There is almost always a certain amount of fill light, even in the darkest scenes. Outdoors on a sunny day fill light is reflected from the sky, the buildings, and the ground. When taking an indoor photo by window light, the fill would be reflected into the shadows by the walls and objects in the room.

Frequently you will want to add fill light to increase the amount of shadow detail in the finished photo. Electronic flash is handy for this purpose, and it will be discussed shortly. But you can also make a simple fill-light reflector by holding or propping up a piece of white poster board, which will reflect main light into the shadows.

Accent lights are usually used only in controlled situations. Such lights are used to highlight specific areas.

How to adjust portrait lighting

When setting up for portraits, you will have better lighting results if you always follow these procedures:

Turn off or block out all extraneous light that could interfere with your controlled lighting plan.

Set the main light. Determine the height, angle, and quality you want. Remember, light should come from above the subject. Don't make the common mistake of placing the light at your subject's eye level or below. This will cause unnatural shadows.

Set the fill light so it sheds light into the shadows the camera sees. Don't worry about shadows out of view of your lens. Adjust the level of the fill light for the effect you desire.

Set the accent light. Frequently this is a small light placed above and behind your subject to accent the hair and to provide background separation.

When making close-up portraits, don't allow your subject to slouch, particularly if he or she is sitting on a stool or in a chair. Watch out for shadows on the background near the person's head. If they occur, increase the distance between the subject and the background.

An angled pose is more complimentary than a straight-on shot, which often looks as if it belongs on a WANTED poster.

One thing you'll notice as you work with portrait lighting is that film doesn't record an image in quite the same way as it appears to the eye. Shadows may photograph with less detail than you thought. This is because film doesn't have the same brightness range as an eye. Nor is there a brain built into the film to interpret and modify visual input.

The experienced photographer has learned to see as the film sees. And as you work with controlled lighting, you, too, will build skill in visualizing the effects of light on film.

PORTRAITS WITH NATURAL LIGHT

You will undoubtedly take many portraits with natural light. With modern high-speed films, the natural light of a scene is often quite sufficient for photography. It works well with children and candid situations, since people are more comfortable with natural light than with hot photofloods and flashing bulbs. Natural light also makes it easier for your subject to forget about the camera. Plus, it requires no batteries, no recycle times, and no extra equipment.

Using natural light outdoors

Outdoors your first encounter with natural light will probably be with the direct rays from the sun. Before fast films and auto-exposure cameras, photographers were well-advised to keep the sun at their backs. However, this method is not only outdated, but it frequently spoils the pleasant feelings photographers want to capture. It also forces your subject to look directly into the sun. This will make him or her squint, and the results hardly compliment a person's features.

To solve this problem, turn your subject at an angle to the sun, or even put the sun behind the subject. Such backlighting can produce a nice effect. When doing close-ups with this type of light, you may need to fill in the shadows. This can easily be done with a flash, as you will learn at the end of this chapter.

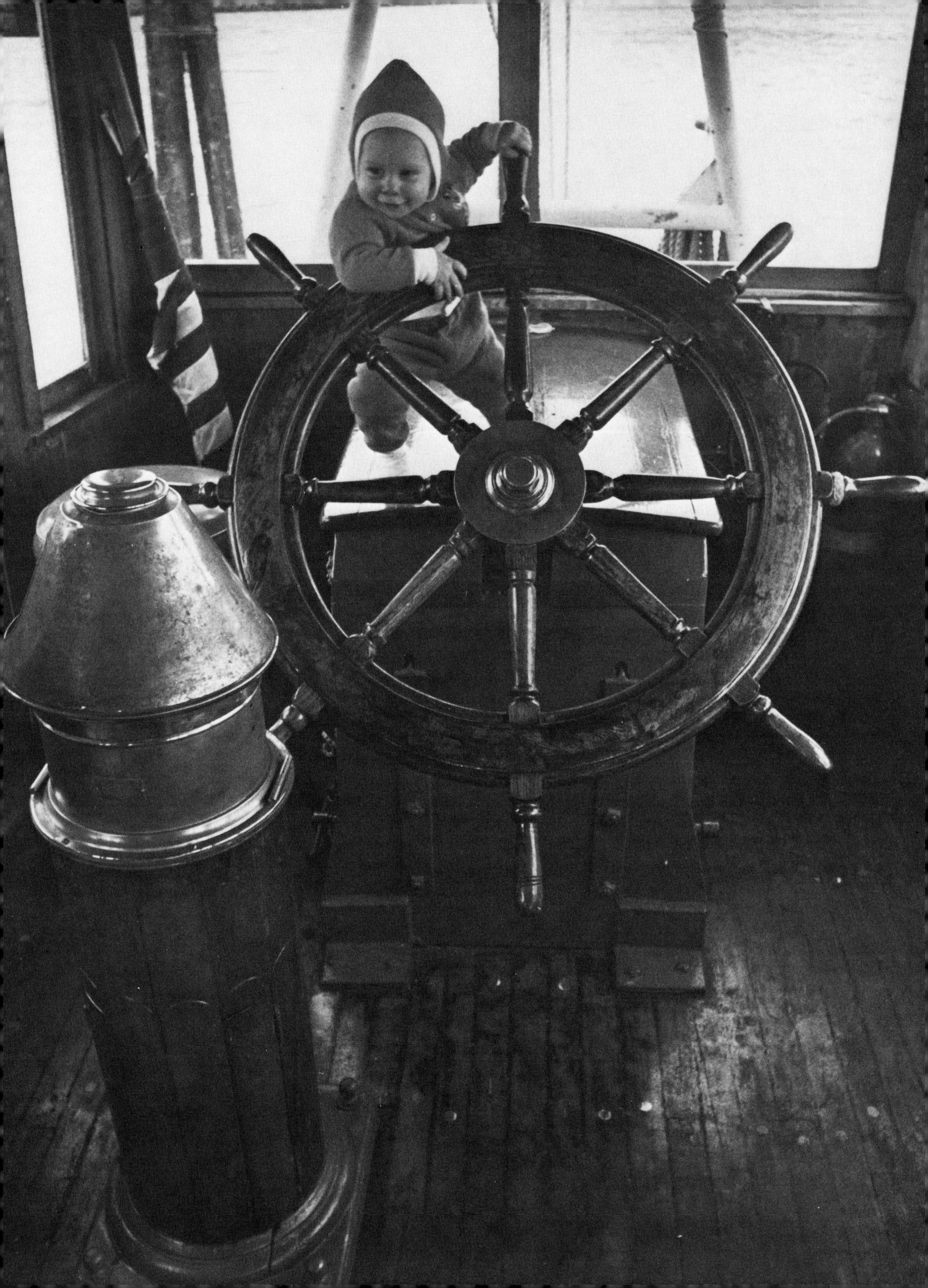

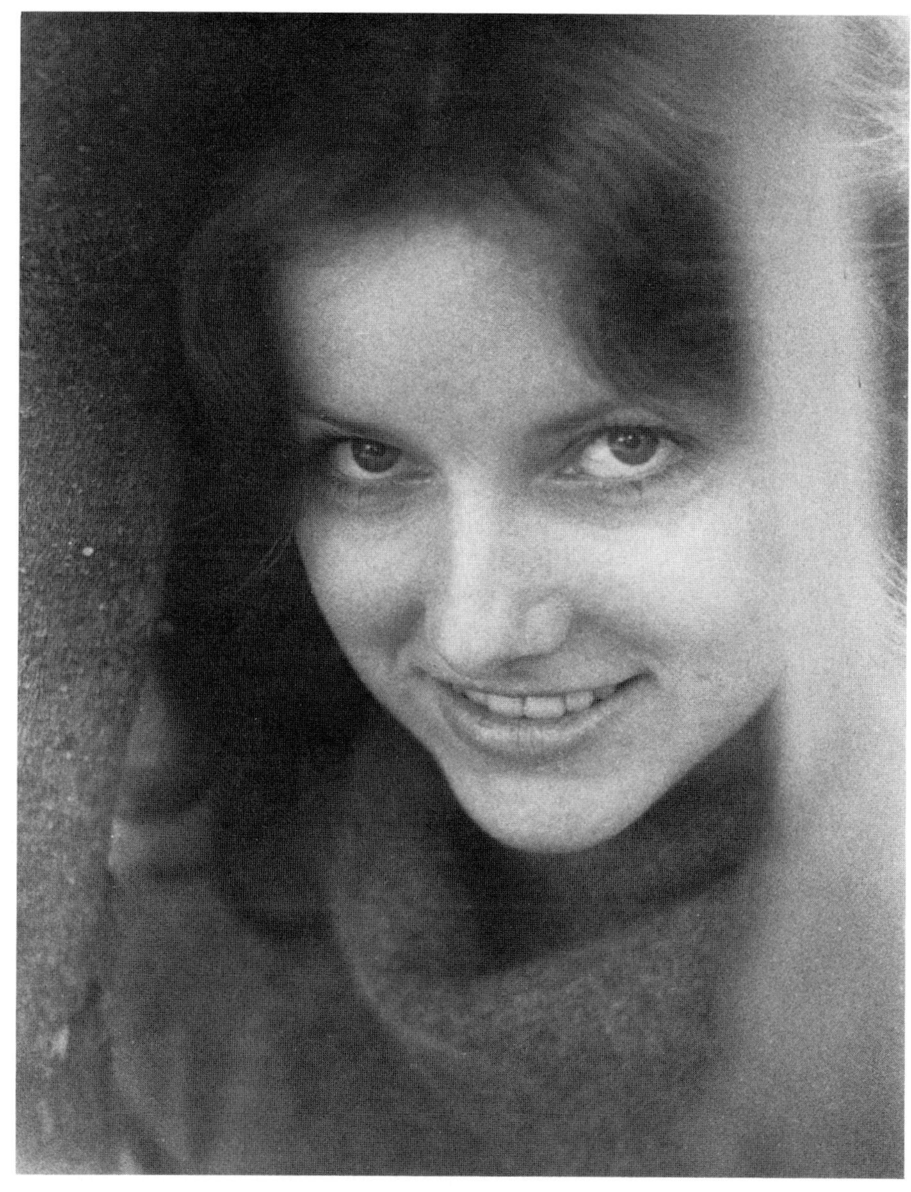

This outdoor portrait was made in open shade through a soft-focus filter. You can make your own soft-focus filter by coating an old skylight filter with clear nail polish.

Opposite page: *Available light works well for candid shots because your subject can be more comfortable than under hot photofloods or flashing strobes.*

Shade

Another way to avoid the harsh, direct rays of the sun is to move into the shade. Under a tall tree or at the north side of a building are good places for portraiture. But remember that the intensity of the light can drop quickly in dense shade, so be sure you take careful meter readings and adjust your camera settings as necessary.

When working in the shade, you may find that your scene includes a bright, sunny background. This bright background can fool your light meter. Therefore, to avoid an incorrect exposure, move in close to your subject for the meter reading. Then set your camera and move back to compose your photo. Be sure your camera's auto-exposure system is disengaged after you've set the camera to prevent the meter from changing the exposure.

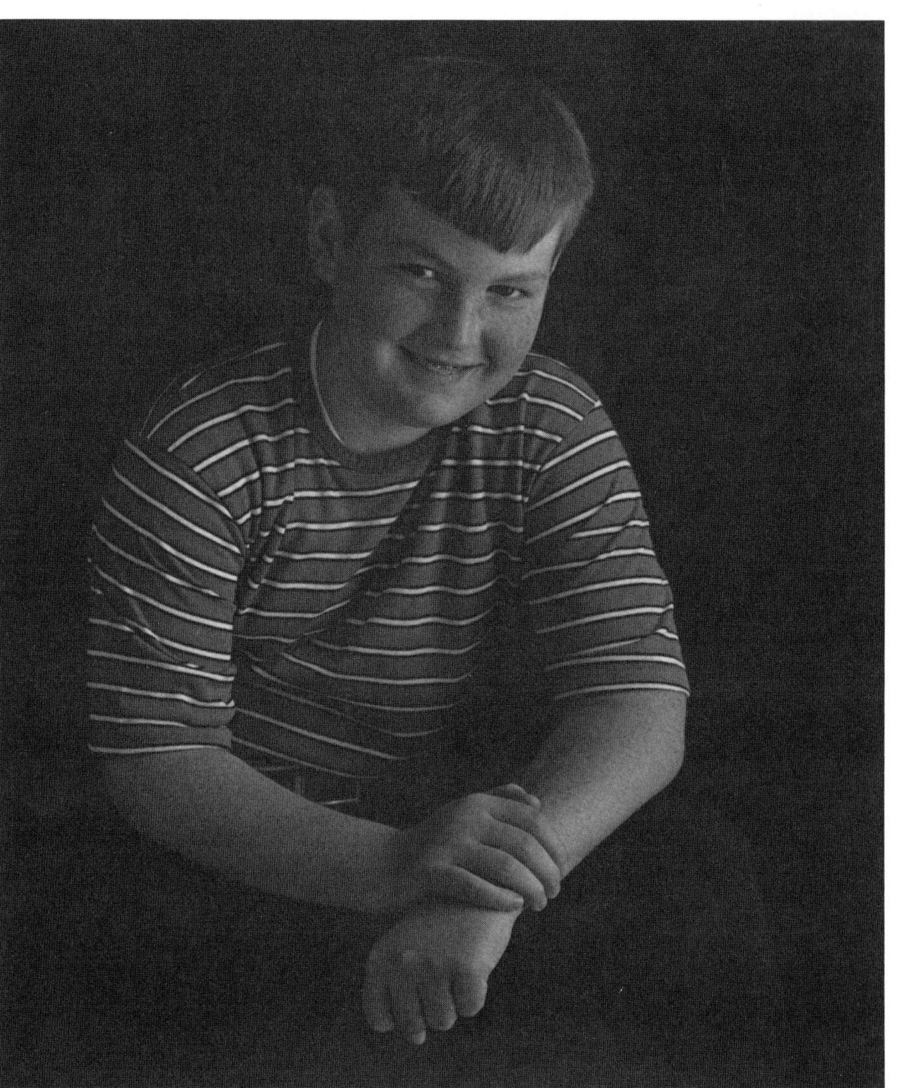

This portrait, made at a family reunion, was lit by diffused light coming through textured glass in a window. A white table cloth was used on the left to reflect a little light into the shadows.

Opposite page: *Unfortunately, many people put their cameras away on cloudy days. But this soft light is excellent for portraiture. Photograph by Joe Norton.*

Hazy, cloudy, and inclement weather

In the earliest days of photography, practitioners put their gear away when the sun wasn't shining. They needed the sun's strong rays because they were working with weak emulsions. Today, however, nonsunny days can be exciting. The light is very kind to people's faces, and colors take on new subtleties. Many moods await the sensitive photographer. Don't give up when the sun doesn't shine.

Using natural light indoors

Indoors, natural light comes from two sources: daylight through the windows and light from the room's light fixtures. The window light produced by indirect rays from the sky is marvelous portrait light. It is soft yet directional. It emphasizes the three-dimensional quality of your subject, is kind to human features, and often creates a warm, friendly feeling. There are several examples of window-light portraits in this chapter to illustrate the qualities of this light.

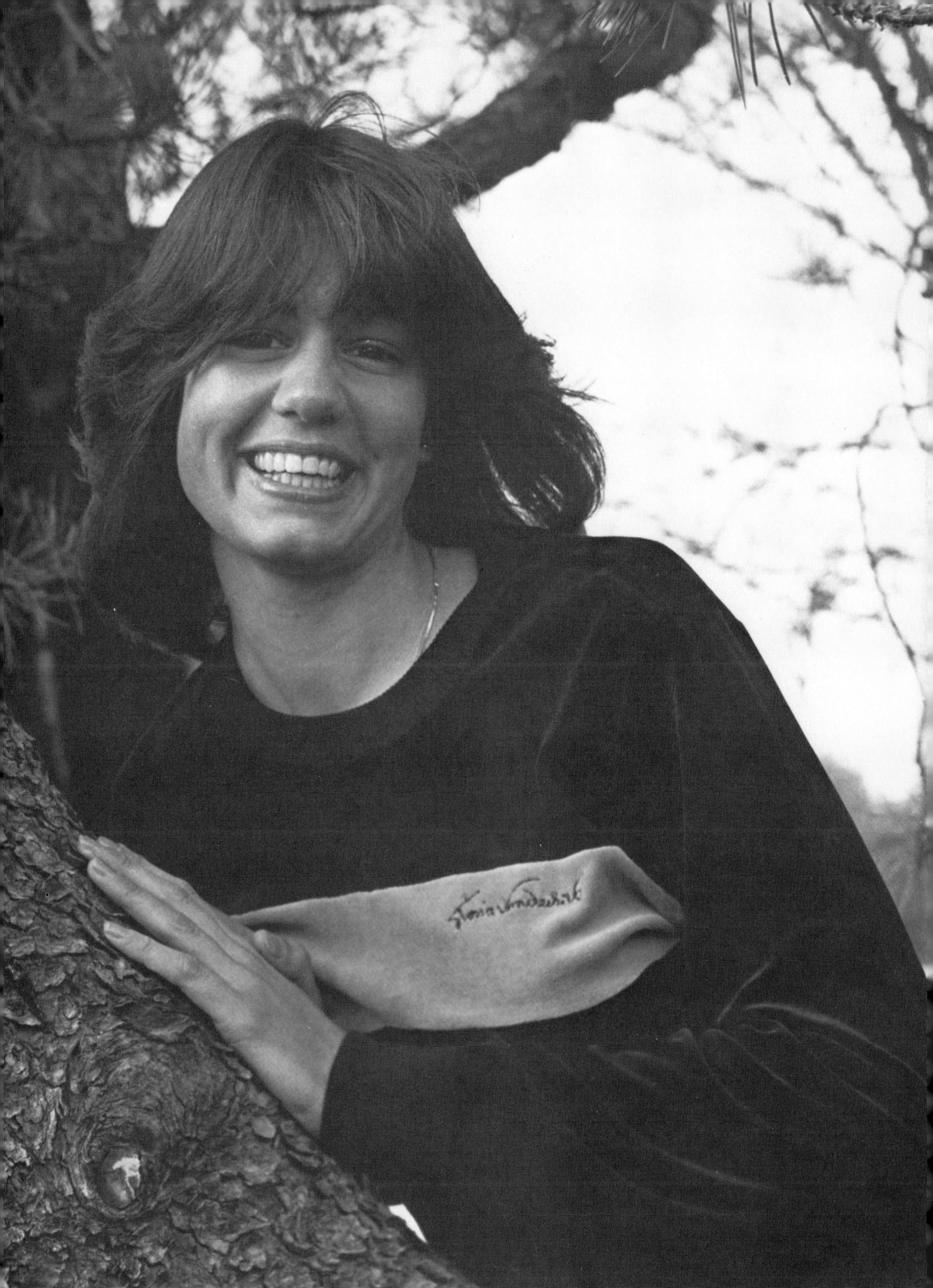

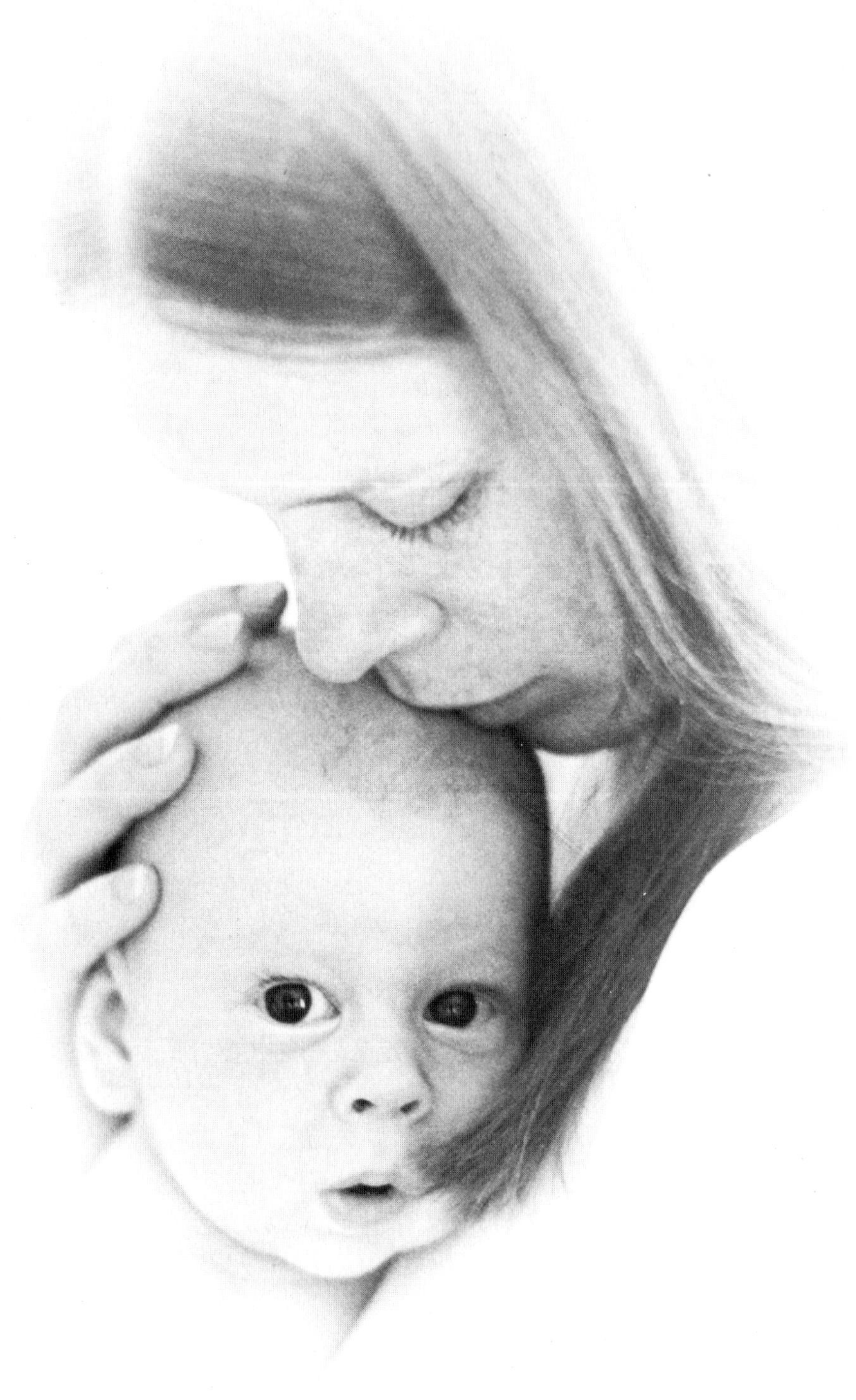

This portrait was made in front of a white wall. The light was soft daylight bouncing around a sunlit room, and the negative was printed as a vignette.

The artificial light from a room's light fixtures is usually too dim for even the fastest films. You can solve this difficulty by replacing the bulbs with brighter ones or with photofloods. But check first, making sure the fixtures can withstand the increased heat.

LIGHT AND COLOR

You may have noticed in some photos that colors don't always look correct. Although everything looked just fine when you made the photos, some indoor shots may have turned out yellow, or some outdoor shots made late in the day may have yellow highlights and blue shadows.

Because the information gathered by your eyes is interpreted by your brain, colors are corrected to what they should look like. Film, however, doesn't make such automatic adjustments. The light from your dining-room lamps looks yellow to the film because it is yellow. In photos, fluorescent lights make things look green because, compared with daylight, the light is green.

Though the use of technically "incorrect" film and light combinations can be creative, accurate color rendition requires an awareness of light sources and how to correct them.

Tungsten sources are those from photofloods and regular household light bulbs. This light seems yellow when compared with daylight. To avoid this yellow color shift, use film designed for tungsten illumination or place an 80B filter over your lens. This filter will remove excess yellow if you are using daylight-balanced films. Another solution is to put blue photofloods into your light fixtures.

When using daylight film under fluorescent light, you should use a FLD filter. When you use tungsten film under fluorescent light, you should use a FLB filter. These filters correct the greenish cast that fluorescent light gives off. In Chapter 7 we will discuss the exposure corrections necessary for filters.

HOW TO USE AN ELECTRONIC FLASH

Many family photos require more light than that available in the scene, and an electronic flash (EF) will add this light.

Exposure

Almost all EFs made today have automatic exposure control. These units measure their own output as light is reflected by the subject. They then cut off that light when the proper level has been reached. To use the typical auto-EF, you must set the exposure-control dial on the unit for the film speed you are using. The dial will then indicate the f/stop to use (or perhaps a choice of f/stops). After that the flash does the rest. Be sure to check the instructions for your particular unit, as there are many variations.

Using a single flash

The most common technique for using a single EF unit is to attach it to the camera. Although this is useful for "grab shots" it does not produce the best results. This is because the light is aimed directly at the subject. Often called flat light, flashes can be unflattering. They can hide the three-dimensional qualities of a subject. Therefore one of the first rules of flash photography is to separate the flash from the camera when possible.

To use a flash detached from a camera (known as off-camera flash), you may have to purchase a PC cord which will connect the unit to the camera's synchronization terminals. For dedicated flash systems, in which the flash is synchronized with the camera's electronic exposure system, there are special cords that maintain the important flash-to-camera connections.

Bounce flash

An effective flash technique, which can be used with most units mounted to the camera, is called bounce flash. By aiming the flash at a broad, light-colored surface, an even, soft light is reflected back to the subject. You can bounce a flash off the ceiling or a wall and the effects are similar to those of natural light.

If your EF has a positionable lamphead or removable sensor, getting the correct exposure is easy with bounce flash.

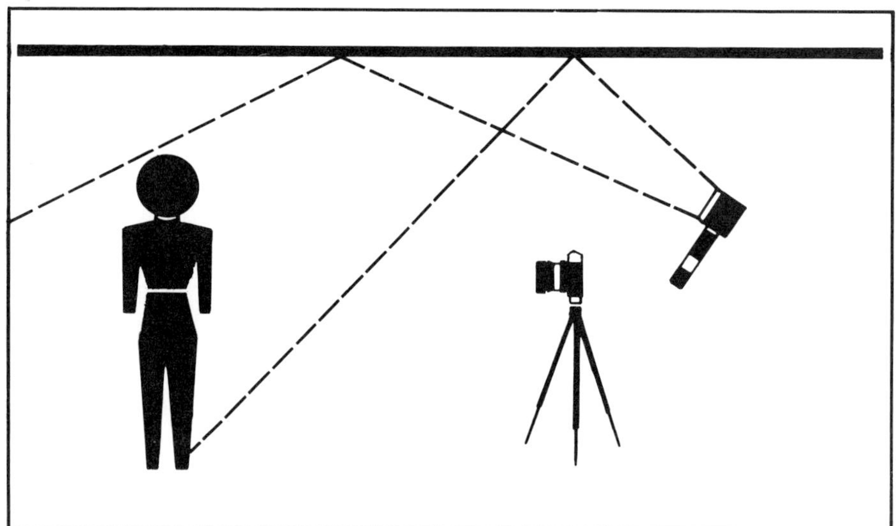

Left: *This illustration shows how to use bounce flash. When using bounce flash, be sure the ceiling is a light color. Dark or high ceilings usually do not reflect enough light. When shooting color film, the ceiling must be pure white, otherwise it will lend a colored cast to the bounced light and the resultant picture.*

Right: *This photo was made with a flash held off to the right side of the camera.*

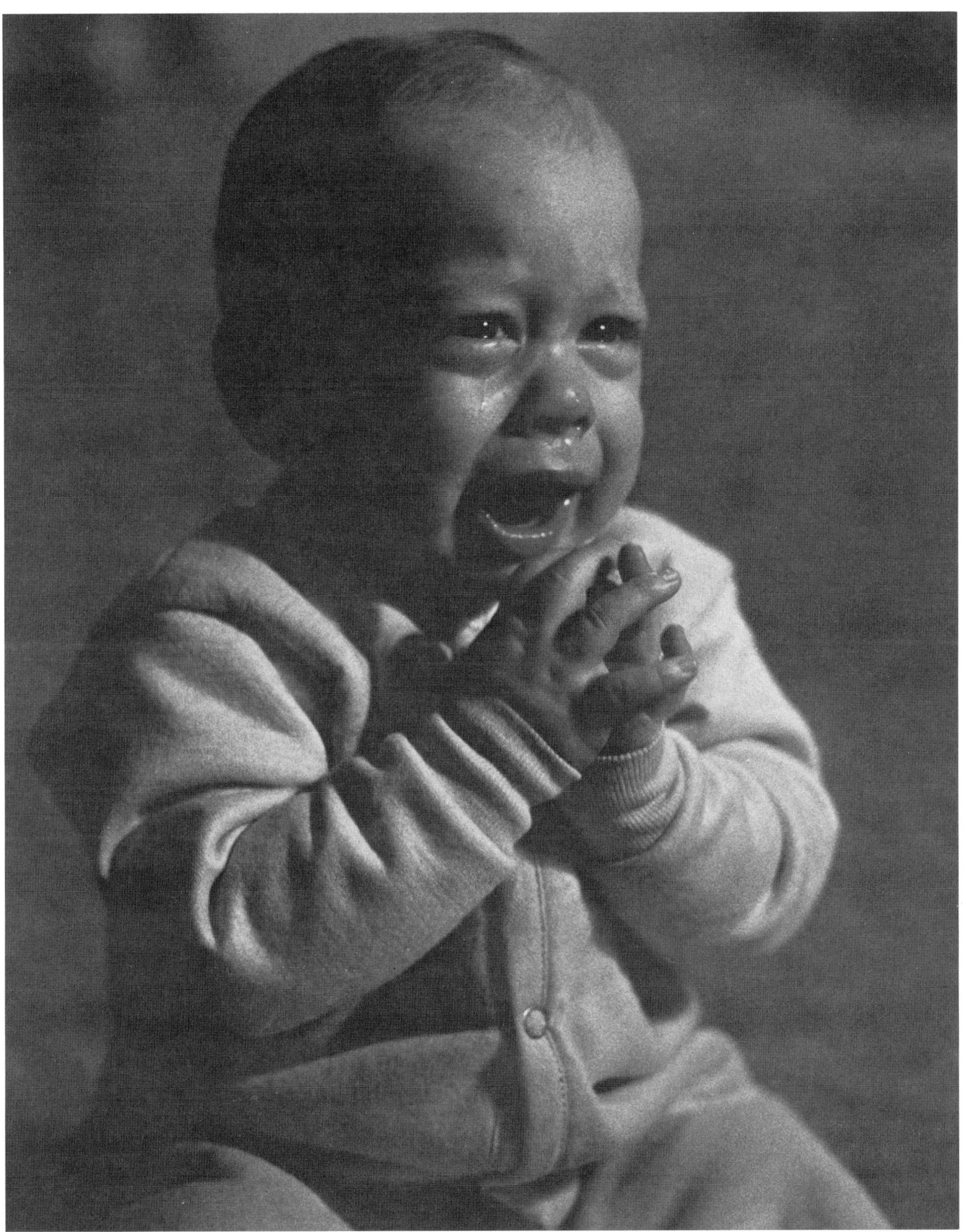

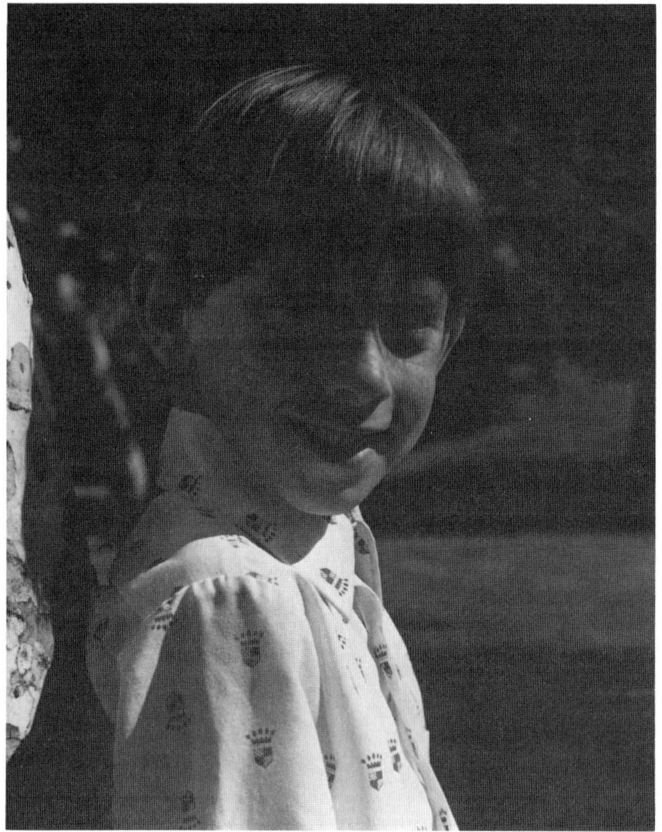

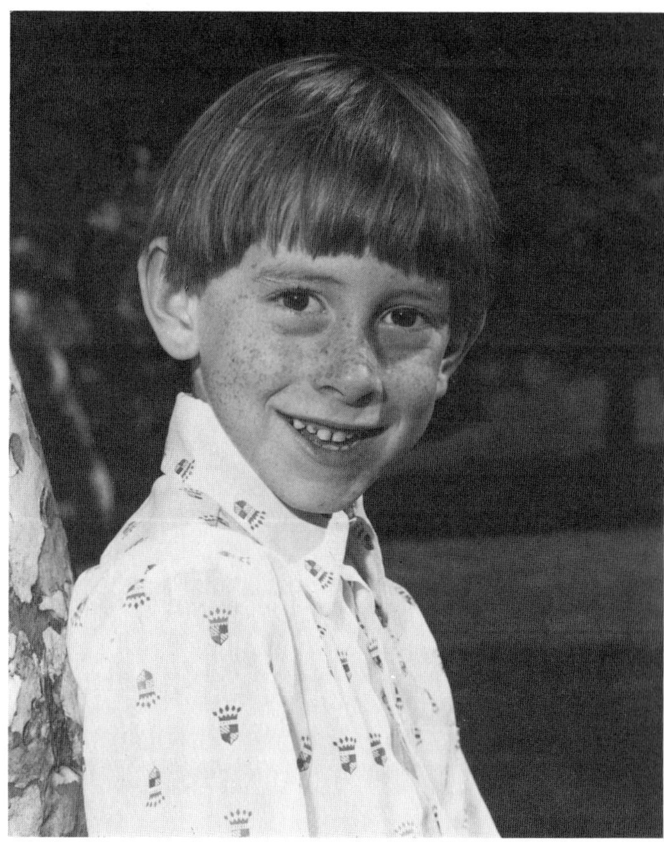

Above left: *This photo was made without any fill-in flash, the left side of the boy's face is lost in shadow.*

Above right: *Here the flash was set for an excessive amount of fill and the natural-light quality is lost. The shirt appears overexposed, and the subtle change from highlight to shadow across the subject's face is completely lost. The electronic flash was set to equal the sunlight exposure.*

Simply aim the sensor at your subject and the flash lamp at the wall or ceiling. If the sensor and the lamp can't be aimed independently, you can calculate the bounce flash exposure by doing the following:

Aim the flash for bounce and set the exposure control on manual.

Estimate the distance from the flash to the bounce surface and back to your subject.

Set the exposure-calculator dial for the above estimated distance.

Read the aperture setting from the exposure-calculator dial and set the lens aperture two stops wider. This increased exposure will compensate for the light the reflecting surface absorbs.

(Note: If you are using an advanced integrated system that meters flash exposure from within the camera, this procedure may be unnecessary. Check your camera's instruction manual.)

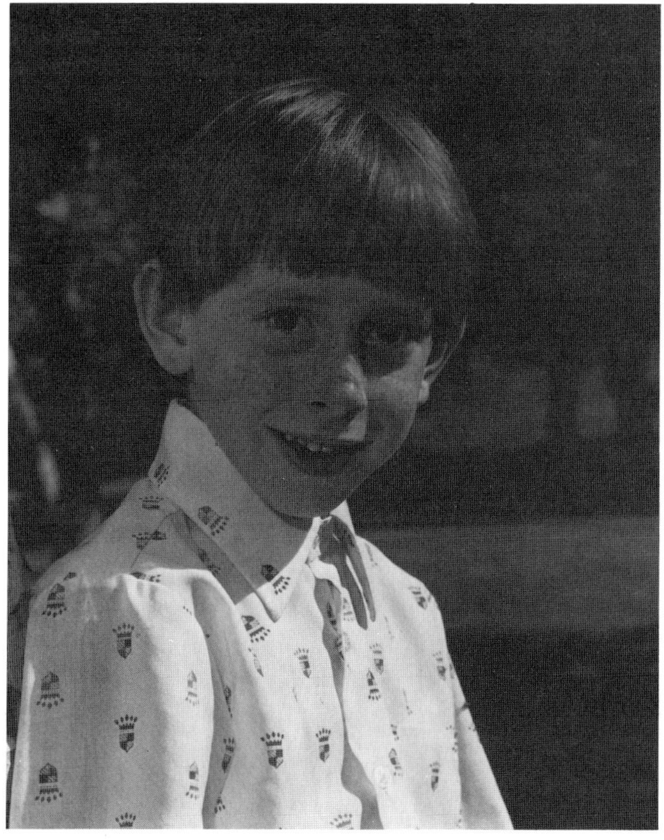

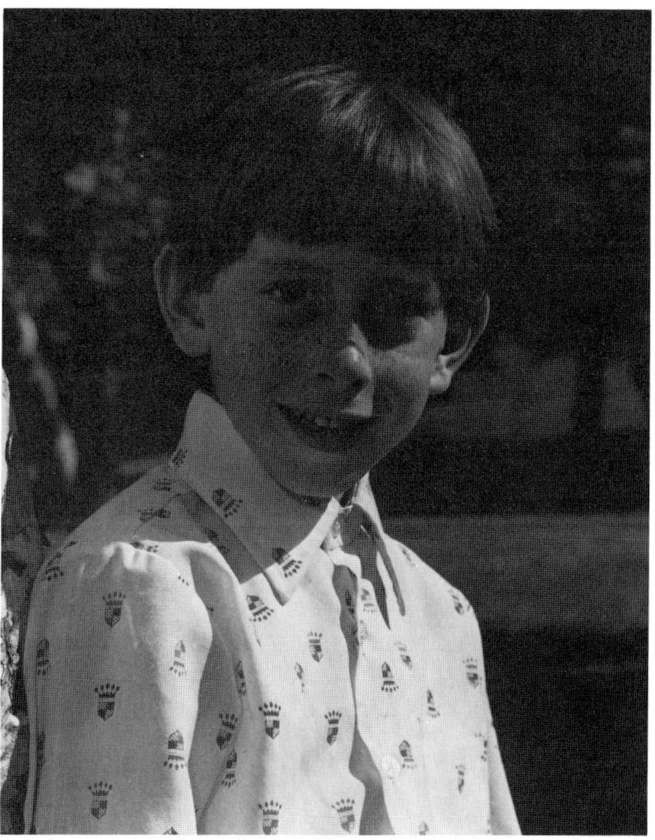

Above left and right: *These two photos show a correct use of flash fill. The shadows are lightened, but the effect of daylight has not been destroyed. In the photo on the left, the flash was set for a 2:1 ratio, and in the photo to the right, the ratio was 3:1. The correct ratio is a matter of taste and intended use.*

Multiple flash

With a little practice electronic flash can be used for such multiple-light setups as portraiture. A detailed discussion of techniques can be found in the *Amphoto Guide to Lighting*.

Two or three auto-flash units can be combined for a very effective portrait system, and their auto-exposure features will greatly simplify your projects.

Using a flash in sunshine

On a sunny day a typical scene will have bright highlights where the sun strikes the subject. But in most circumstances, the shadows will be quite dark. These differences may not be apparent to your eye, however, because human vision often compensates for such variations in brightness.

Since film cannot make interpretative corrections, a photo made under this type of lighting may contain shadows devoid of detail. To correct this problem in close-ups, an electronic flash can be used to add light to the shadows. (The above illustrations show examples of this problem and some possible solutions.)

Listed below are techniques for using a flash as a fill-in light:

Set the shutter for the speed you'd use for a flash.

Check the exposure indicators in the viewfinder to be sure the settings will not result in overexposure.

Attach the flash to the camera; set its exposure control for an f/stop two stops wider than the f/stop the lens will use.

Make your exposures.

This method works because the flash thinks you are using a wider aperture than you really are. Therefore, it puts out less light than is needed for a flash-only exposure. Two stops less is just about right for fill-in flash. You should experiment with flash settings to find the one that pleases you.

If the exposure indicators in the viewfinder signal an overexposure, you can either place a neutral-density filter over the lens or use a slower speed film.

Mistakes with flash

Although an electronic flash is easy to use, it is also easy to make mistakes with this instrument. One of the most common mistakes is using the wrong exposure. Be sure your auto-EF is set for the proper film speed. Also remember that light falls off quickly, so don't expect your flash to carry for more than about 15 feet.

Listed below are points you should remember when using a flash:

Be sure the batteries are strong.

Check flash-to-camera connections.

Clean the battery and flash-connector terminals with a pencil eraser.

Ensure that the auto-flash units have been set for the proper film speed.

Ensure that the camera's shutter speed has been set for flash.

Be sure you stay within the distance range of your flash unit.

TEN TIPS FOR BETTER PORTRAITS

Portraits are a rewarding part of family photography. Whether candid or formal, they help us hold onto the brief moments in our family's history.

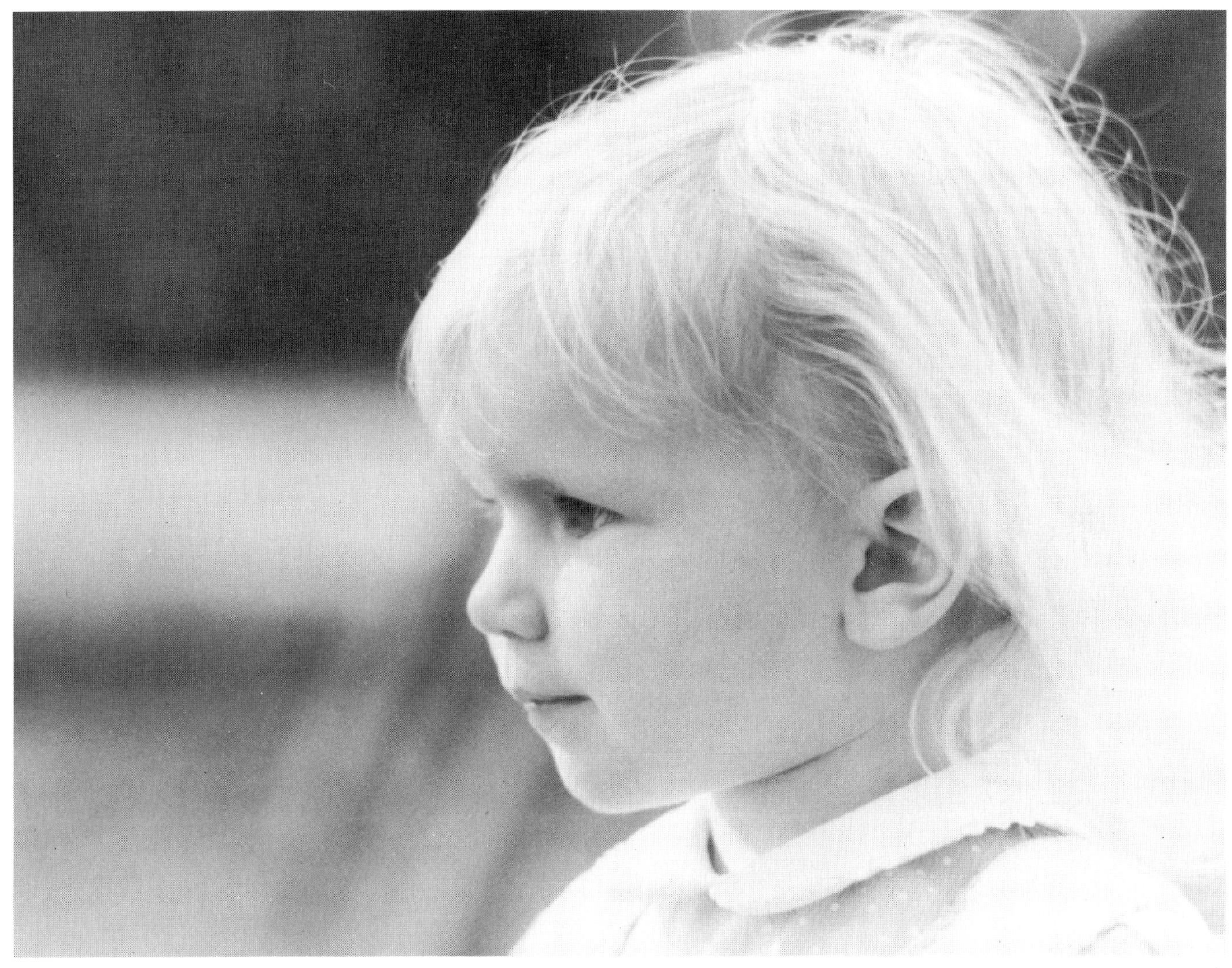

Listed below are ten tips for taking better family portraits:

Be ready

Work quickly

Have fun

Give praise

Have short sessions with breaks

Know when to quit

Avoid bull's-eye vision

Move in close

Include serious, thoughtful expressions

Don't press your family's patience. Use a mannequin or doll for lighting and camera tests and experiments.

CHAPTER SIX

SPECIAL OCCASIONS

Taking special photos of special occasions

The family events most frequently photographed are special occasions—weddings, parties, holidays, and reunions. These are times when the camera is as much a part of the festivities as the refreshments. Only the photos remain long after the food has disappeared.

One frequent challenge on such special occasions is when the photographer must also be host or hostess, maid, butler, cook, bartender, *and* photographer. Needless to say, when this happens the camera is frequently pushed aside for other business. So try to avoid giving yourself too many roles at the event. Delegate responsibility, not only so you can enjoy the event, but so you can take photos without too many distractions.

Also, be wary of the perfect-picture attitude. Don't become so concerned with technical details that you overlook important picture opportunities. Try for the best, but don't refrain from taking photos just because they might be slightly flawed.

USE TWO APPROACHES

Shoot both candid and posed photos. Candid photos capture the spontaneous flavor of an event, while posed photos allow you to show relationships and specific situations. When shooting candids, work quickly, move in close, and anticipate what is about to happen.

By the way, don't leave yourself out of the photos. A family photo collection is not complete if an important person is missing. Get other people to take some photos for you. And if they don't understand photography, just set the camera for them and show them how to release the shutter.

Furthermore, don't forget to round out your coverage with photos of the little things that may not be attracting everyone's attention. Look for quiet moods—children who have fallen asleep in a corner and older people who may have withdrawn from the high-energy events.

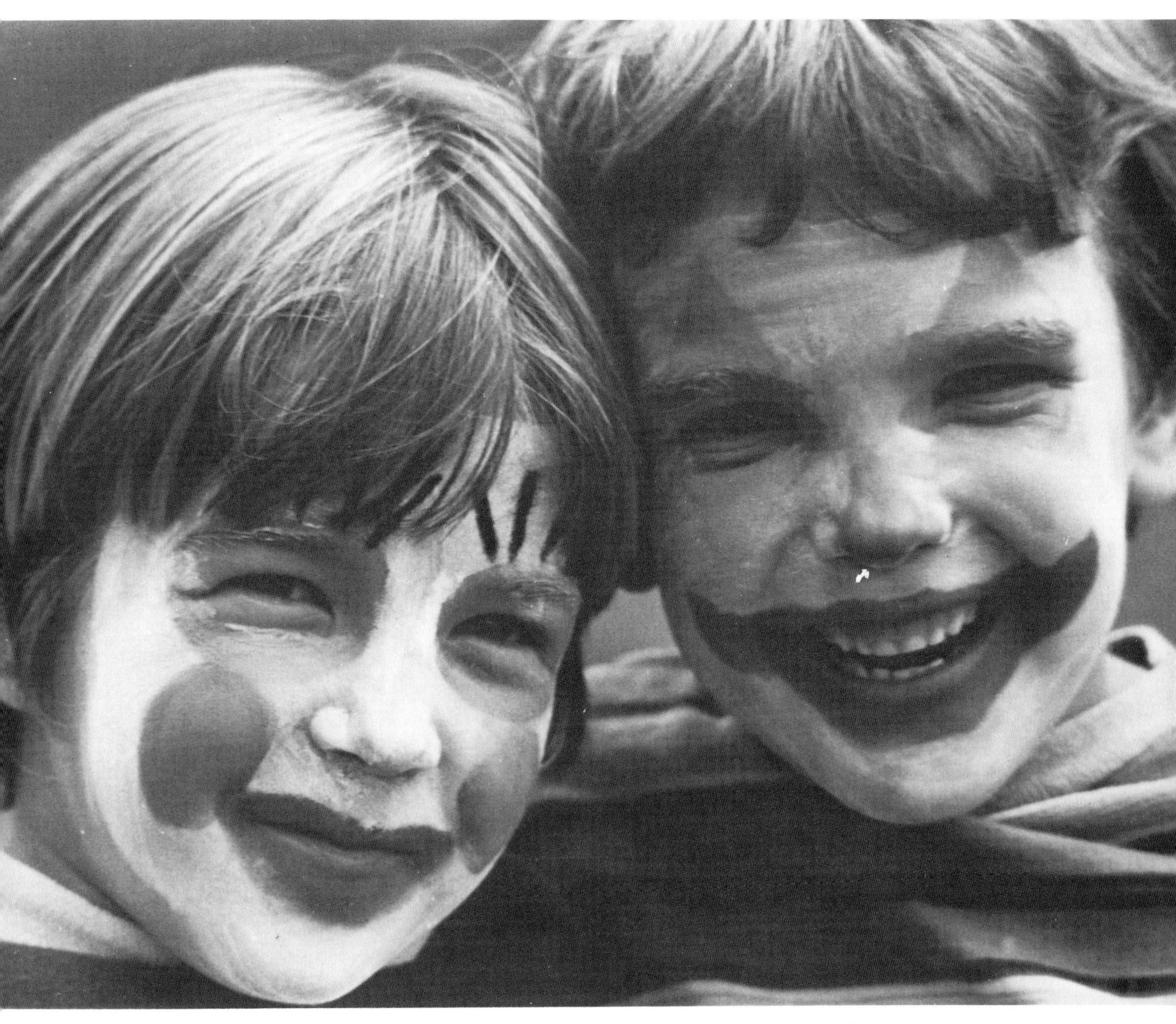

When you want to make a close-up portrait of two people in costume, have them put their heads together like this. Photograph by Audrey Vittitoe.

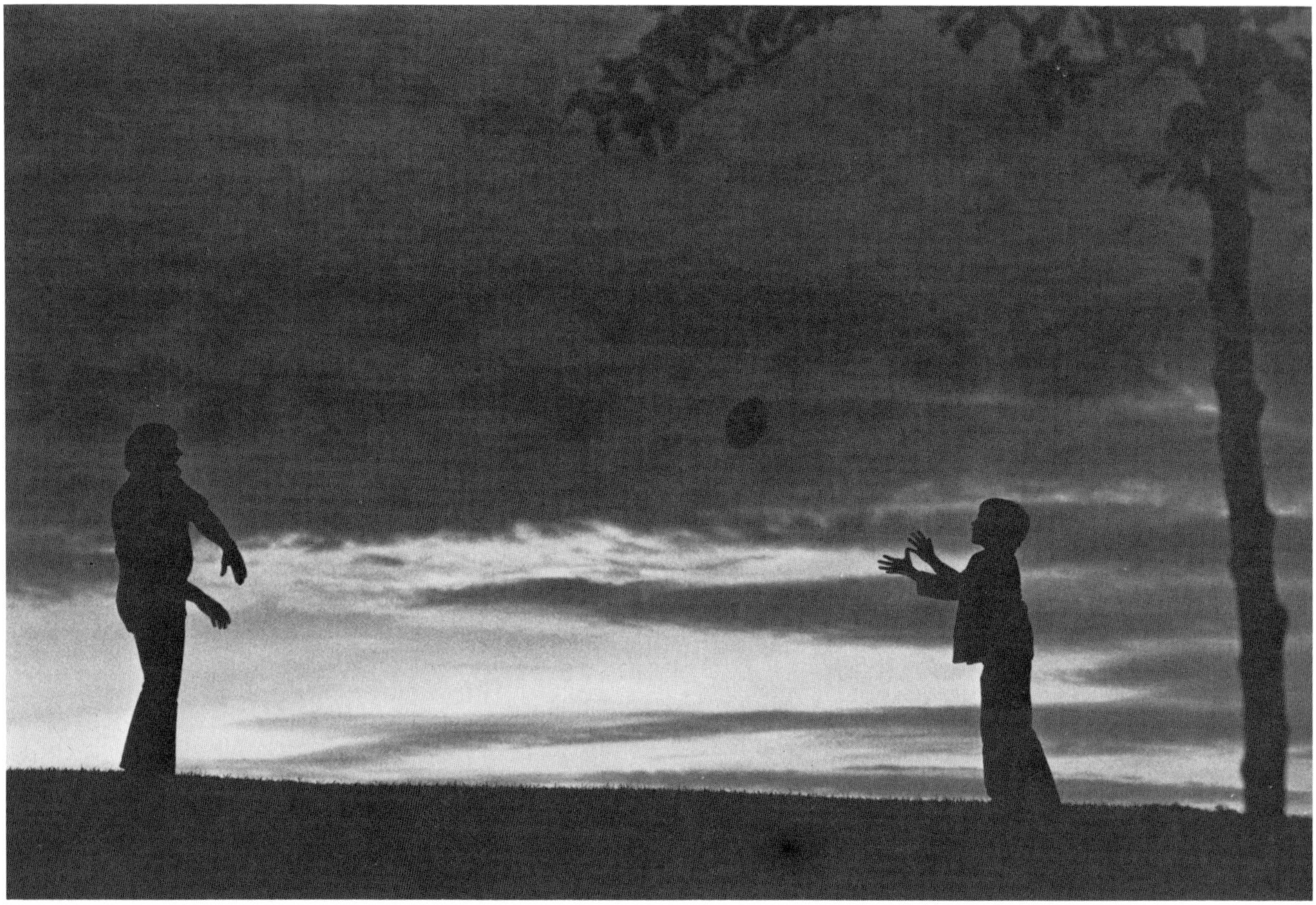

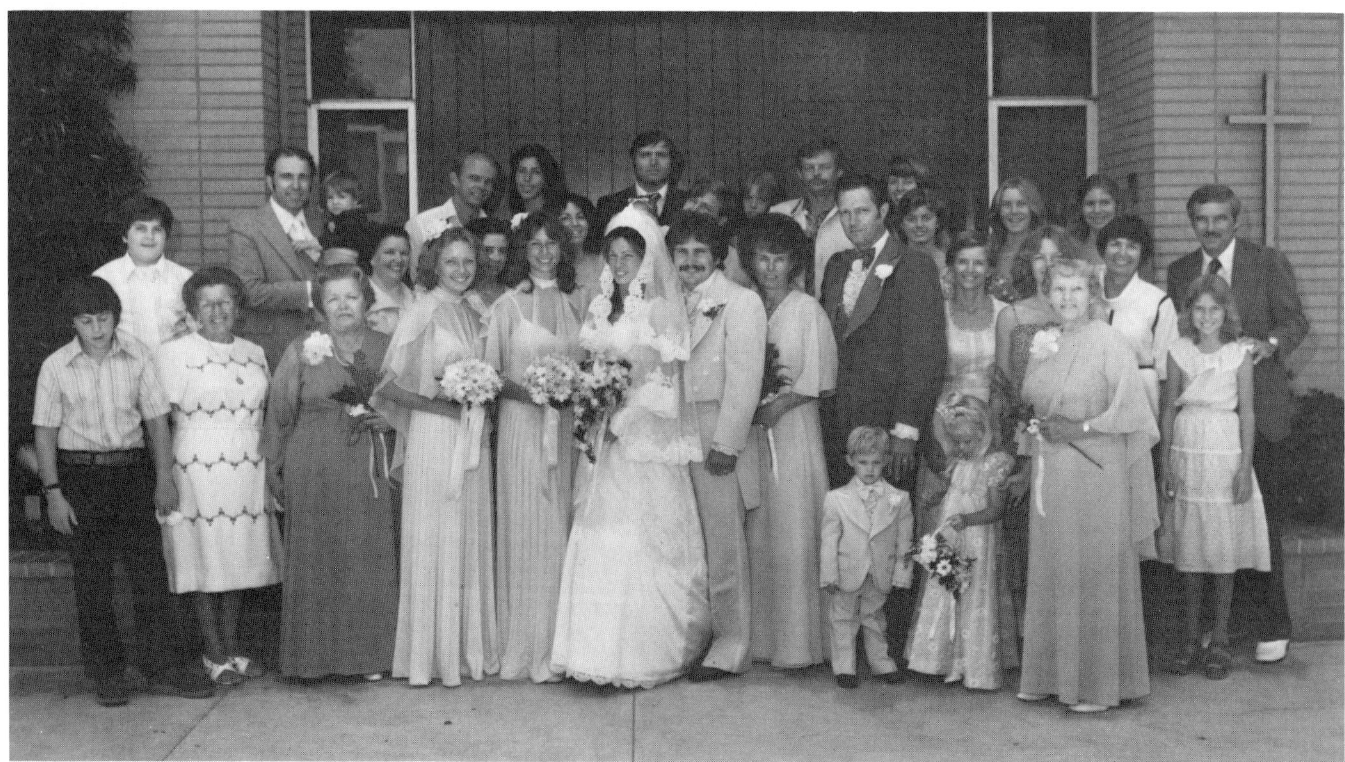

THE FAMILY REUNION

Reunions are a time for remembering old family stories, catching up on recent events, and taking important photos for the visual family tree.

In addition to the candid shots, you should take a group photo. If the reunion involves more than a dozen people, plan ahead for the photo by doing the following:

Set a time and place for the session, and be sure everyone has this information.

Check in advance that you can encompass the whole crowd in your viewfinder.

Make sure the background distractions won't spoil your shooting.

Don't have the sun glaring into eyes, causing squinting.

Make sure sufficient light will be available. (Don't expect a pocket-sized flash to be effective beyond 10 feet.)

This shot may look candid, but it required a bit of planning. First, a location was found on a slight rise where a low camera angle would prevent houses in the background from being visible. Then the film was deliberately underexposed to create the dark mood.

When photographing a large group, such as a reunion or wedding party, look for a wide step on which the people in the back can stand.

Try to find a location with some steps or one that can be set up with choir risers. Otherwise people at the back of the group may be hidden by those in front. It takes more time than you may think to arrange a large group, and if they get impatient, the task will become even more difficult. Therefore, plan in advance how you will arrange them.

If the group is large, you should also consider the problem of traffic. To prevent a problem in a confined area, have everyone line up by height in another area. Then lead them into place, tall ones first. Have the tall people take the last row. Then when it is full, the shorter people should make a new row in front.

If you are a member of the family, you should also be in the photo. So set up the shot by putting the camera on a tripod. Have either the self-timer or a helper release the shutter.

Posing smaller groups

By building a pyramid around an arm chair, you can easily pose smaller groups. Try to place family members' heads on different levels, and keep people close together so there won't be large gaps. Otherwise it will look as if someone who was supposed to be there stepped out before the photo was made.

Four generations

A must photo at family reunions is a carefully made photo of four or more generations. Set up this type of photo as you would any other group photo. But make close-ups as well as medium-distance shots.

Copying old prints

It is a good idea for everyone to bring old family photos to reunions. Then you can use an instant-print camera with a close-up attachment to make on-the-spot copies for family members who want them. An SLR is an excellent camera for making copy negatives or slides from these heirloom photos. You can simply take a photo into the bright sun and hold it so the sun doesn't glare off its surface. Then focus the camera carefully and shoot the print.

Although there are special techniques for dealing with damaged photos, they are beyond the scope of this book. If you are faced with problem prints, check photography books in your library or in a bookstore for more information.

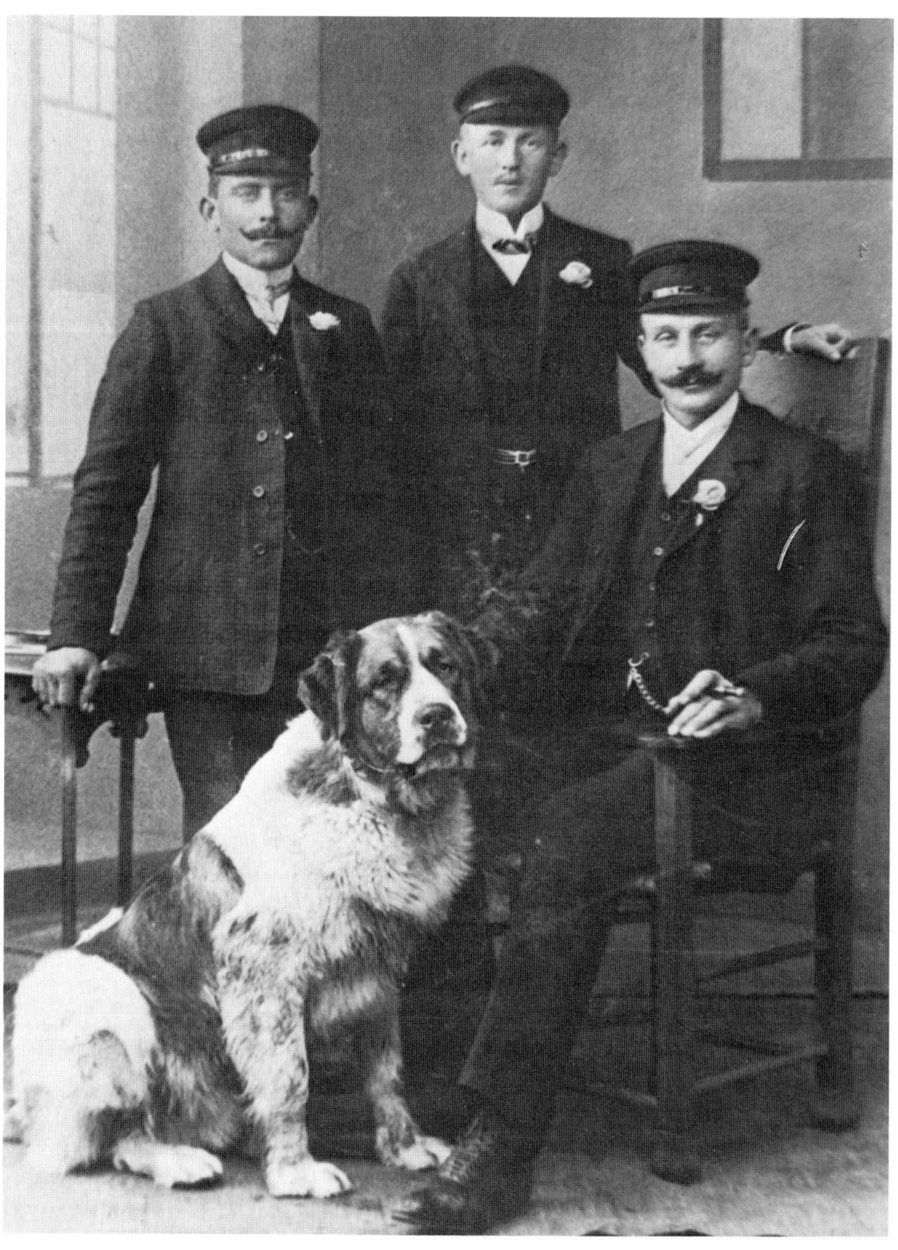

When planning family reunions, ask everyone to bring their heirloom photos. You can copy them and assemble a photographic family tree. A 35mm SLR loaded with ASA 125 film will produce acceptable copies, or you can use an instant-print camera for on-the-spot results.

THE SCHOOL PLAY AND FAMILY ATHLETES

Photographing a school play or pageant is particularly important if your child is a participant. So arrange to attend a dress rehearsal. Then you can move about and get onto the stage for close-ups. Sometimes schools with active drama departments even schedule special rehearsals for this purpose. Be sure to take advantage of the stage lighting if it is an artistically lit production.

Be careful about taking photos during performances. In formal settings photography is often a sign of poor theater manners, since it can be a distraction to other members of the audience. On the other hand, it is common for parents to take a few snapshots at a grammar-school Christmas pag-

For most sports, a telephoto lens helps you take better action shots, while keeping out of the action. Photograph by Michael O'Connor.

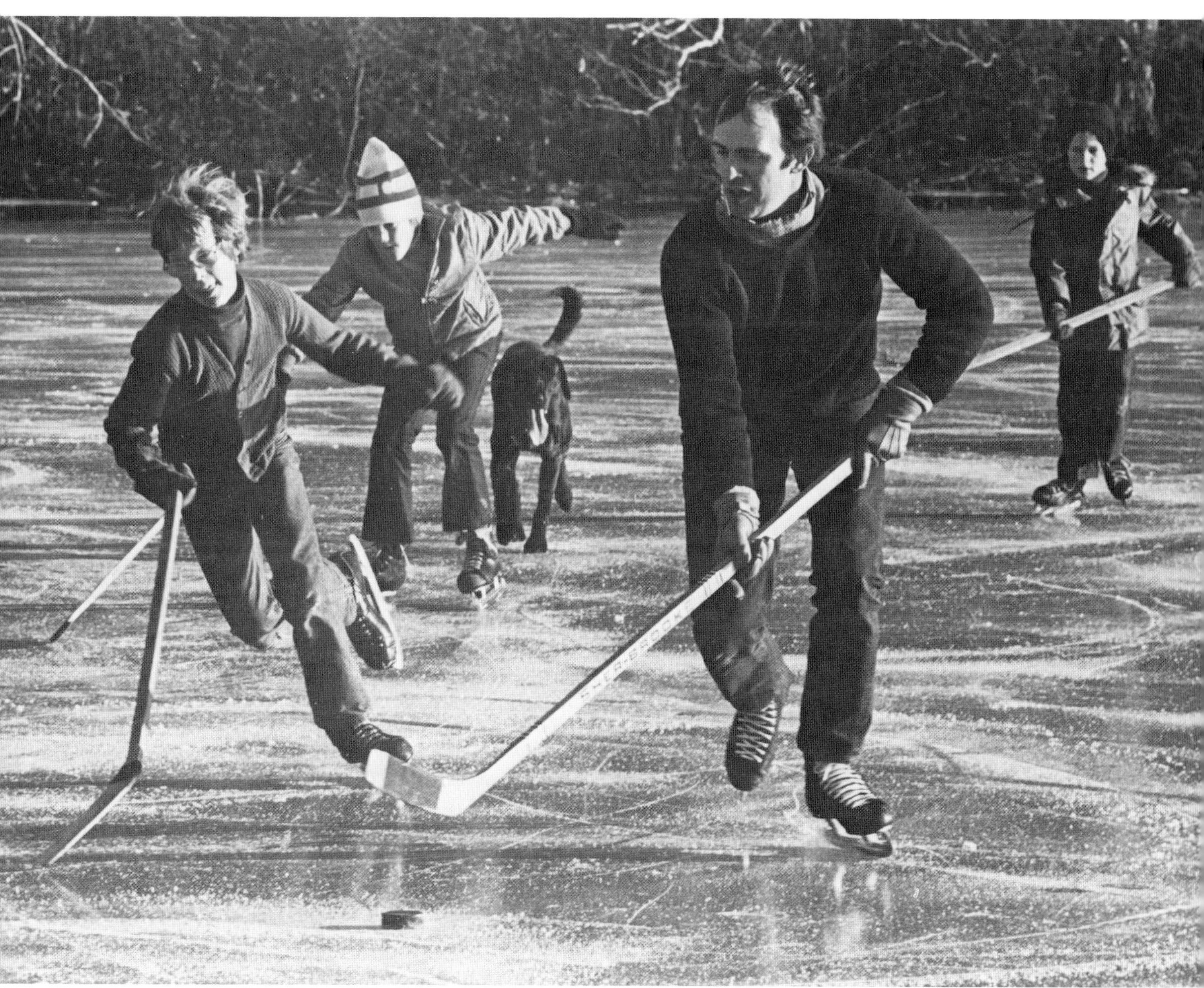

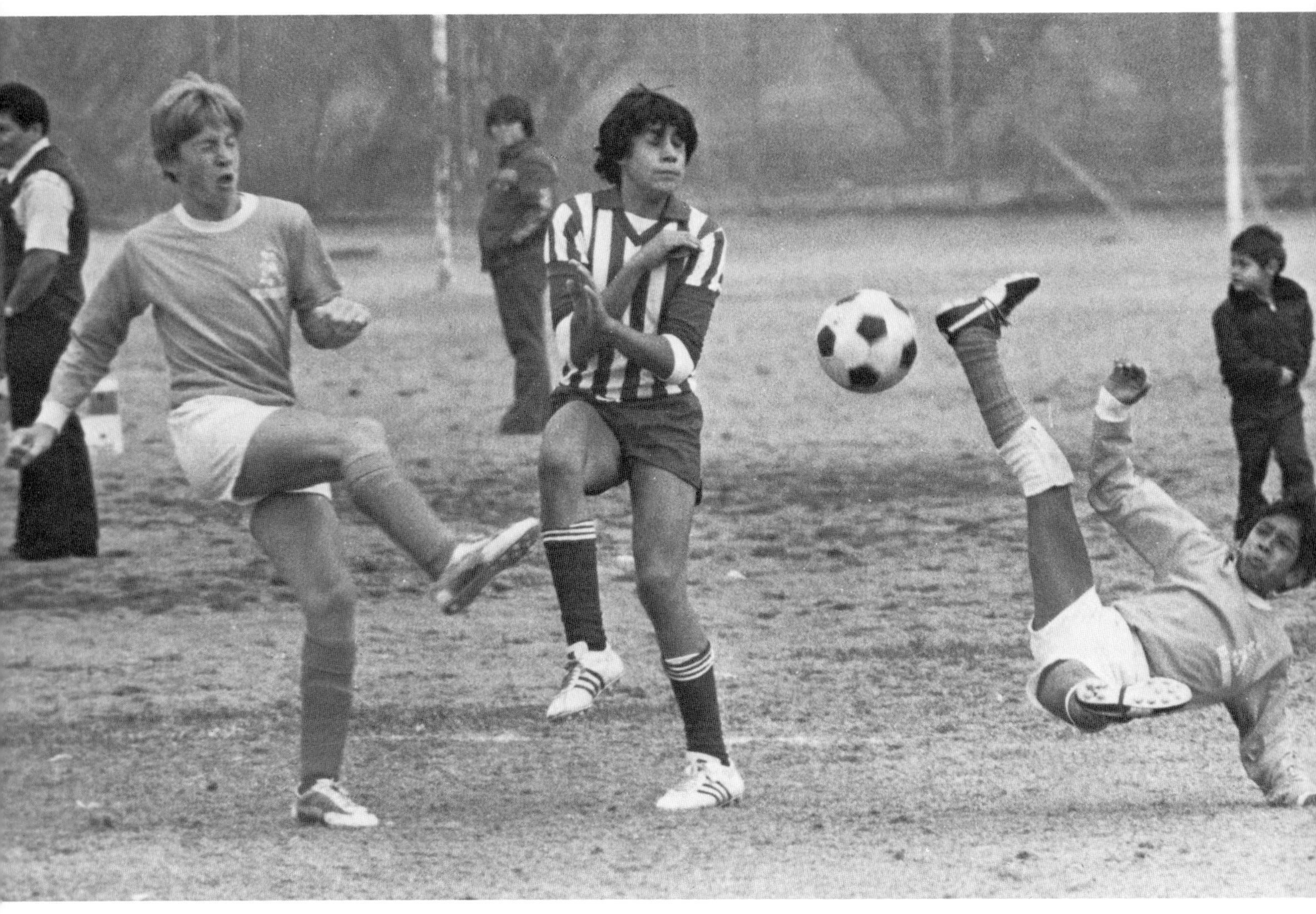

Photos of your child participating in his or her favorite sport can show an important facet of the child's personality. Photograph by Eusevio Arias.

eant. So use discretion and follow announced rules.

When photographing from the audience would not be objectionable, you should use high-speed film and a telephoto lens. Remember, too, that flash will cause a disruption and it will probably not be effective because of the distance between the audience and the stage.

Family athletes

When someone is involved in sports, he and his activity should be included in the photo collection. For most sports, telephoto lenses and auto-winders or motor drives will get the best results.

Listed below are some tips for shooting team sports:

Baseball: Stand behind the first-base line. Use a 200 to 300mm lens for a full-size diamond; a 105mm for little-league diamonds. Practice focusing quickly on second base, third, and home plate so you can react quickly when action happens.

Soccer: Stand behind and slightly to the side of one of the goals. This is because action wanders all over the field. Then wait for the action to come to you. Moderate telephoto lenses or zooms are good choices here.

Football: Get on the sidelines if you can, and try to stay a few yards ahead of the ball. Fourth down is when you are likely to see a pass, so move downfield before the play begins if you want a photo of the receiver. If shooting from the stands, you will need a very long telephoto lens—500mm or more. These can sometimes be rented from camera shops.

Swimming: Prefocus on a spot and wait for the swimmer to come into range. Watch exposure carefully; outdoor pools reflect a lot of light, and overexposure is a hazard. Again, telephoto lenses are needed for close-up action.

Basketball: Most of the action happens at the basket. The usual position for photographers is near the basket, where normal lenses are quite effective. For exciting but hard to catch shots, try for some mid-court action and blocking efforts in addition to the usual jump shots. A midrange telephoto or zoom lens works well for these photos.

If you want to photograph a game or meet from the sidelines, be sure to check with the coach in advance. For obvious reasons the game organizers cannot always allow everyone to crowd the sidelines to take photos. You might, however, be able to become the official team photographer, trading prints for the advantage of a close-up view.

GRADUATIONS AND RELIGIOUS CEREMONIES

Here are some tips for photographing these important milestones:

For cap-and-gown and religious confirmation gown photos, take them in advance. Frequently gown garments must be turned in immediately after the ceremony, amidst crowds and confusion. Also, you may not be allowed to take photographs during a certain religious ceremony, so find out about these rules beforehand.

For the actual ceremony, check out photographic vantage points in advance. Limited seating is common, and you may have to arrive quite early for the best spot.

For photographing from your seat, you will probably need a telephoto lens.

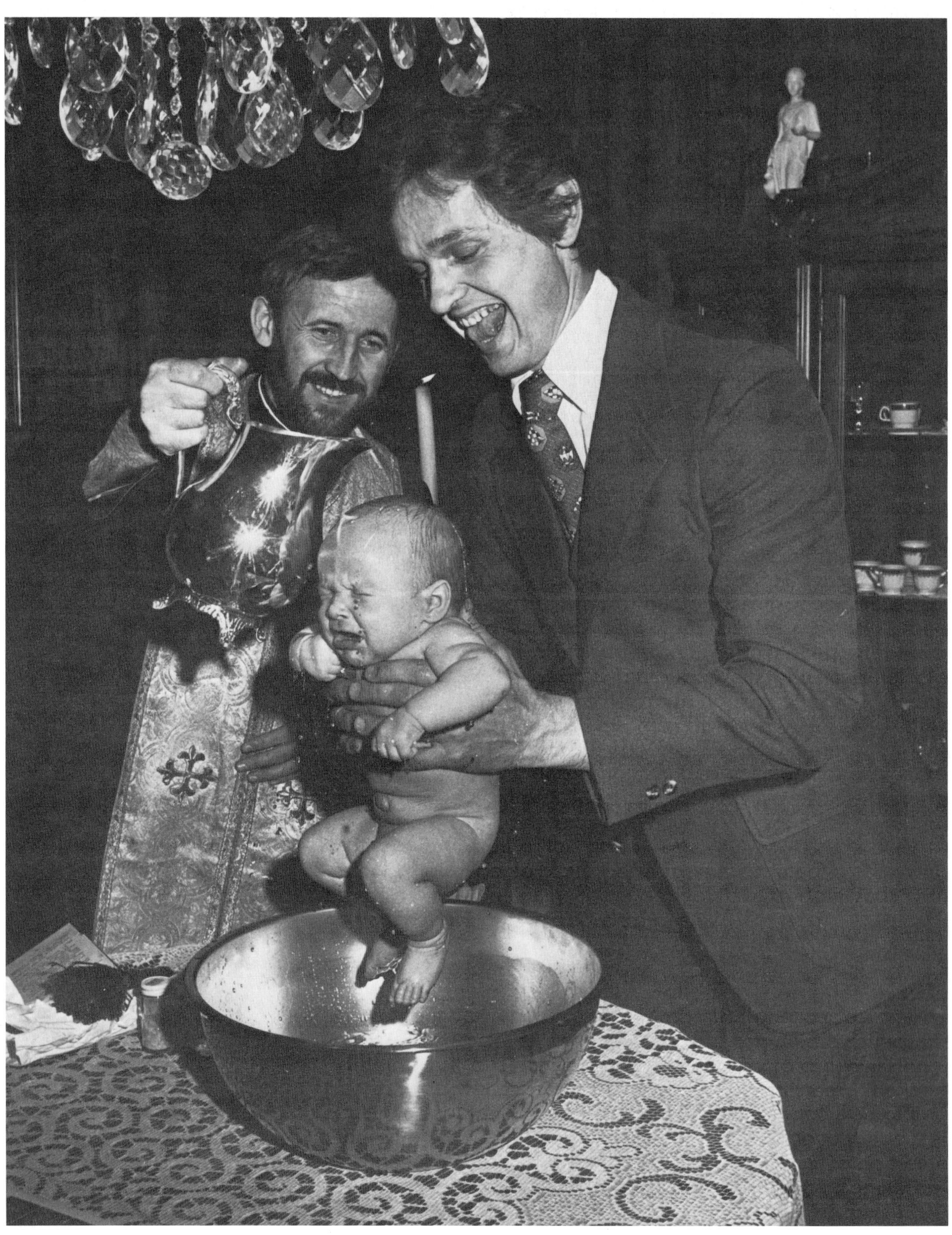

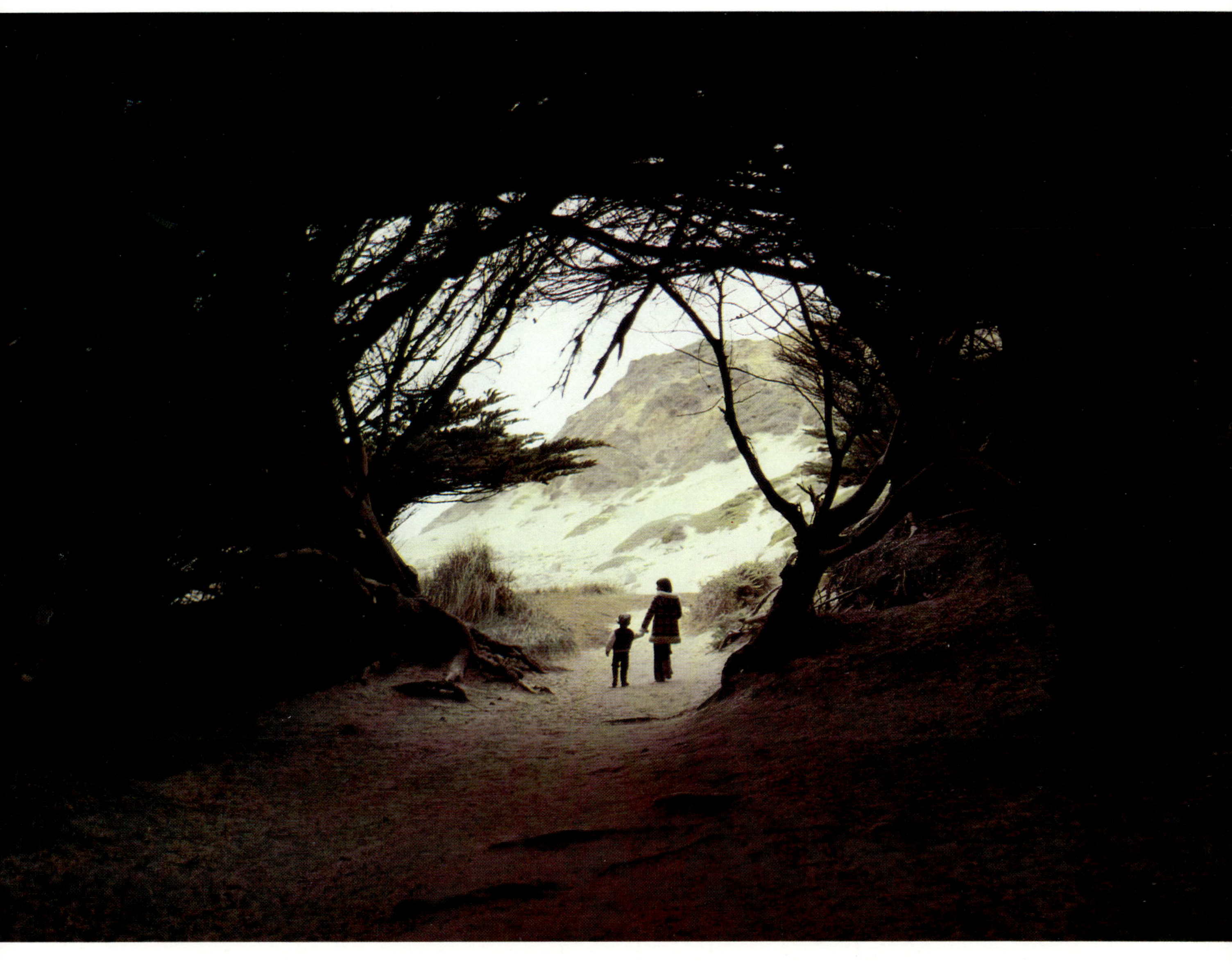

Above: *Photograph by Rod Luna.*

Left: *Check out photographic vantage points before the ceremony begins. Photograph by Dr. Edward F. Leone, a KINSA winner.*

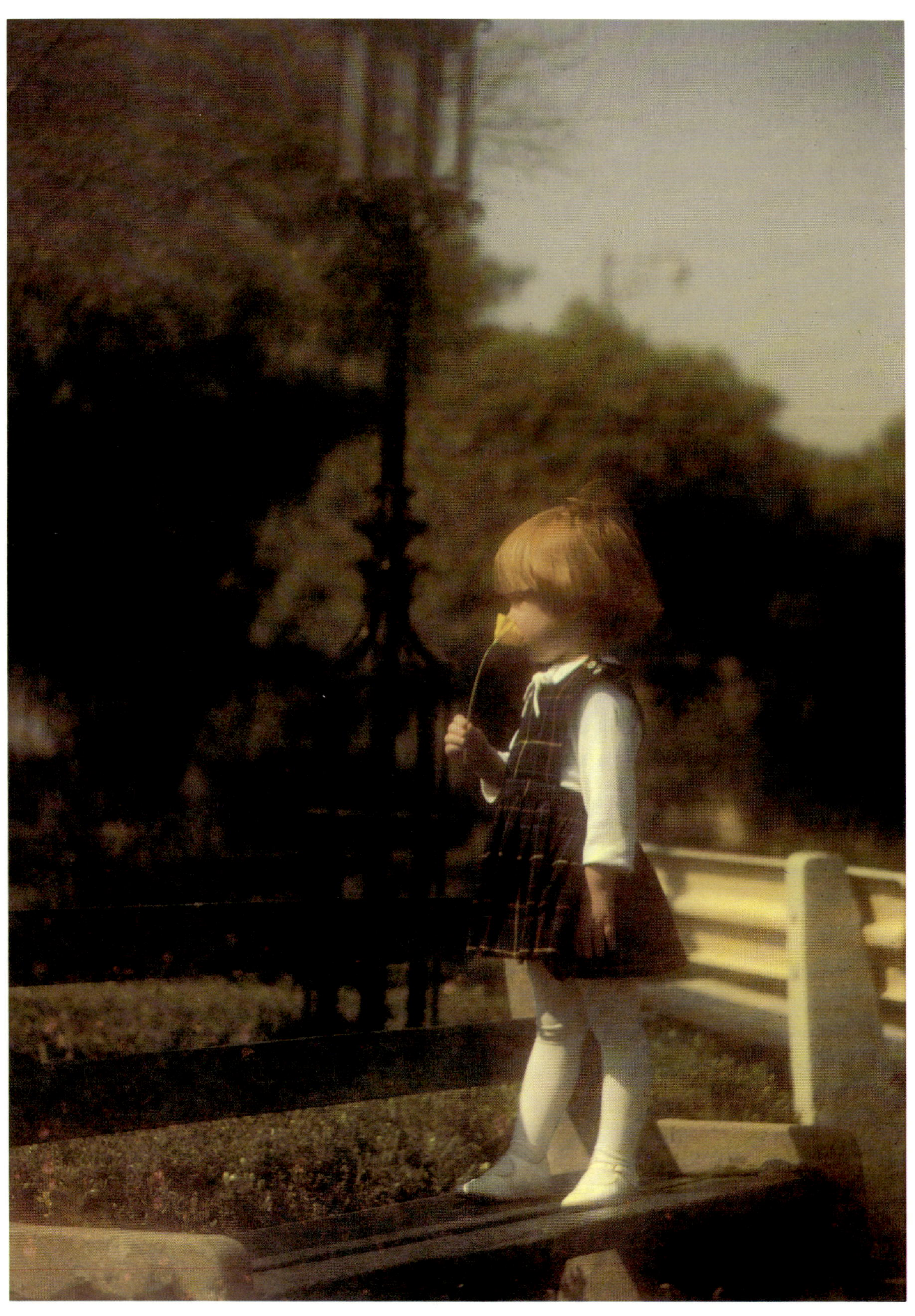

Both a K2 filter and a diffusing filter were used to create the dreamy, romantic feeling in this photograph by Mary Ann Lewis.

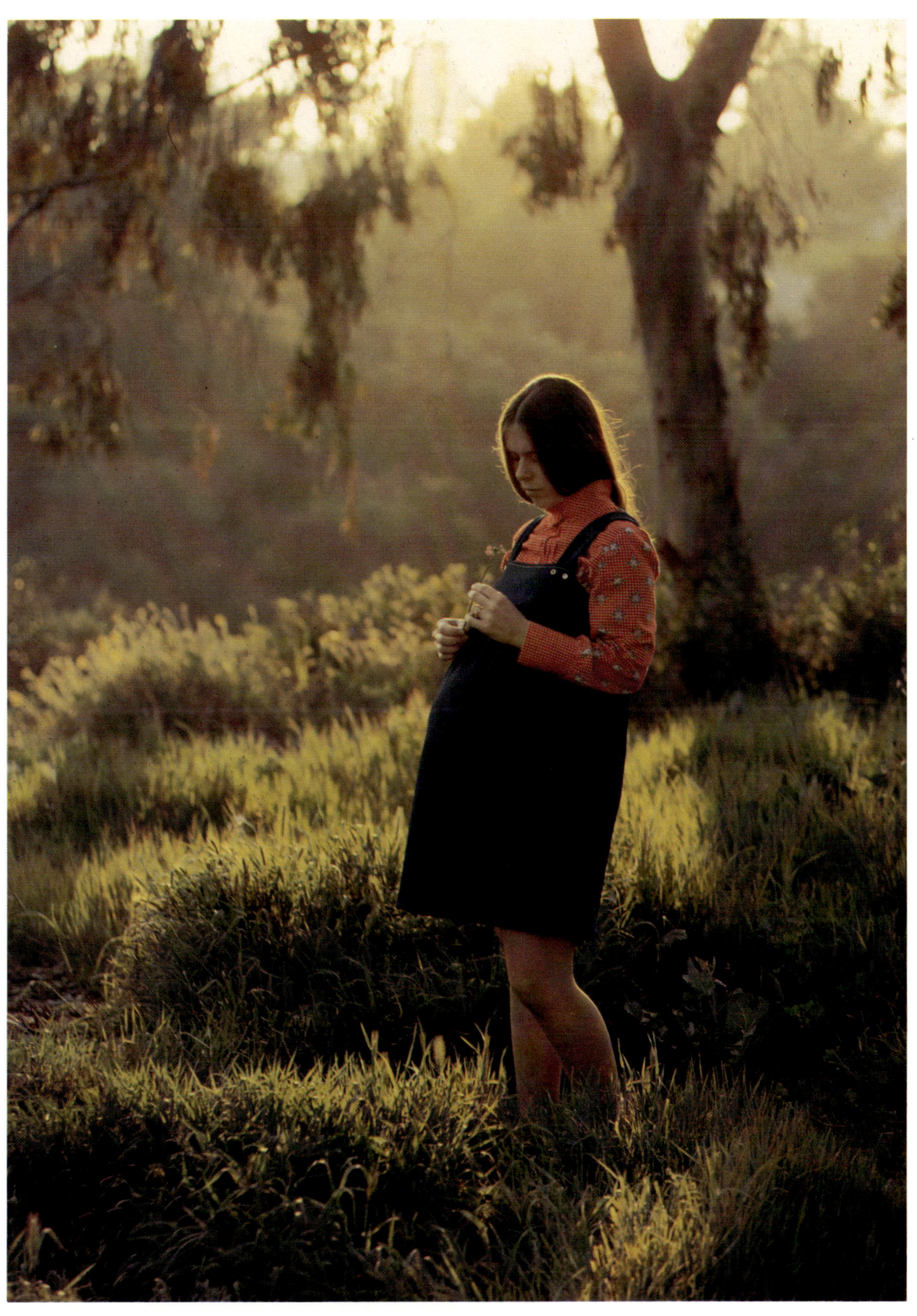

Late afternoon sunlight, slight backlighting, and the narrow depth of field of a telephoto lens all added to the warm feeling of this picture.

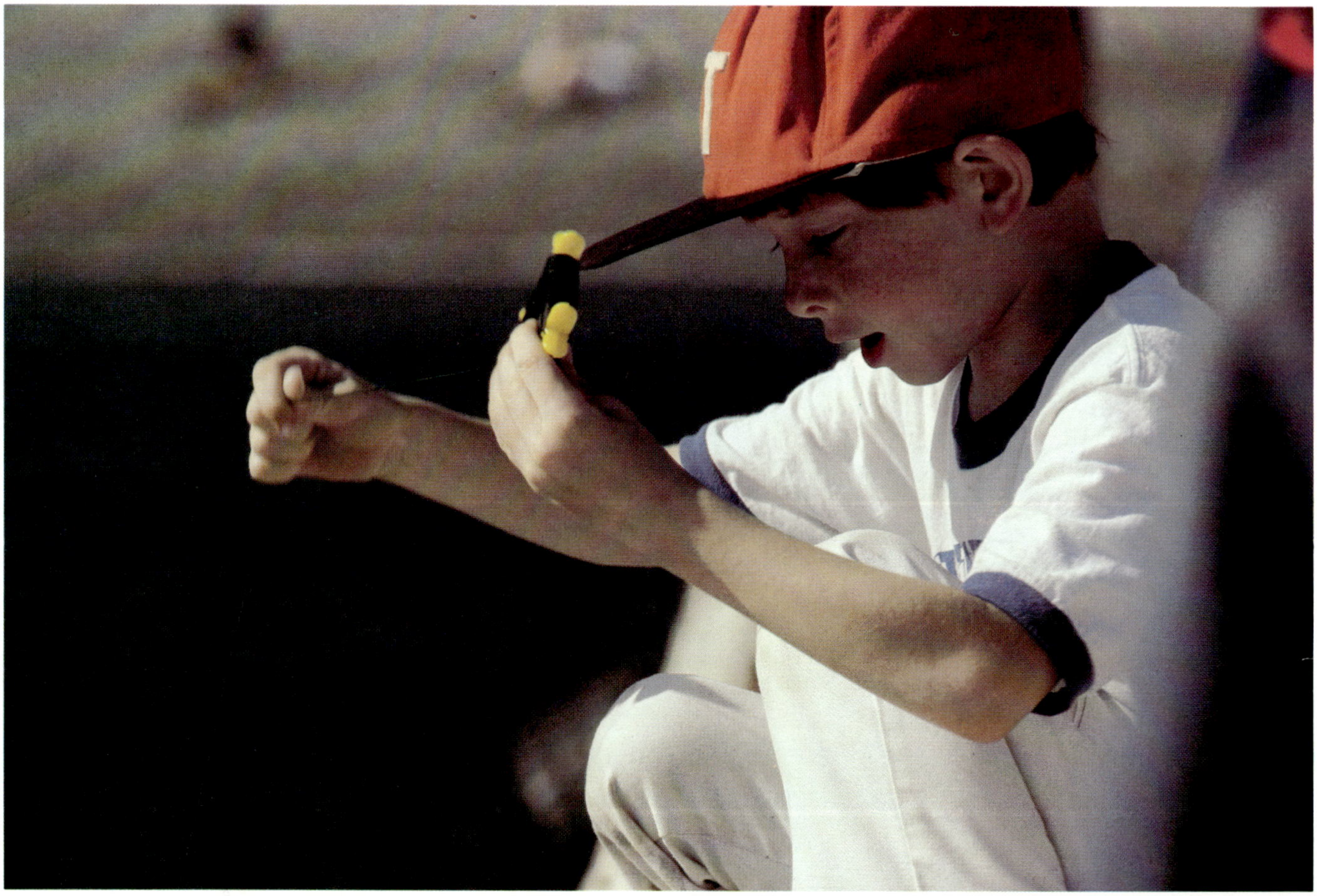

Above: *Although I was standing some distance away, a telephoto lens enabled me to get close enough to the fishing boy to get a good, tight, candid shot.*

Right: *Backlighting can be used to add dramatic highlights to human hair. Be careful to compensate for such backlit situations, however, or your subject's face may be too dark.*

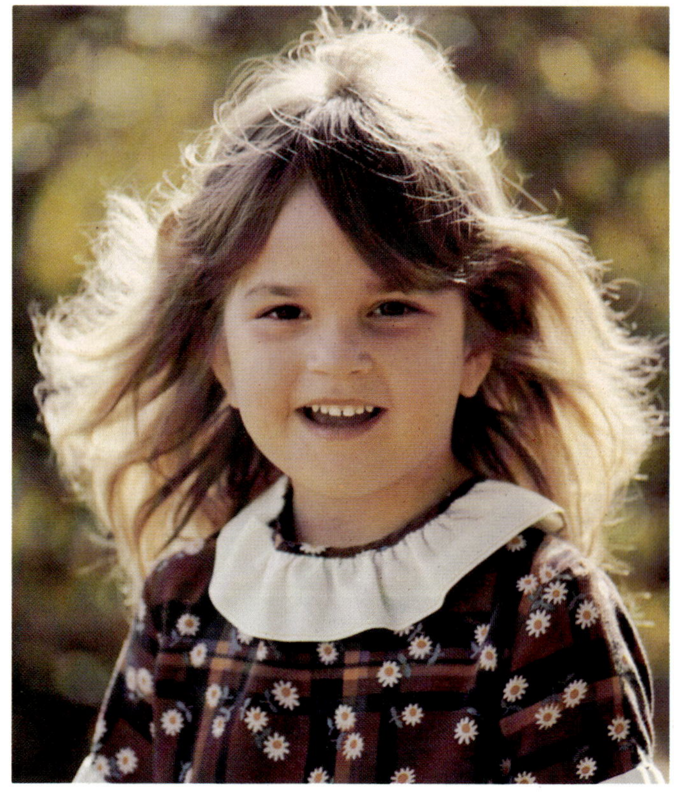

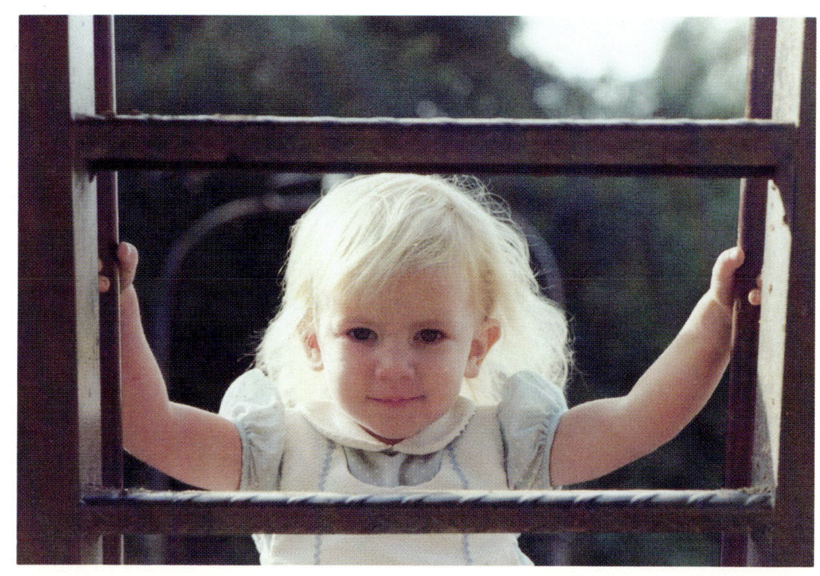

Left: *Another example of backlighting. Notice how the dark background makes the highlights in the hair even stronger.*

Below: *Always keep your camera handy and ready—you wouldn't want to miss a precious moment like this. Photograph by Rod Luna.*

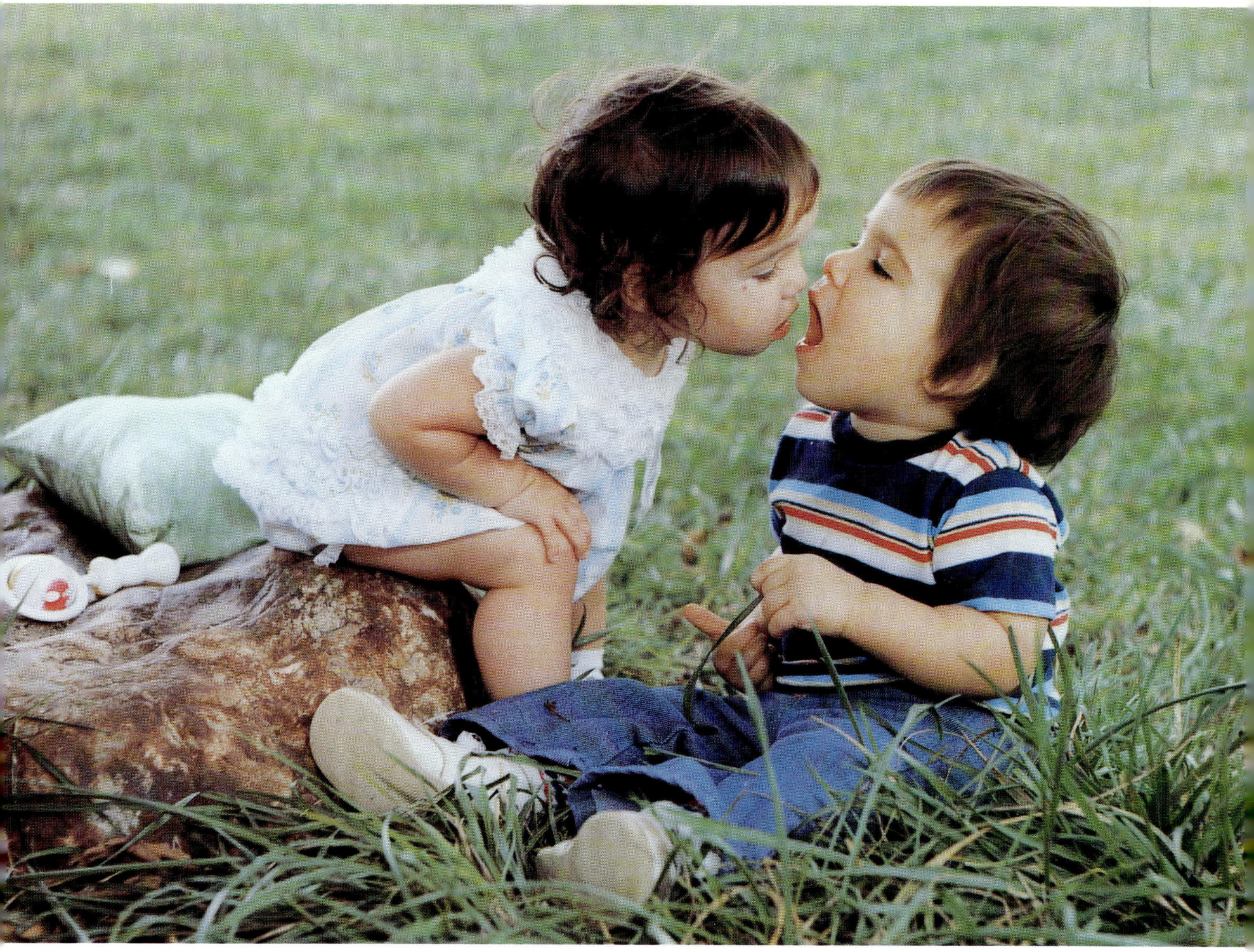

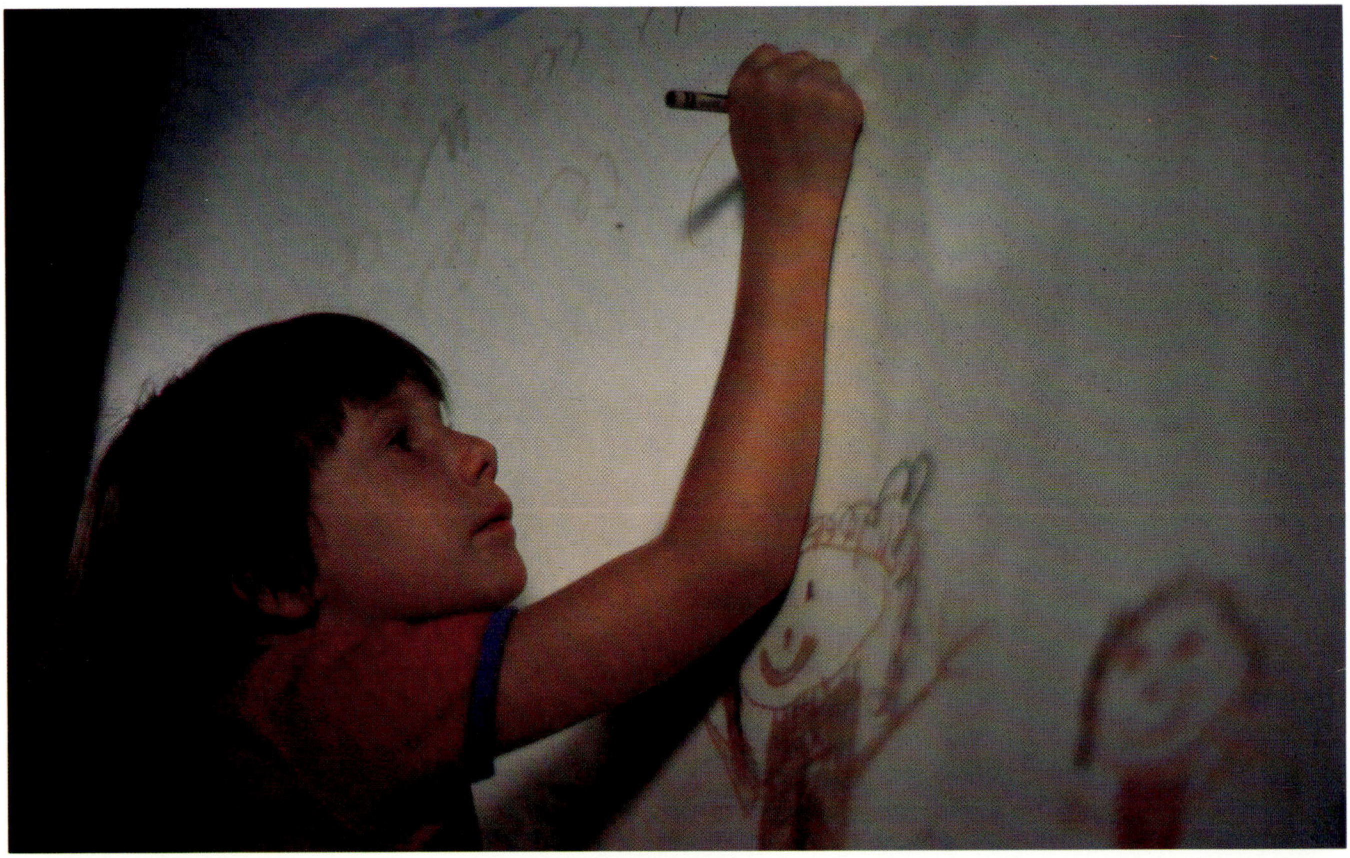

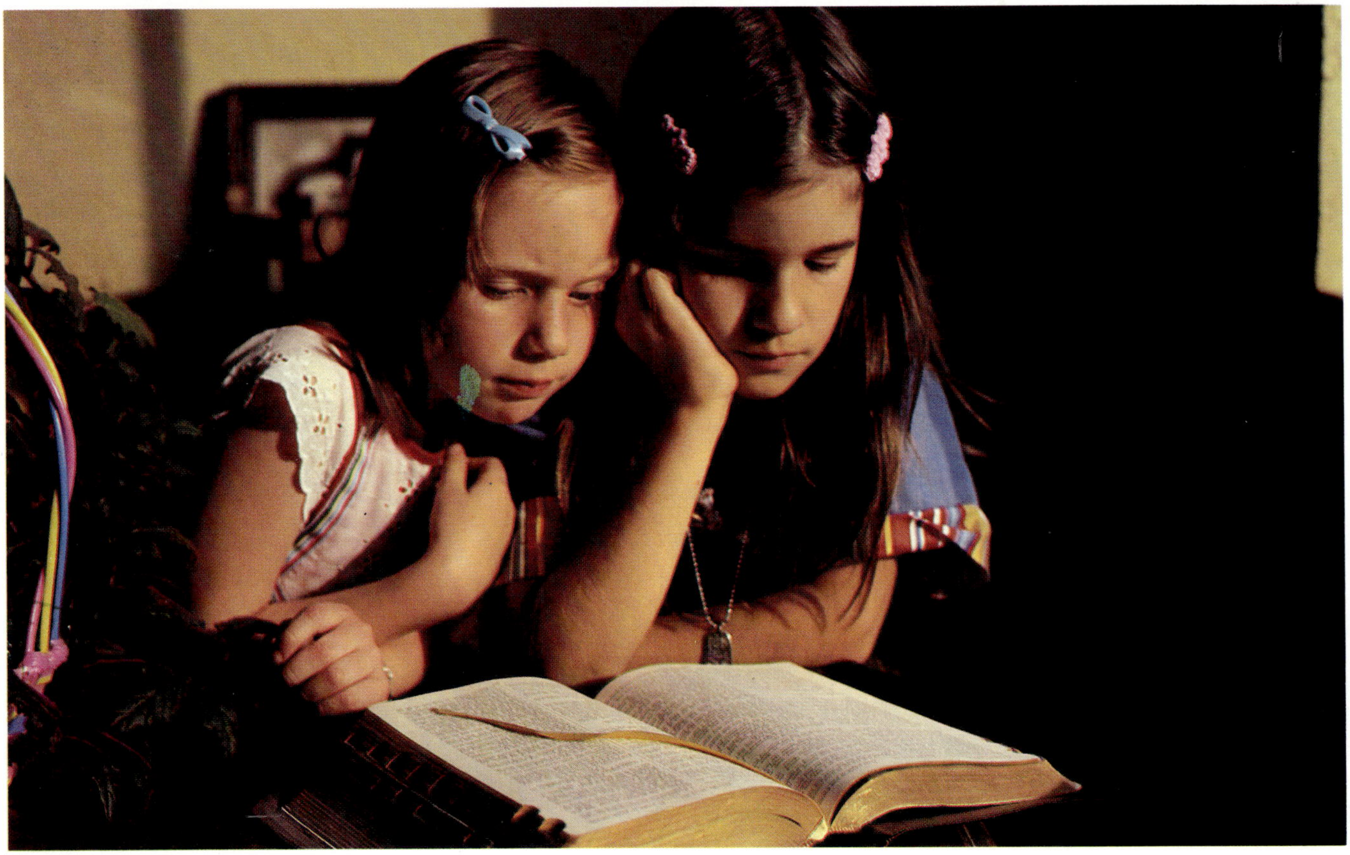

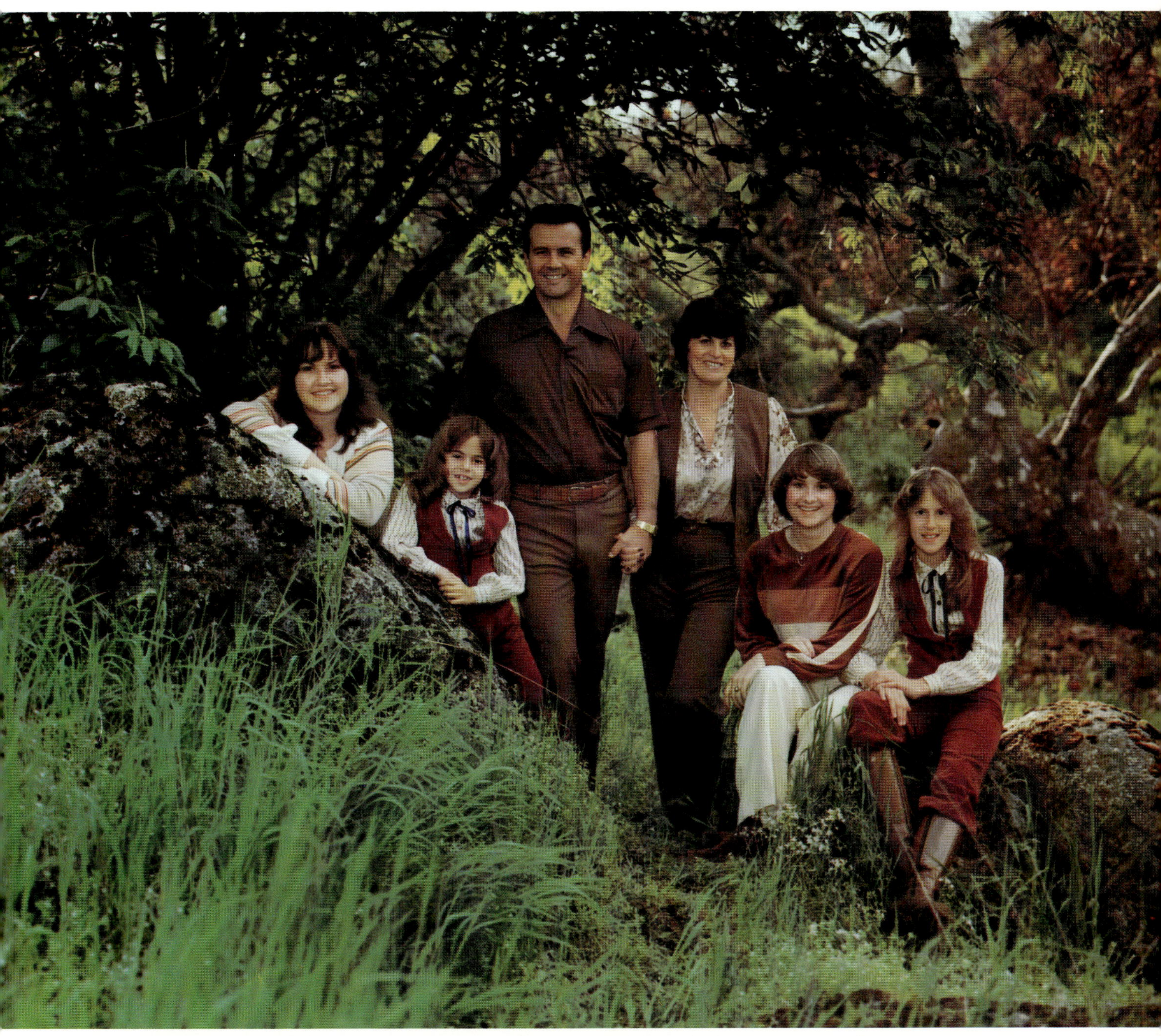

Top left: *Bouncing the light from your flash unit off of light-colored ceiling or wall produces softer shadows and a more "natural" look in the photograph. Photograph by Rod Luna.*

Left: *Rod Luna used only the light from a window to create this interesting "set up" shot.*

Above: *Careful attention to detail makes this family portrait by Robert and Colleen Scheidt, a success. The clothing is color coordinated, the faces are placed at different levels, and the background is neutral enough to not distract from the subject.*

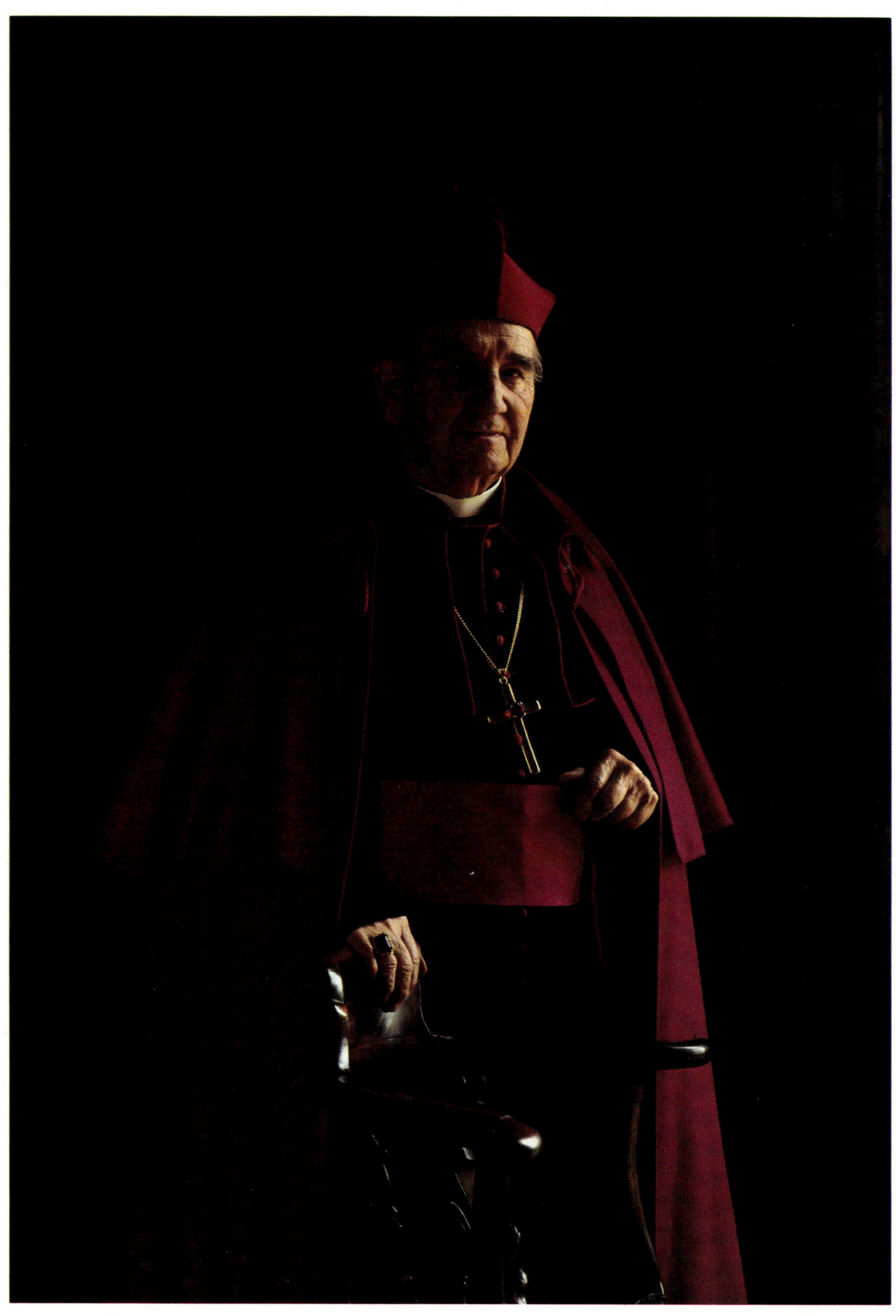

I used window light and a reflector (for fill light) in order to best show the clergyman's vestments.

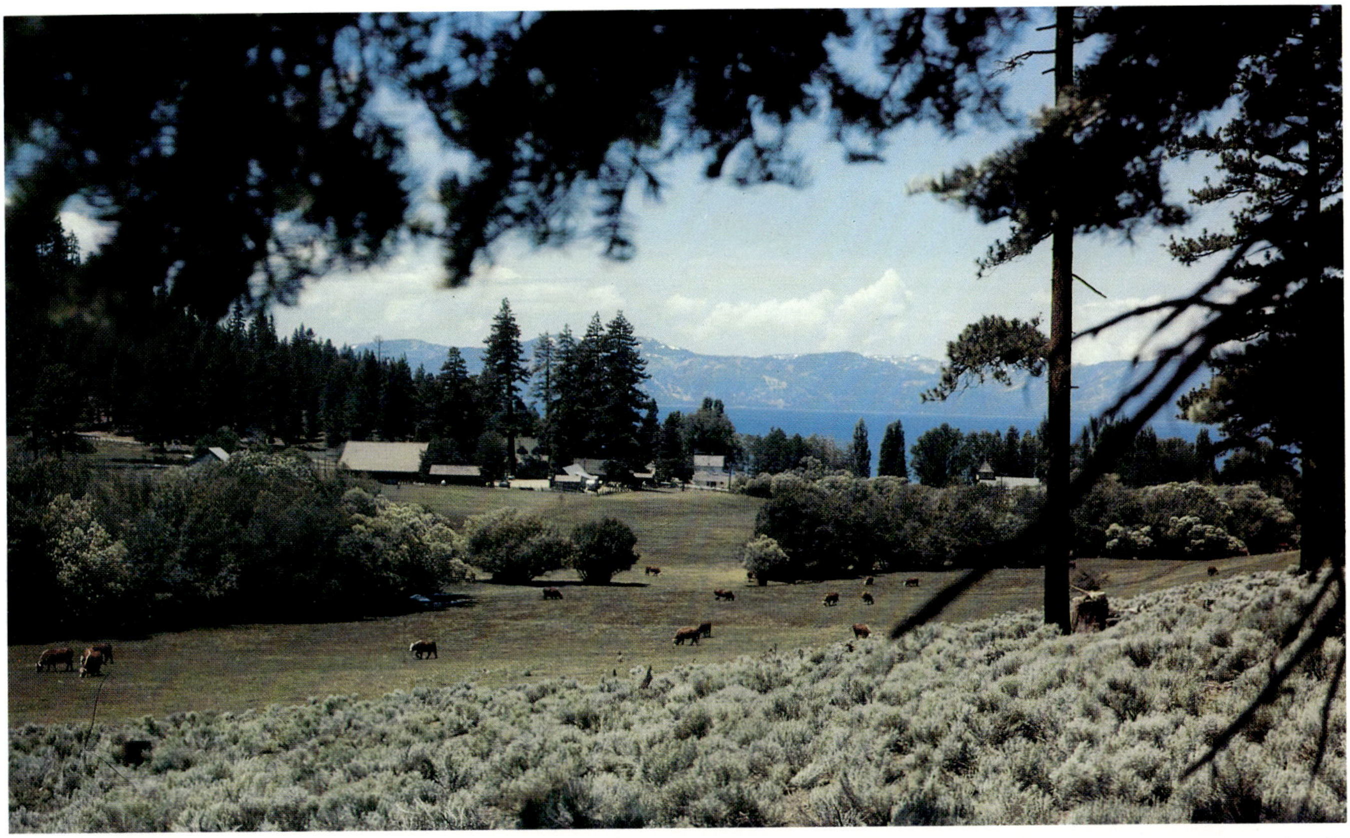

The tree branches in the foreground of this photograph of Lake Tahoe provide a frame for the scene as well as depth.

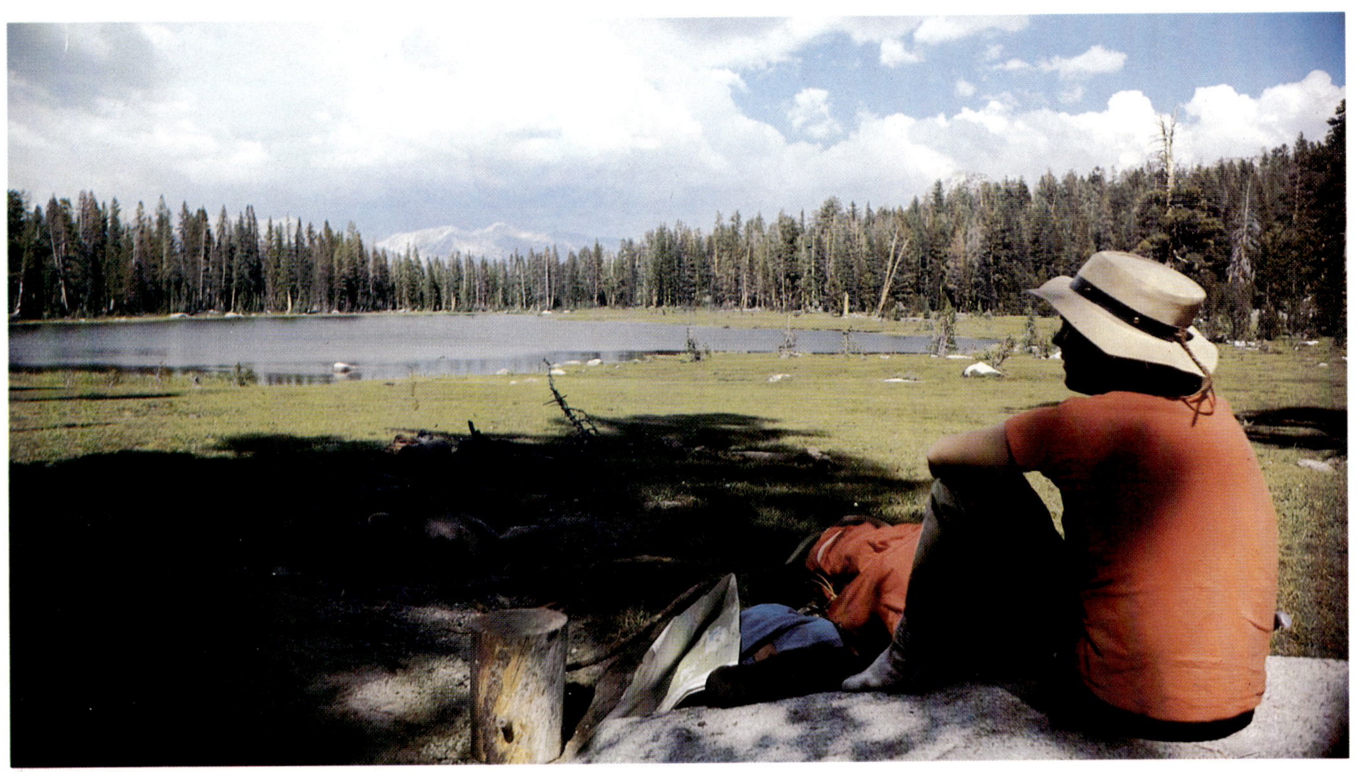

By including a person in this scenic shot, I was able to show the scale and depth of the scenery.

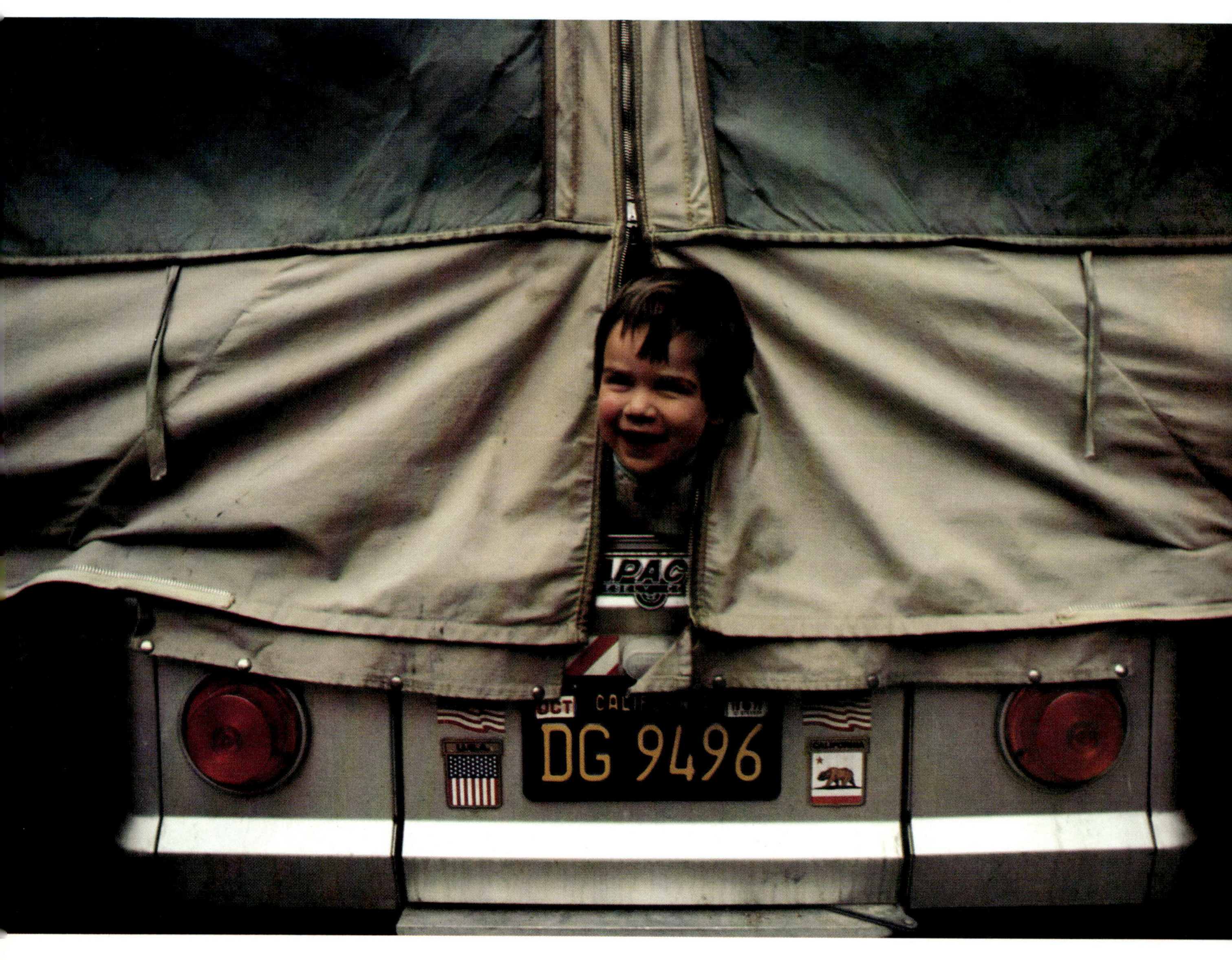

You have to be alert to capture fleeting moments like this. Photograph by Rod Luna.

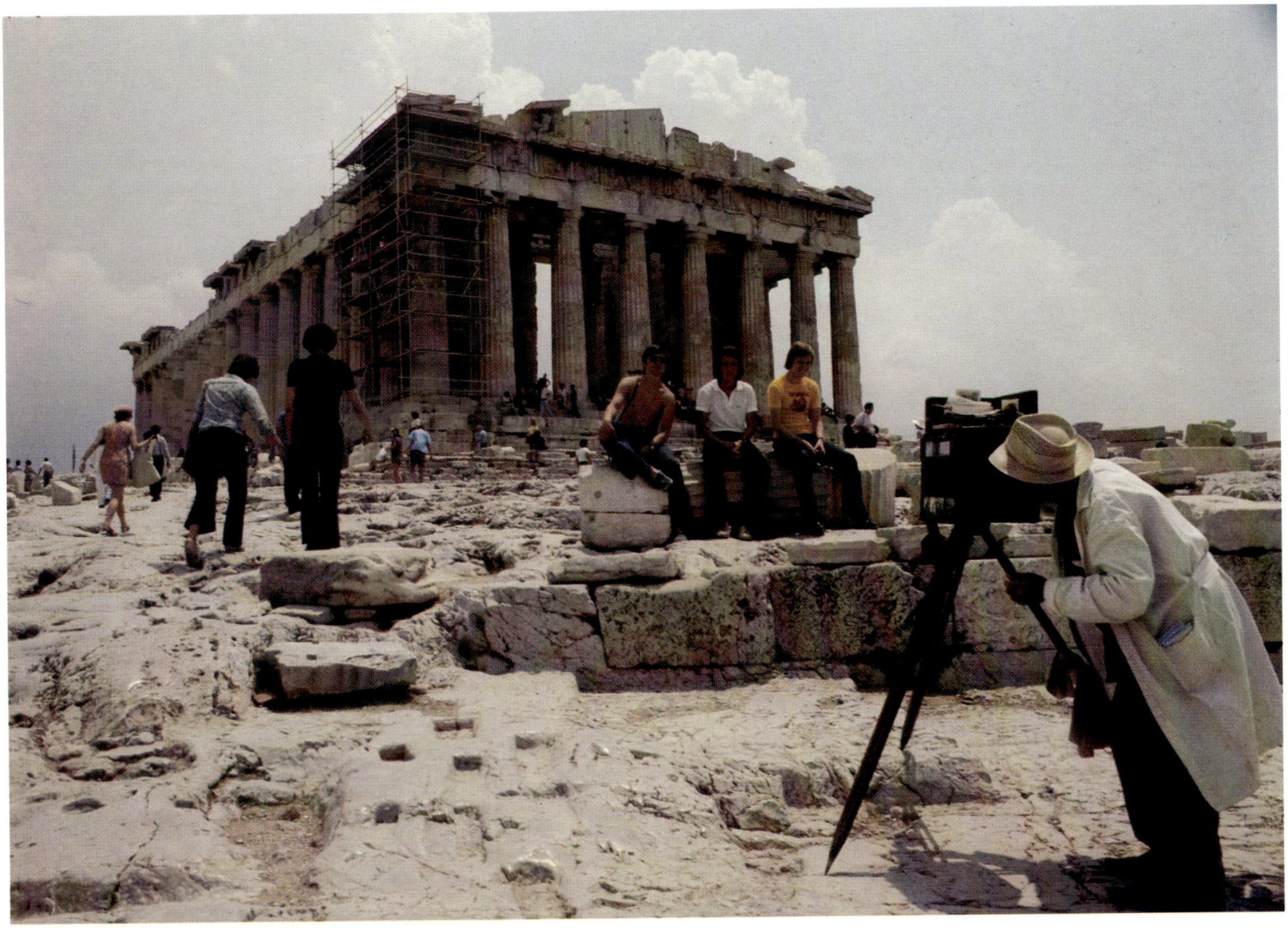

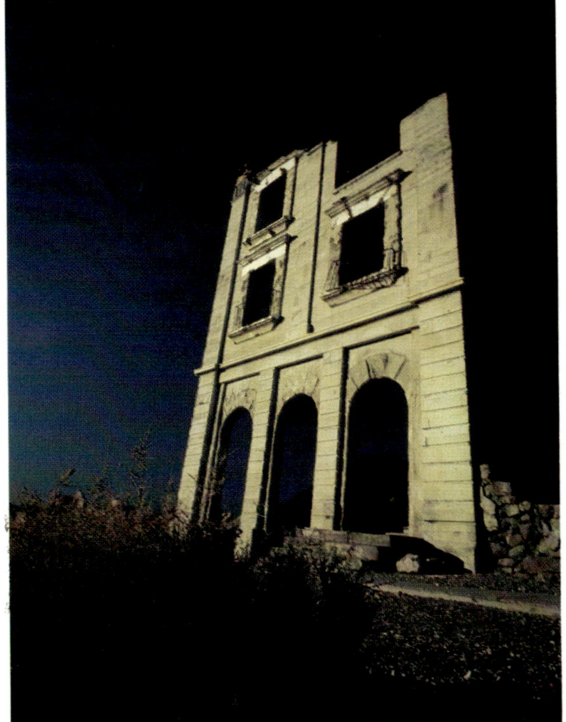

Above: *Including peripheral objects (such as the souvenir maker) can often make a more interesting image out of a popular subject.*

Left: *I used a polarizing filter to darken the sky in this shot. Polarizing filters can often add life to an otherwise flat sky.*

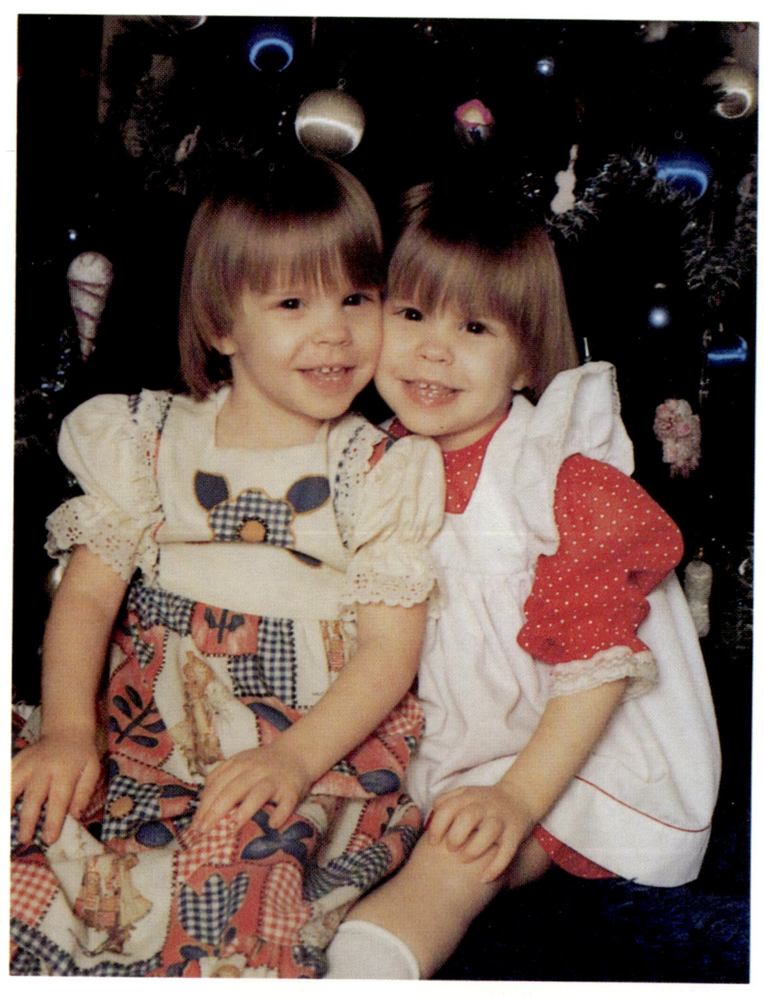

These three photographs are successful holiday pictures because they include visual symbols of the particular holiday. Photograph on the left by Brian Mercer. Photograph below by Liz Burpee. Photograph on the right by William Garrity, a KINSA winner.

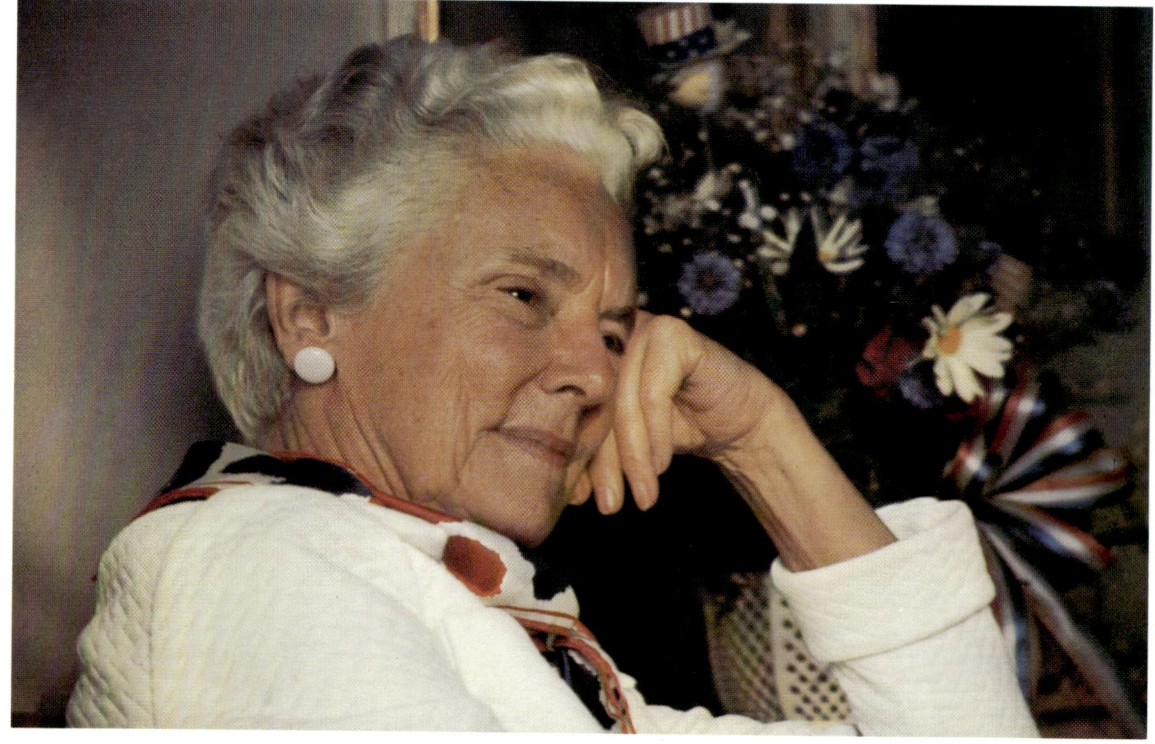

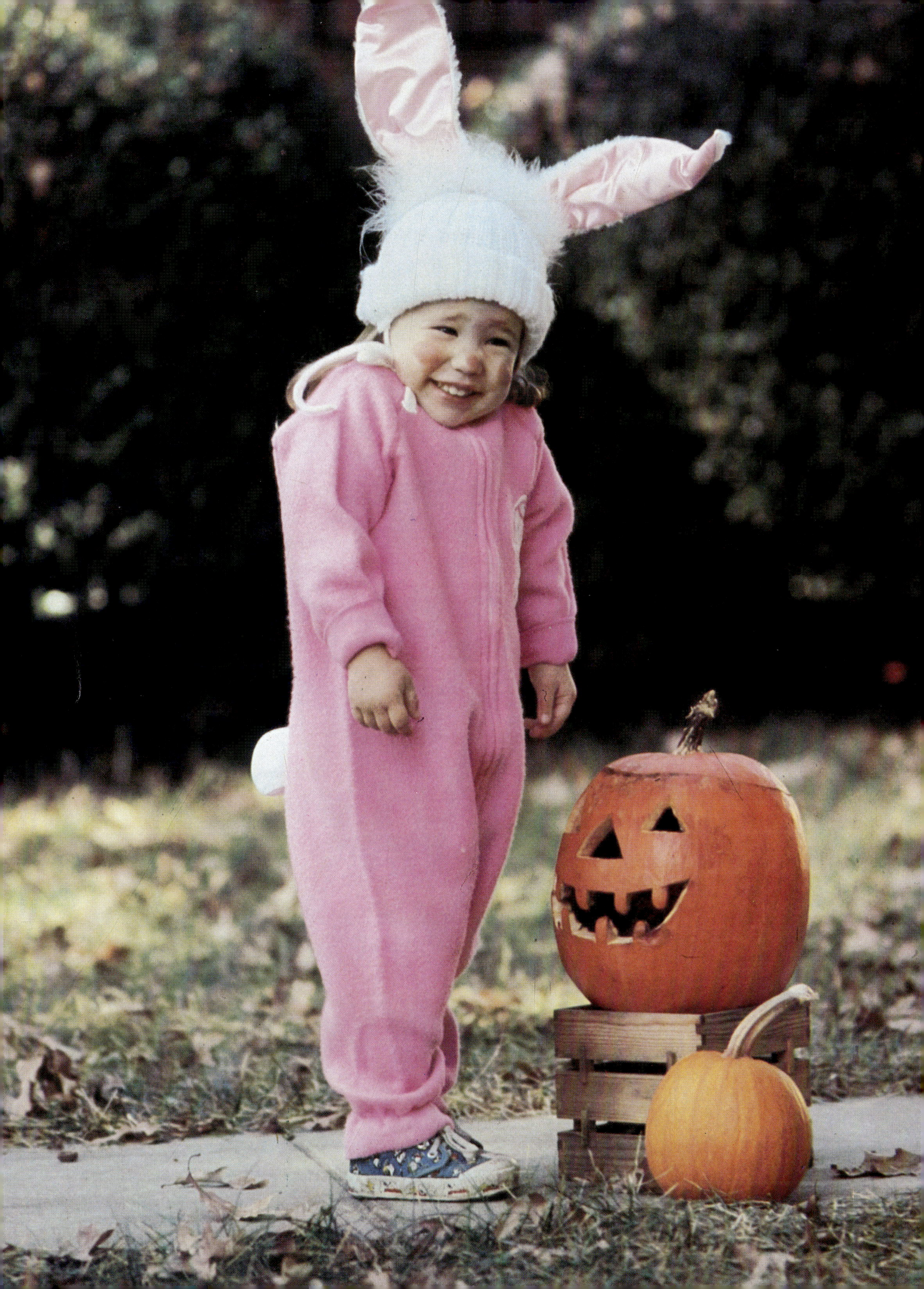

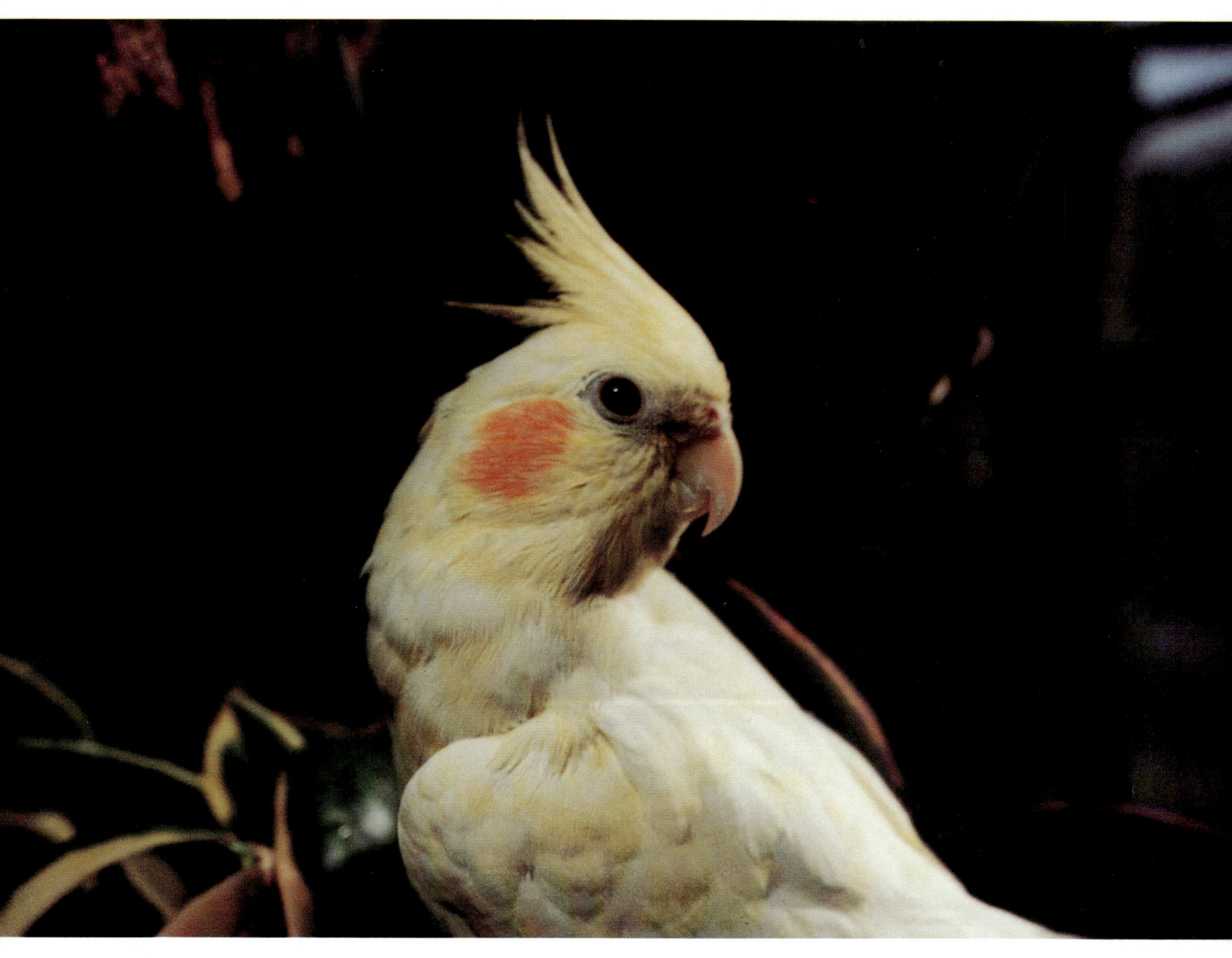

Richard Tiffen used a close-up attachment and a fill flash to produce this striking photograph of a pet cockatiel.

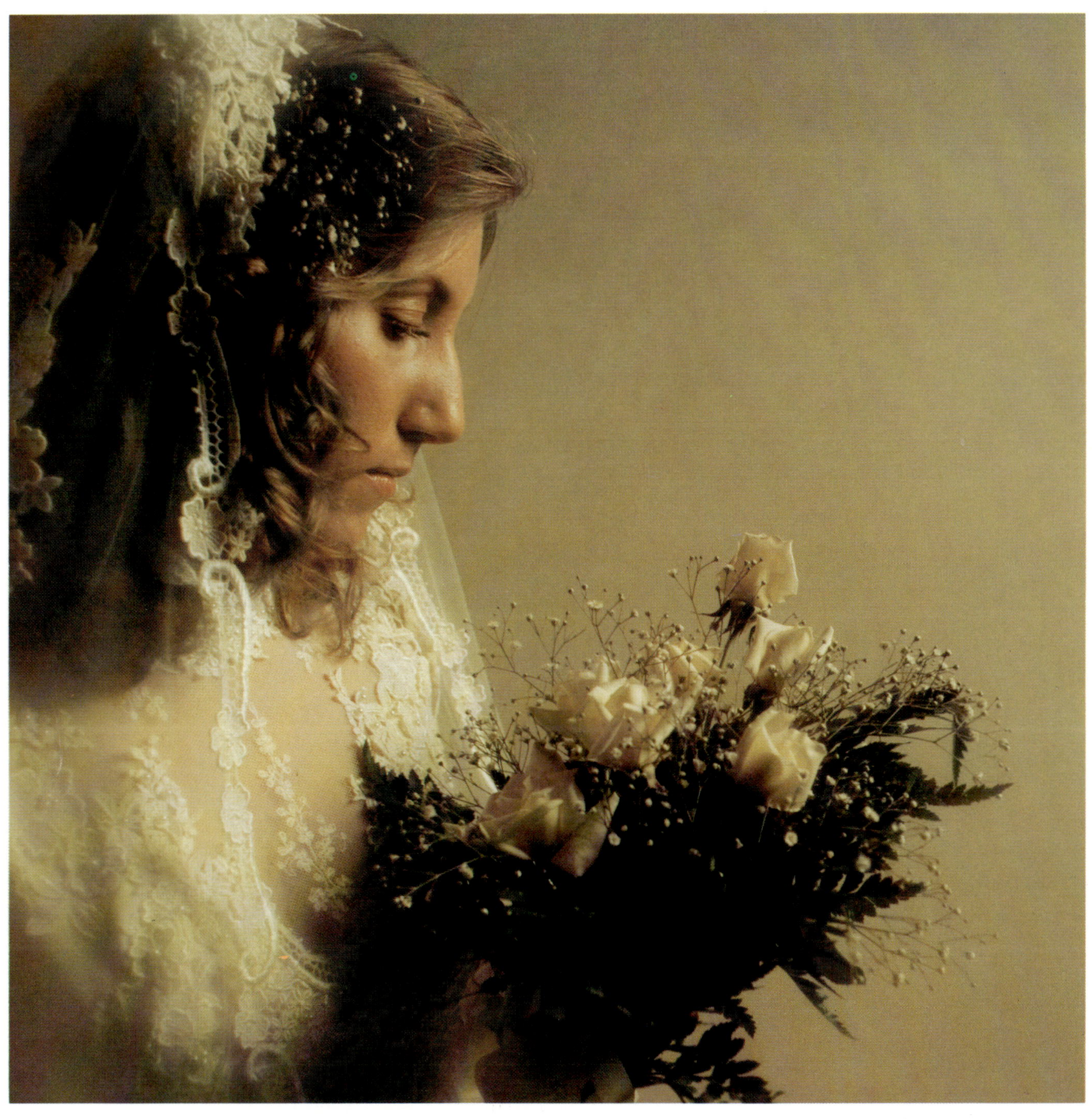

This wedding photograph is a good example of the soft tone produced by bounce flash. A slight diffusing filter was also used.

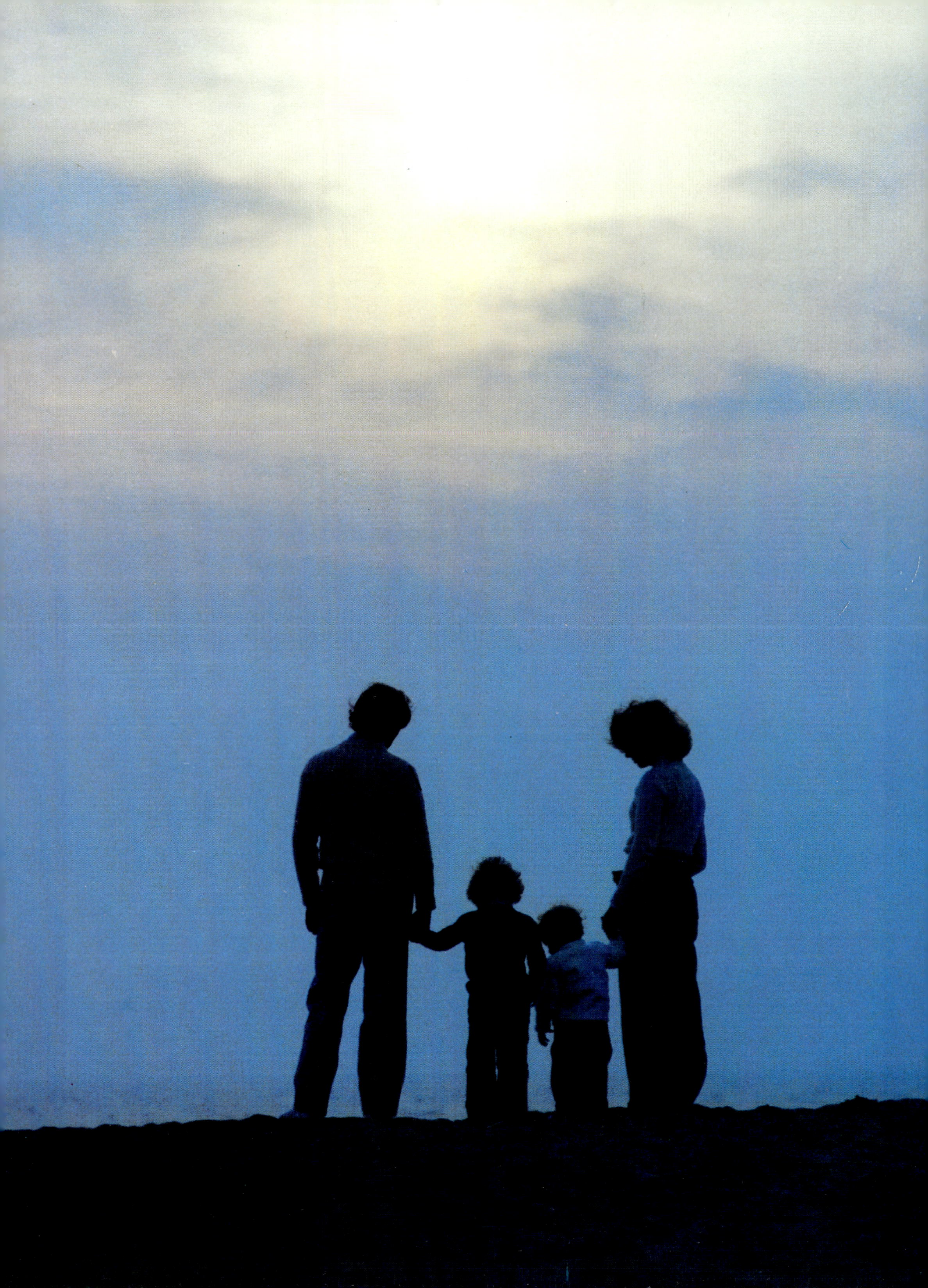

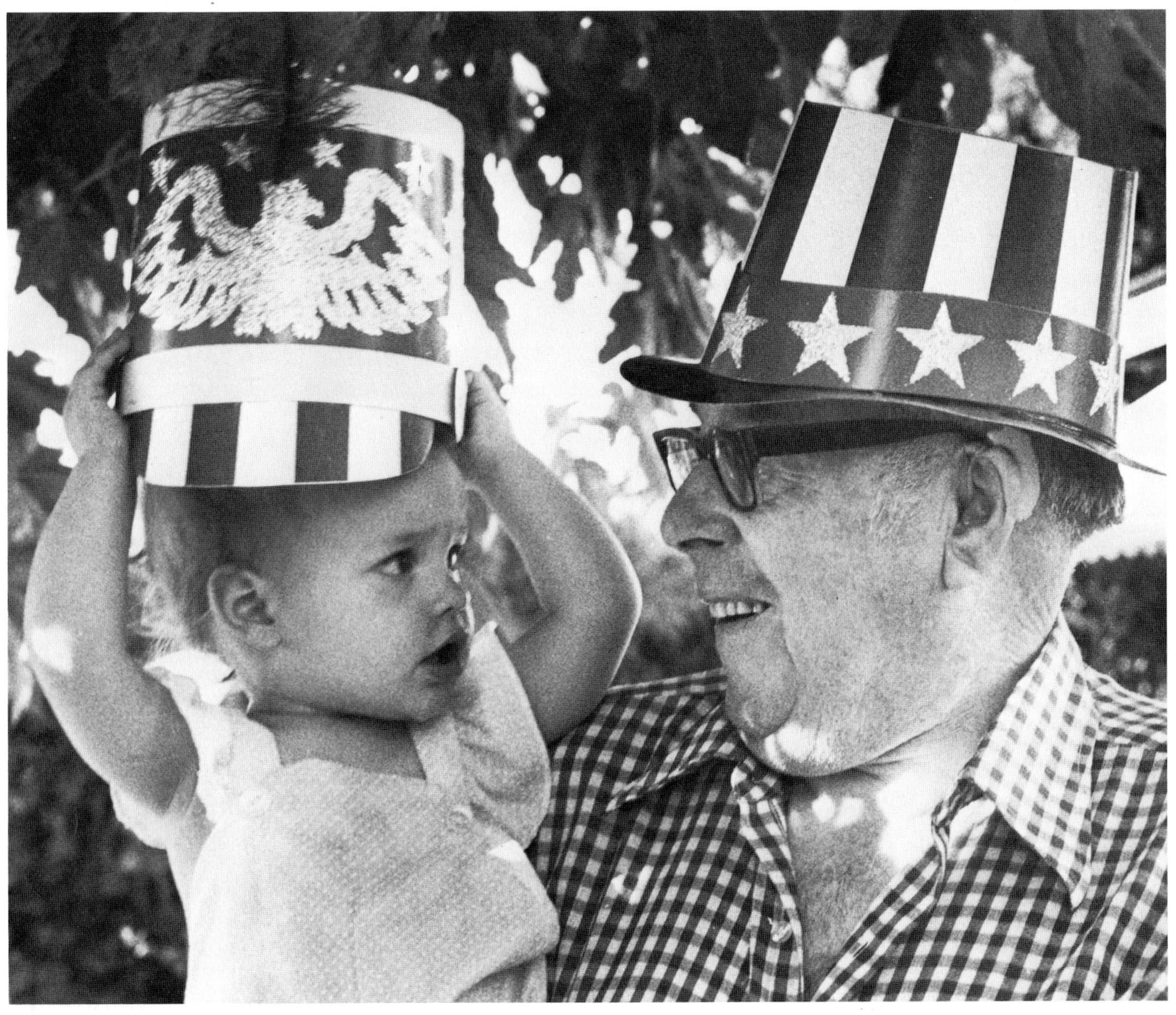

Above: *A fresh approach to a Fourth of July photo. Photograph by Mrs. Elizabeth Nichols, a KINSA winner.*

HOLIDAYS

Holidays—such as the Fourth of July, Christmas, and Thanksgiving—are sources of many happy family memories. In your photos try to show family members engaged in the traditions of the day. There are many visual symbols of holidays. Watch for them and use them to tell the story.

There may be special Christmas-tree ornaments, for example, that have been in the family for years. Photos of the children hanging these ornaments can be precious, particularly if they are candid and show the excitement of the day. Symbols of the Fourth of July are usually flags, apple pies, and bands playing in the park. Your family may have its own traditions on that day—fishing, picnicking, or just relaxing. Whatever your traditions, you and your children will appreciate a photo story of your holidays together.

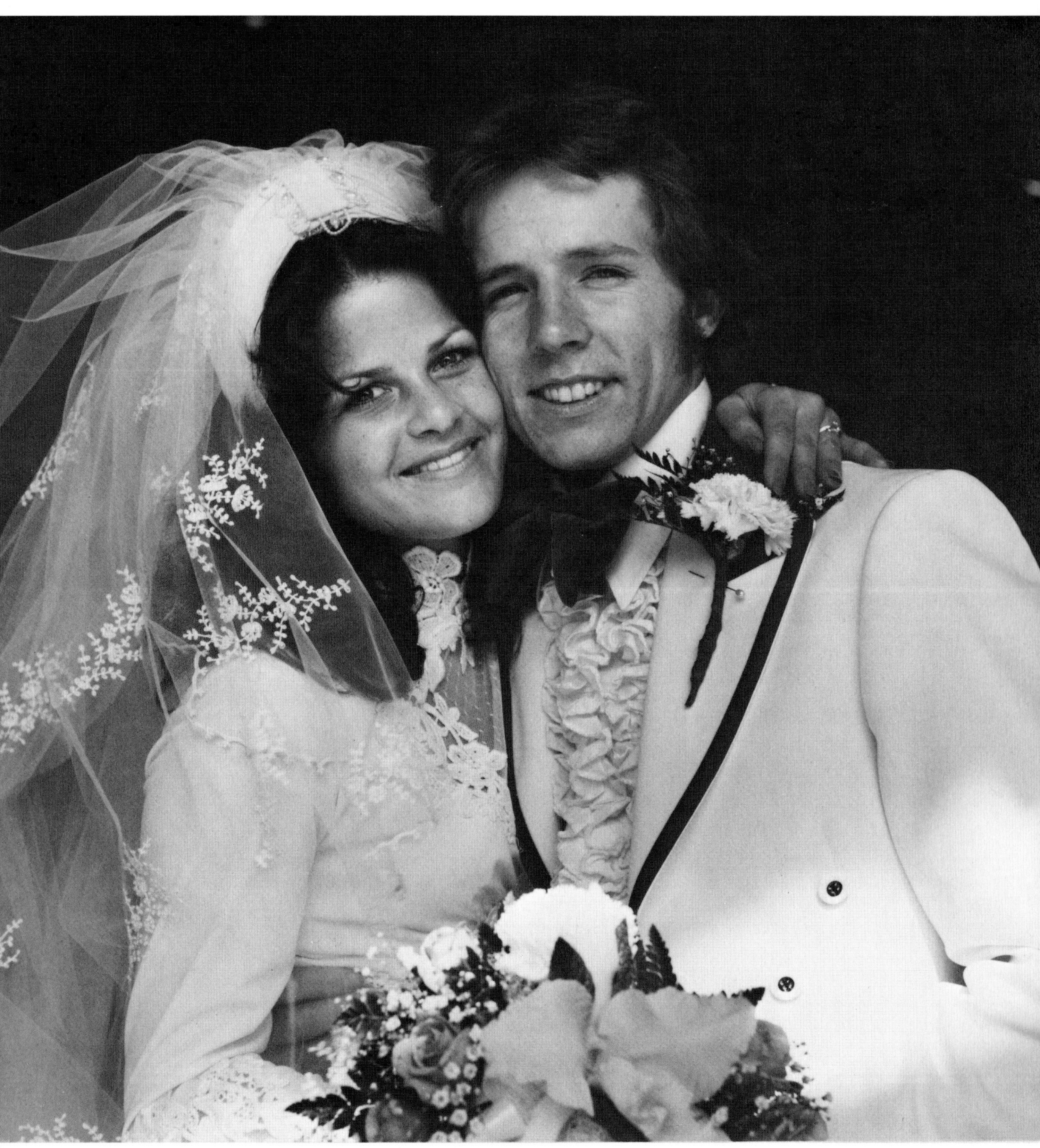

This portrait of the bride and groom was made by the soft light of open shade. Notice how the subject contrasts with the background. Photograph by John Burra.

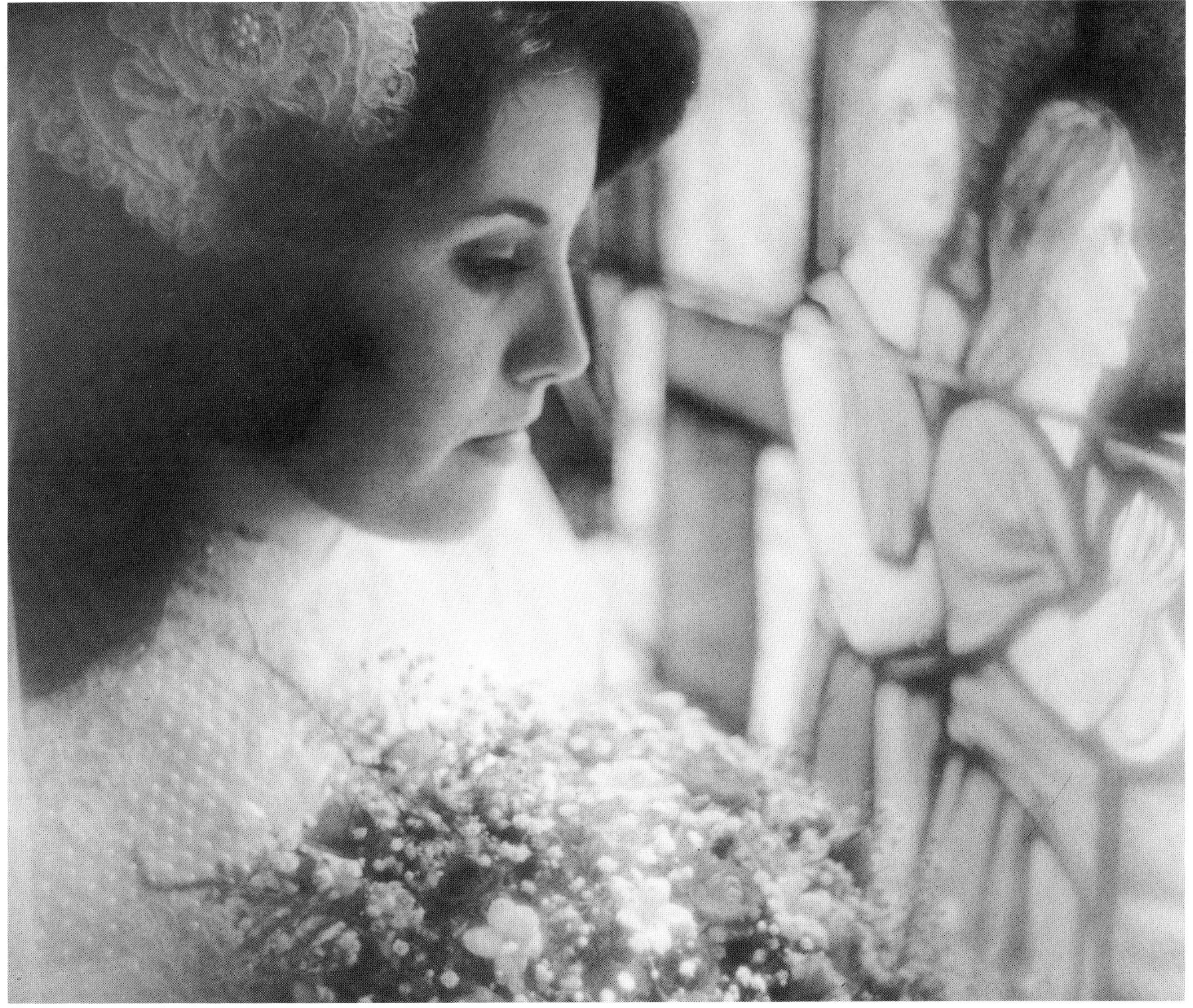

Your coverage of a wedding should include a close-up of the bride. In this photo, the stained-glass windows were used both as a soft light source and an interesting background element.

WEDDINGS AND PARTIES

Sometimes it seems as if there are as many cameras as guests at weddings and parties. Look for the unposed moments. At these events a fast-acting photographer can take many good photos.

Be sure to include the clowning that is bound to occur when people are having a good time. If you want to take posed photos, do so at the beginning of the event. Everything is fresh then, whereas later people will have scattered and flowers will have wilted.

If a professional photographer has been hired for the event, do not interfere with his work. Remember, he is the official photographer and he has a job to do. He may be on a tight schedule and have other assignments to meet. There will be plenty of time during the event for your pictures.

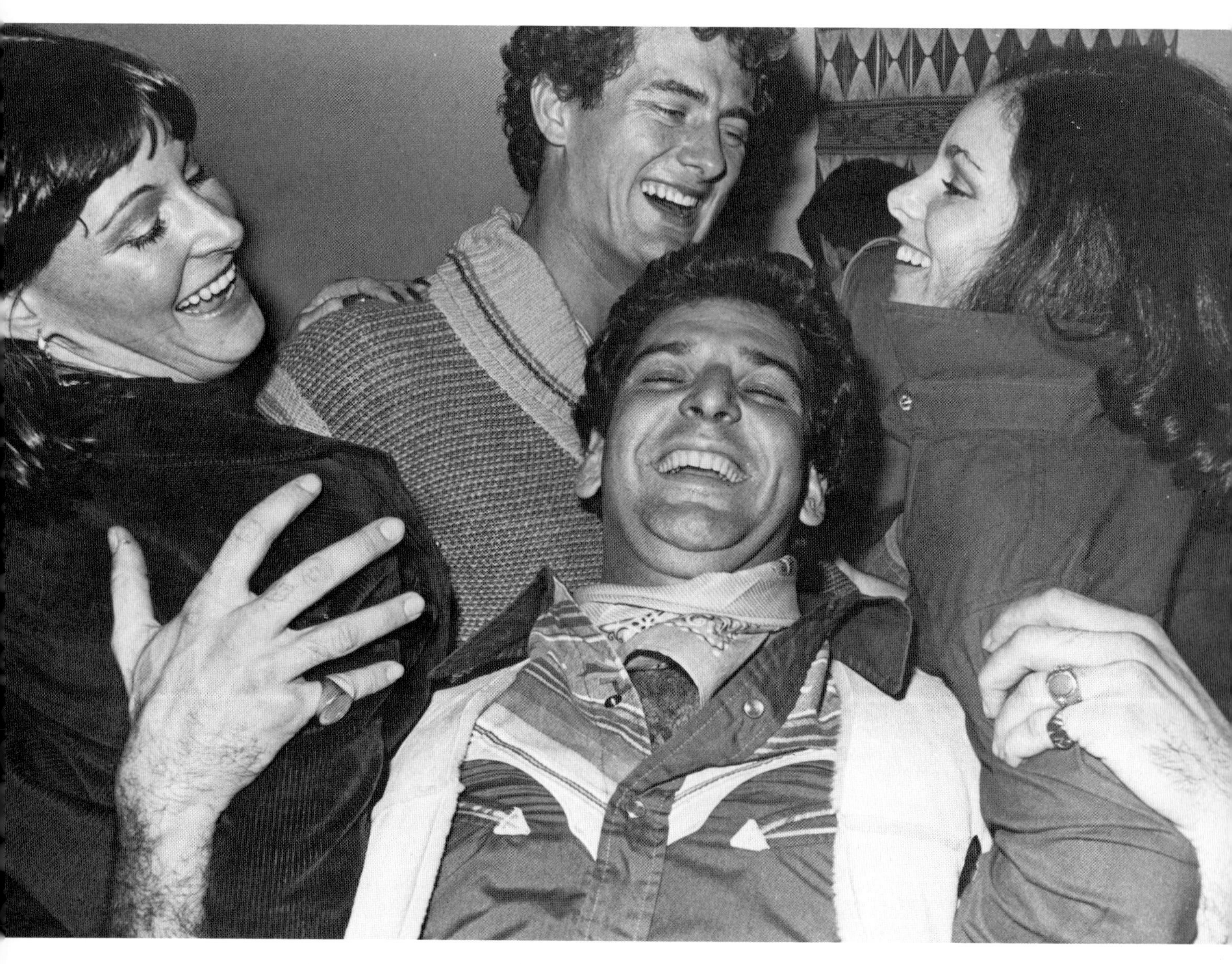

Have your camera and flash ready to record the lively moments of a party. Photograph by Michael O'Connor.

Special tips for weddings
Listed below are tips for photographing weddings:

Be sure your camera is working, your batteries are fresh, and the meter is set for the correct film speed. If you are using a flash, also set the shutter to the correct speed.

Watch out for cluttered backgrounds when taking photos of the bride, especially in the dressing room.

Be sure to take some full-length poses that will show off the bride's gown.

Find out rules in advance. Most religions do not allow photographs to be taken during the ceremony.

Be on the alert for tears of joy, hugs, and kisses. Emotions are highest immediately after the ceremony.

Make sure everyone is facing the camera when taking group photos at tables. Ask those people whose backs are toward you to get up and stand behind the people sitting at the far edge of the table.

Take many photographs and enjoy yourself. But don't try to assume the entire responsibility. Encourage the bride and groom to hire an experienced professional photographer.

I once attended a wedding where the host provided film for all the guests. When everyone finished shooting the rolls, they left them with the host, who then processed the film. This made for a marvelous, comprehensive collection of snapshots.

CHAPTER SEVEN

CAMERAS ON ADVENTURE

The camera was used by travelers even before Daguerre's practical method of photography. Early voyagers used an optical device called *camera obscura* as an aid in making sketches of the places they visited. They then brought the sketches home in order to share their adventures with friends.

Today you are carrying on that image-making tradition. In fact, it is quite possible that your interest in photography began with vacation pictures and a desire to make better visual notes of the happy, exciting times you and your family enjoyed.

WHAT EQUIPMENT TO TAKE

Deciding what equipment to take depends partially on the kind of trip you are planning and partially on the types of photos you intend to take. If you will be carrying your gear at all times, you will want to keep the weight to a minimum. Traveling by vehicle will allow you to take accessories you may use only occasionally. If there are specific photos you want to take, such as close-ups of flowers, then be sure to include a lens with close-up capabilities.

My minimum travel kit contains:

2 camera bodies (1 for black and white, 1 for color)

70–210mm close-focusing zoom lens

35mm wide angle lens

clamp pod

orange, red, and polarizing filters

spare batteries for camera

film (average of 1 roll per day)

notebook and pen

lens tissue

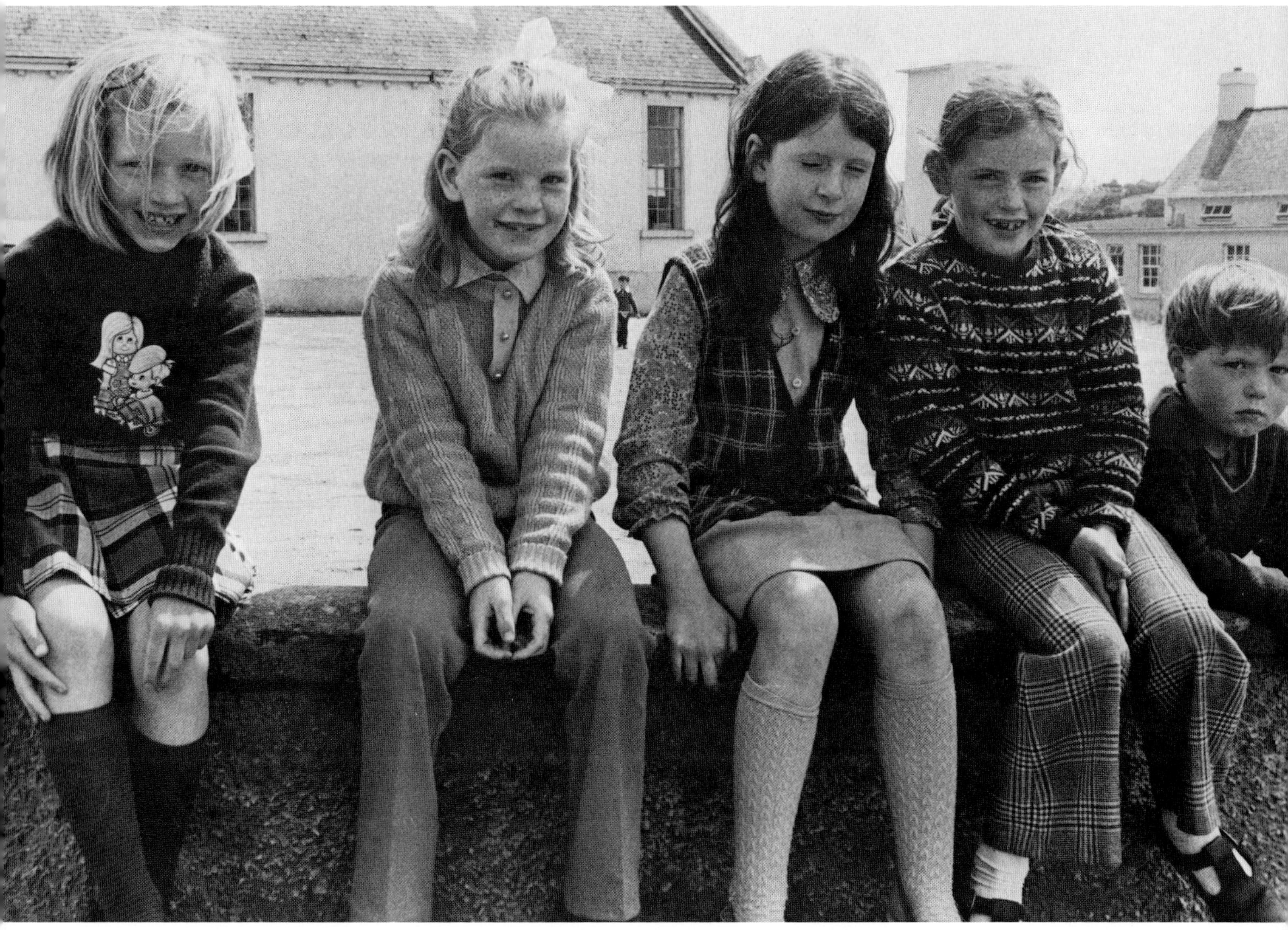

You don't want to miss a great shot like these children in Ireland, due to camera malfunction. Before you leave on a trip, shoot a test roll and put fresh batteries in all equipment. Photograph by Michael O'Connor.

When traveling by car, there is usually space for a few extras. Although not used regularly, they do sometimes come in handy. These extras usually include:

special-effect filters (star, soft focus, etc.)

cable release

tripod

flash with spare sync cord and batteries

300mm telephoto lens

21mm wide angle lens

large ear syringe (for cleaning cameras)

Of course this list will vary with your individual preferences, but do avoid taking everything you own with you. You will find that about 90 percent of your needs can be met with the basic kit.

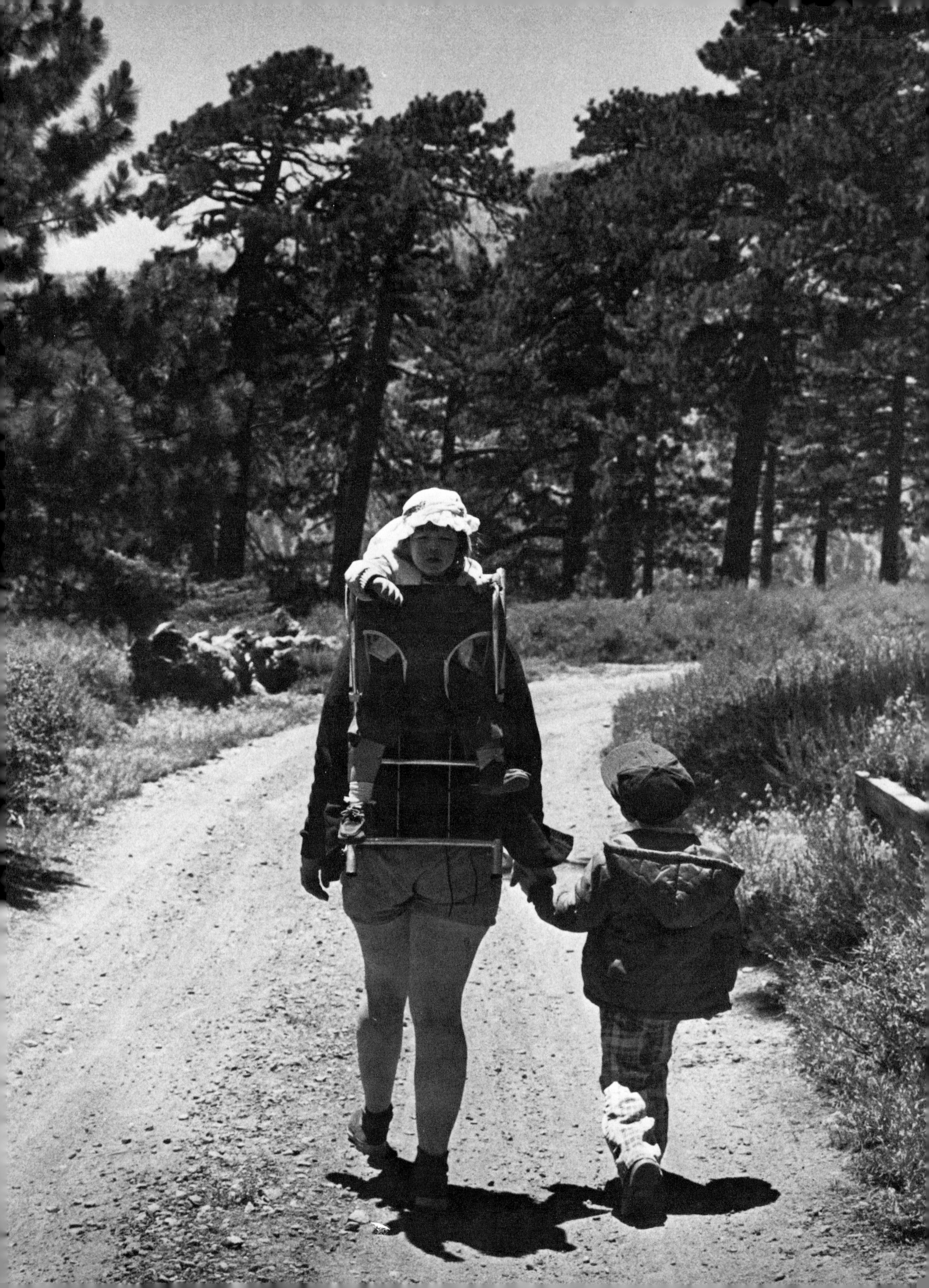

Test before you go
One of my friends took a long European trip and shot forty rolls of film. But because the camera malfunctioned, thirty-eight of those rolls were blank. If he had tested his camera before leaving, he would have known that the light meter wasn't working. Don't take chances. Shoot a test roll in each camera before you leave, and start your trip with fresh batteries in all equipment.

Equipment and foreign travel
When traveling to foreign countries, use the same equipment list as for any other trip. However, be sure to check the gear with the U.S. customs officials *before* you depart. They will give you a certificate verifying your ownership of the equipment. This certificate will save you from possible import duties on your return.

Almost all foreign countries welcome tourists and their cameras. However, don't arrive looking too much like a professional photographer. Some countries place restrictions on professional photographers. If you arrive with several shiny aluminum cases full of cameras and film, border officials may not accept your pleas of amateur status. The result may be a fee or some other restriction.

Film is generally available in other countries, but you may have to settle for brands you are unfamiliar with. Therefore it is better to take enough film with you to last the trip. Although some countries have limits on how many rolls you can bring in, you will rarely have trouble if you spread the rolls around in your luggage.

Film processing abroad is subject to erratic quality control, so bring your exposed rolls back with you for development. On extended trips you can arrange to send your film back, a roll at a time. It should be promptly processed and checked by someone at home for signs of camera malfunction.

COMPREHENSIVE COVERAGE

When photographing your adventures, whether they be to exotic countries or to the local recreation area, be sure to provide a full photo story. Your coverage can easily take a chronological approach. Begin with preparations and departure, then move to arrival, points of interest, return trip, and unpacking.

When making your photo story, be sure to include all aspects of the event. If you have ever seen photo coverage of a Himalayan mountain ascent, a raft trip, or a bicycle trip, you have probably seen photos of hard times as well as the good, the trivial as well as the major. Although your trip may not be quite so adventuresome, be sure to include the fatigue and the flat tires as well as the fun.

Opposite page: This illustrates a good opening shot for a chronological approach to recording an adventure.

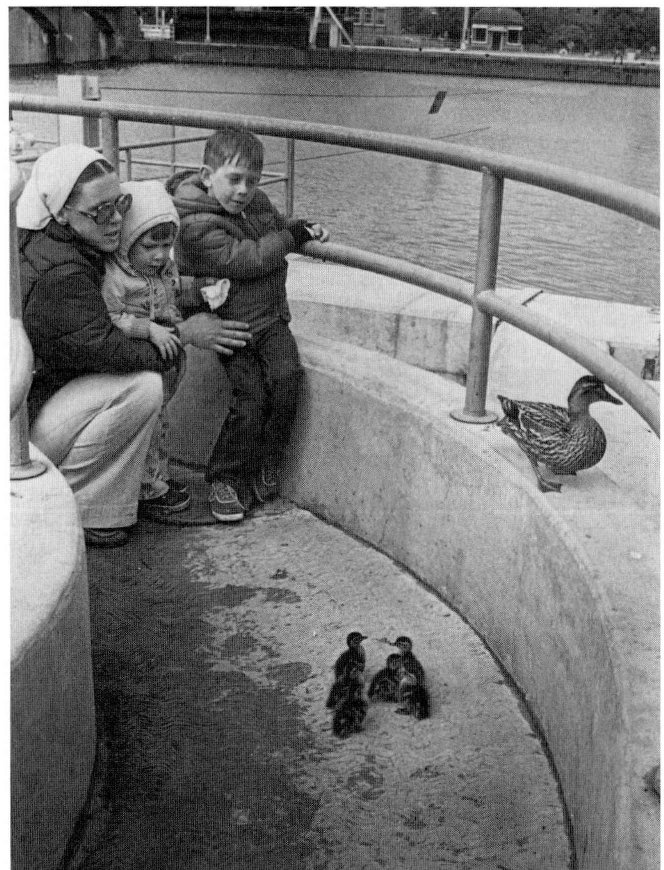

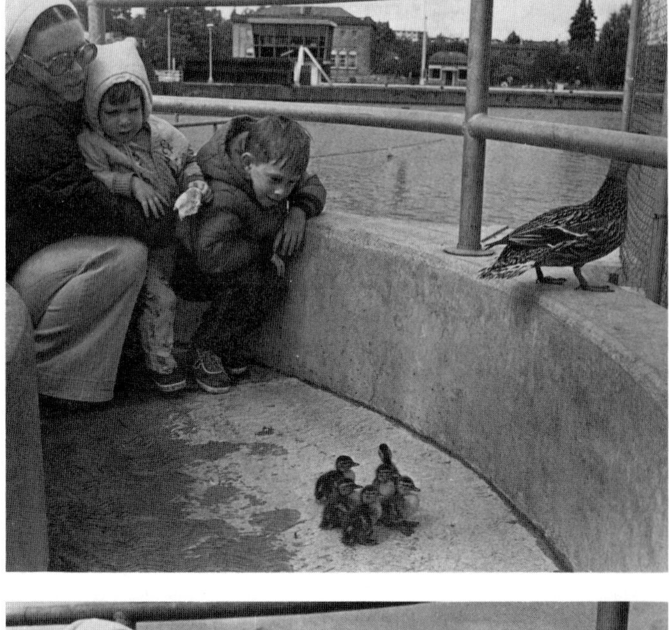

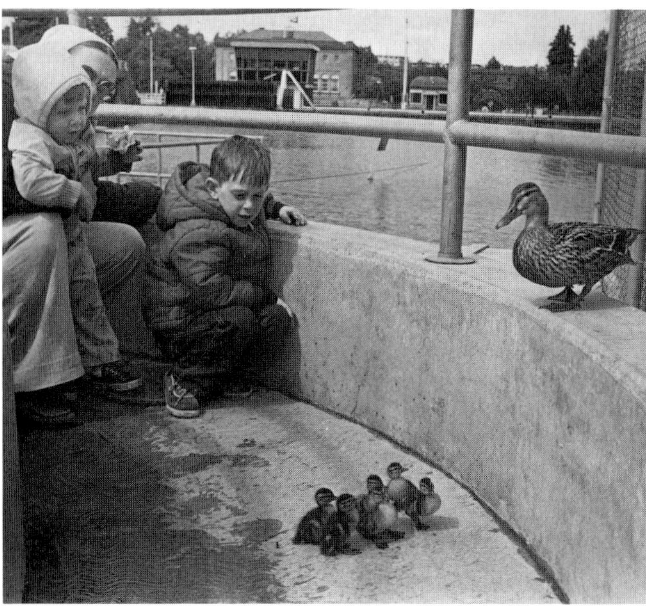

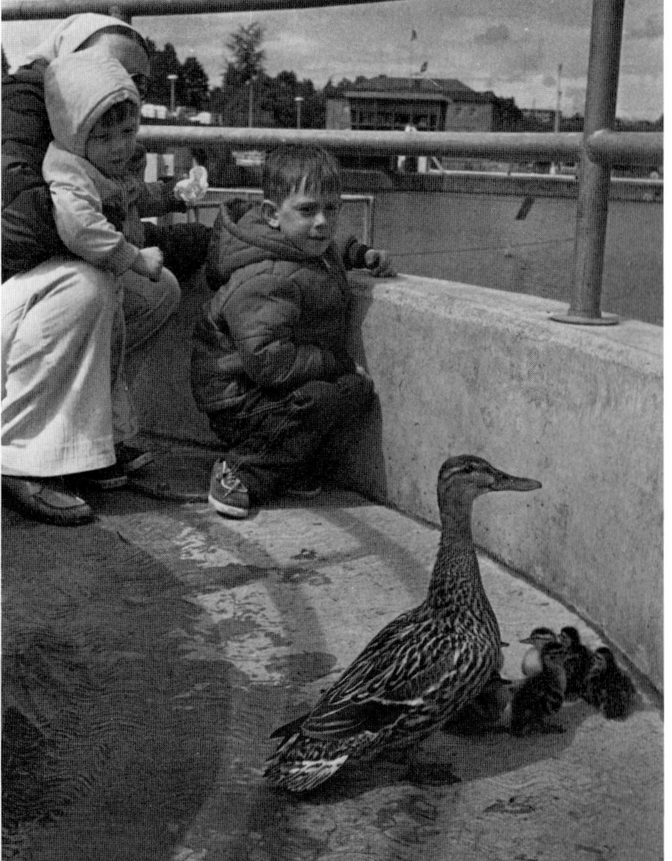

Do not wait for the perfect shot, because the situation may not improve. Be prepared to shoot many photos in the hopes that one will be successful. The first shot, top left, *does not emphasize the ducklings. To correct this, the photographer squatted down for a low angle;* top right. *Just at that moment, the mother duck's head was hidden by the railing. In the photo on the* bottom left, *the mother duck turned around, but the woman's face is hidden by the little girl. Things deteriorated,* bottom right, *when the mother duck hopped down to protect her young. Some compromise is frequently necessary in these candid situations.*

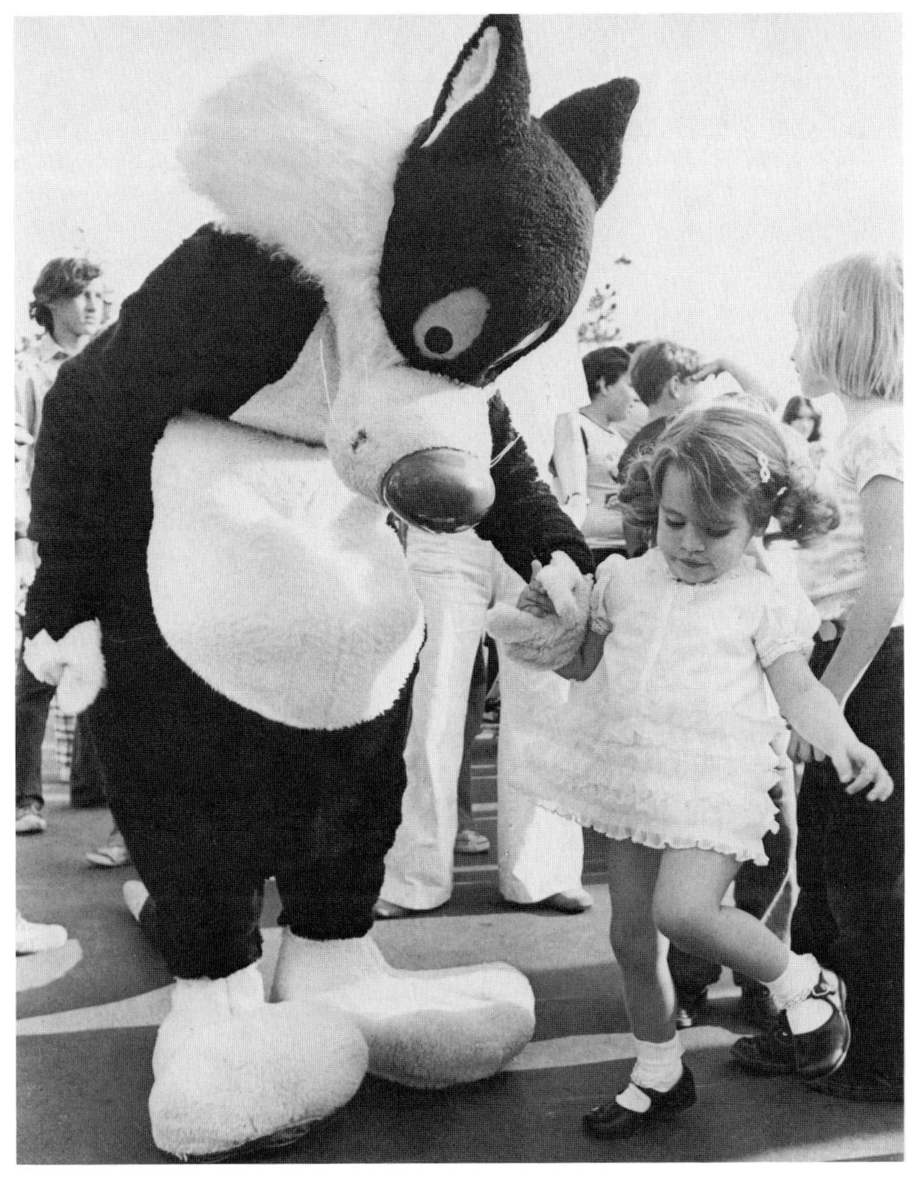

You can make photos of an amusement park more exciting by showing your family actively enjoying one of its features. Photograph courtesy of Marriott's Great America.

Don't quit shooting if the weather turns foul either. Weather can be full of visual excitement, and if it affects your trip, the results should be included in your story.

The three-shot technique

When shooting your story, remember a technique used by professional filmmakers. It will add interest to your report. This technique can be stated thus: long shot, medium shot, close-up.

The long shot is an overall view of the scene. It shows locale. A medium shot narrows attention to a specific area, and the close-up shot moves in on details and shows expressions.

By using this technique you will avoid taking too many photos at the same distance from the subject. Such coverage can be boring and lacking in impact.

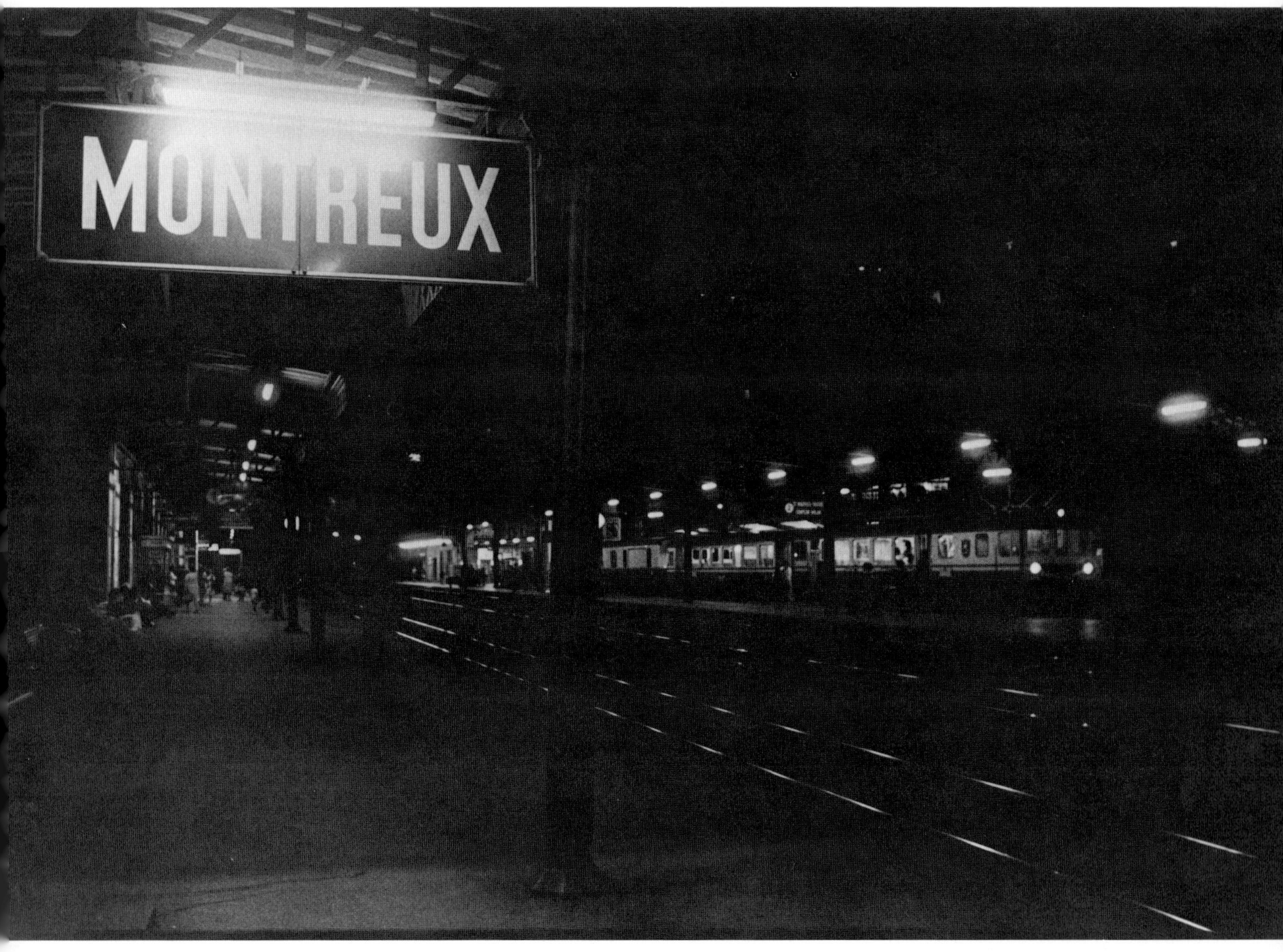

Above: *Look for street and railway signs that you can photograph and use as titles for your completed story. Photograph by Michael O'Connor.*

Right: *Including a person when you are photographing natural phenomena can give the viewer an idea of the scale of the scene.*

At points of interest

To keep your photographic record from becoming dull and repetitious, avoid the tendency of posing your family. Instead, show them actively exploring some point of interest or enjoying its features.

Be sure to use the composition tips we have discussed and remember that foreground framing is an effective way to add depth to your photos. Also, keep an eye out for signs you can photograph and use as titles for your completed story. Almost every national park and monument has such signs posted at their entrances. Clever photographers can find ready-made titles in street signs, road maps, buildings signs, and mileage markers.

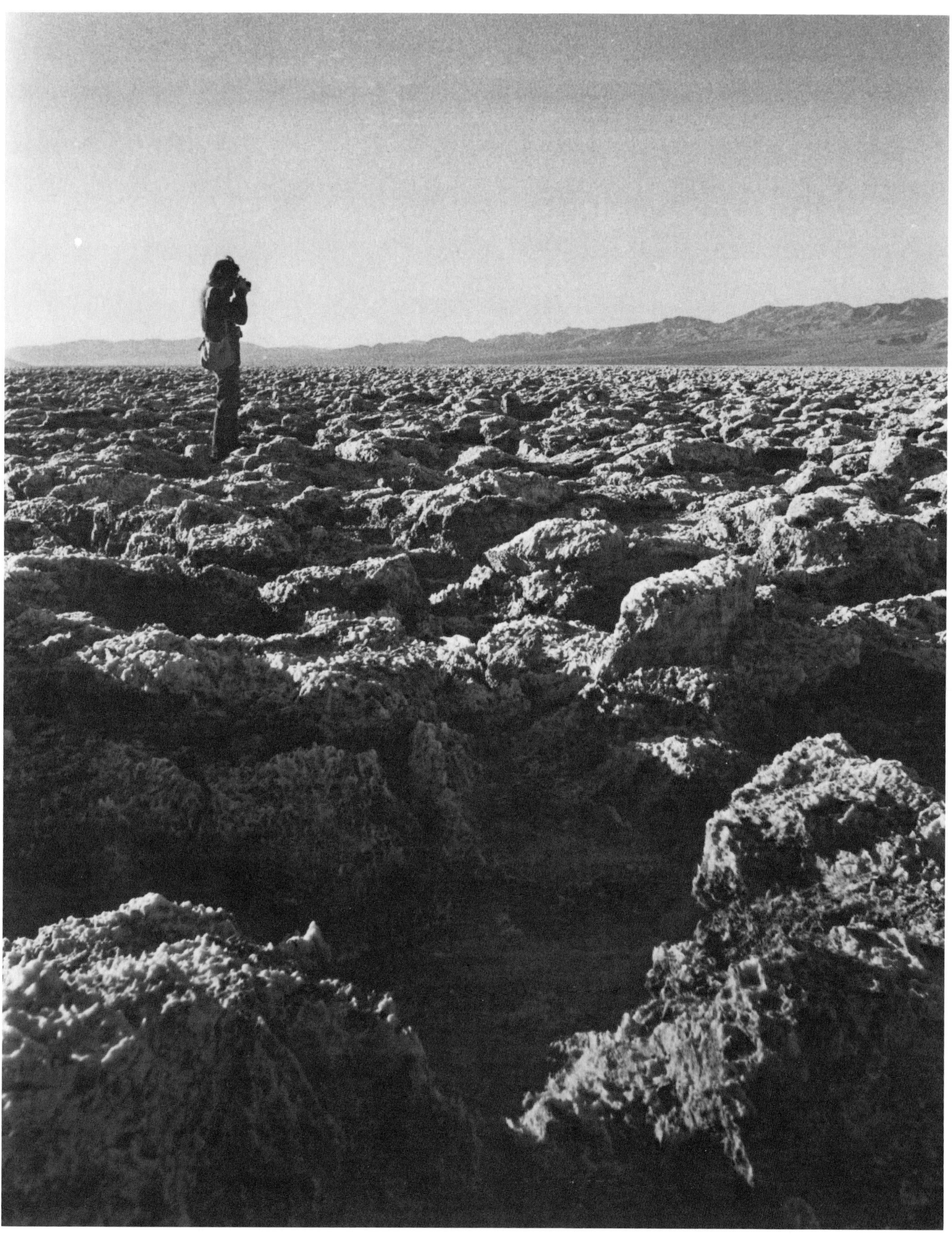

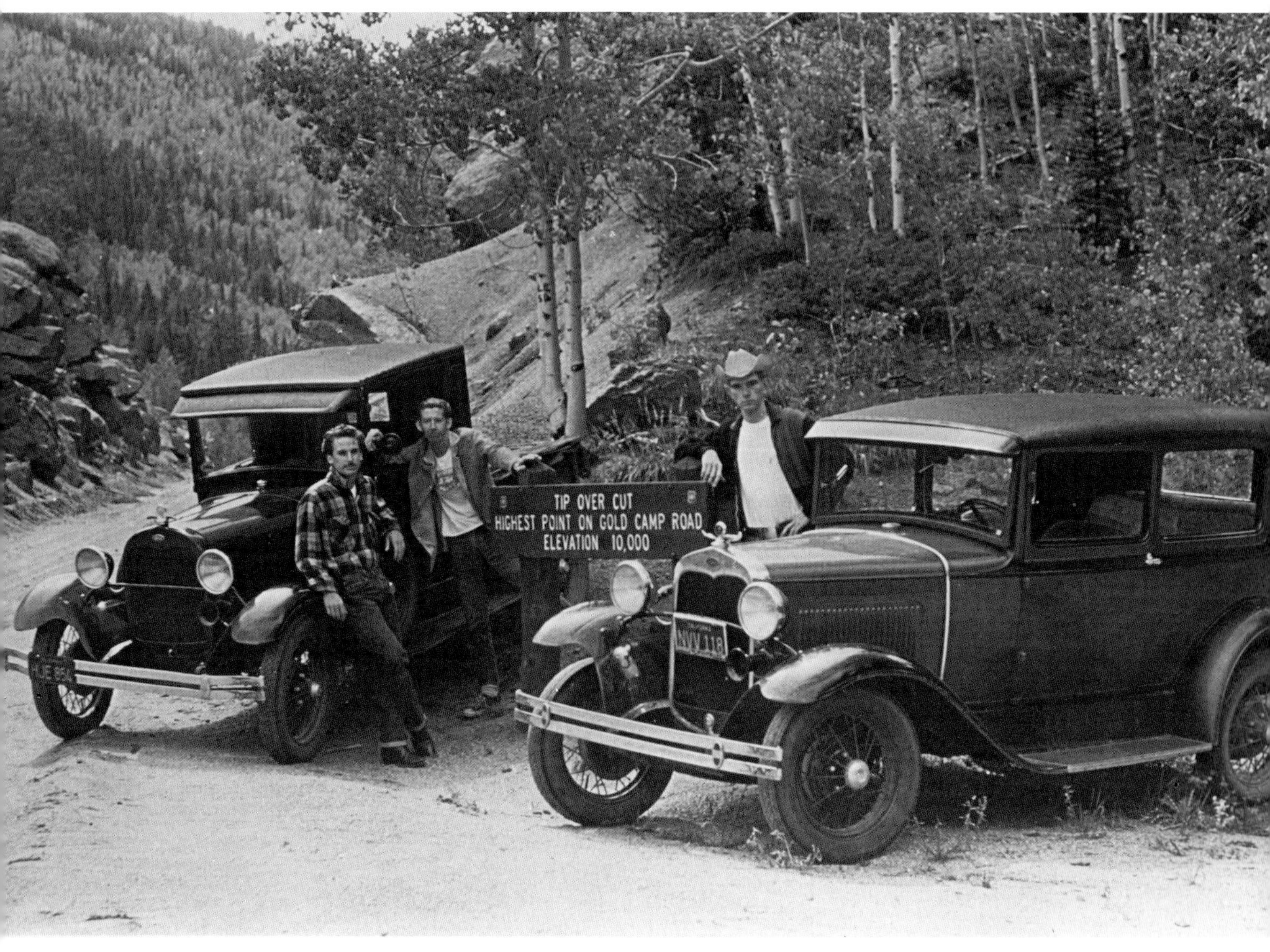

For a more accurately composed picture, stop your car to take that picture.

AUTO AND RV ADVENTURES

When traveling in a car, keep a camera handy for those moments that may not present themselves again. For example, your child may fall asleep in a funny position, or you may see something ahead that won't wait for a second look.

When you see something along the road that you want to photograph, stop the car to take the picture. Photos made from moving vehicles almost always have blurred foregrounds, and you cannot accurately control the composition when you are hurtling down the highway. Do shoot some photos, however, that show the movement of the car and the view out the windshield.

Cameras and hot weather

You have probably heard the admonition about keeping your camera in the glove compartment. Excess heat there can spoil your film and damage your camera. Under the seat can be even hotter in the summer, since the exhaust pipe passes immediately beneath the floor. A good place for your camera bag is on the shady side of the seat. The gear is easily reachable yet safe from heat.

A good place to keep your film is in an ice chest or refrigerator, and in fact this is good policy at home for those extra rolls. But be sure the film has a chance to warm up before you open the package. Otherwise, condensation on the surface of the film can occur and ruin your photos.

SPECIAL TIPS FOR SPECIAL TRIPS

When taking your camera to the beach, observe a few precautions. They will keep your camera safe and improve your photos. It should be obvious that the camera must be protected from sand, but ocean spray is often not so noticeable. Yet it can leave a film on your lens. Use a haze or skylight filter for protection and be sure to wipe the camera thoroughly when you leave.

When loading film, protect the cassette from direct sun by turning your back and loading the camera in your shadow.

River raft trips

On raft trips the possibility of getting sand into your camera increases. For such a trip it would be wise to buy an underwater housing for your camera. Or you might even want one

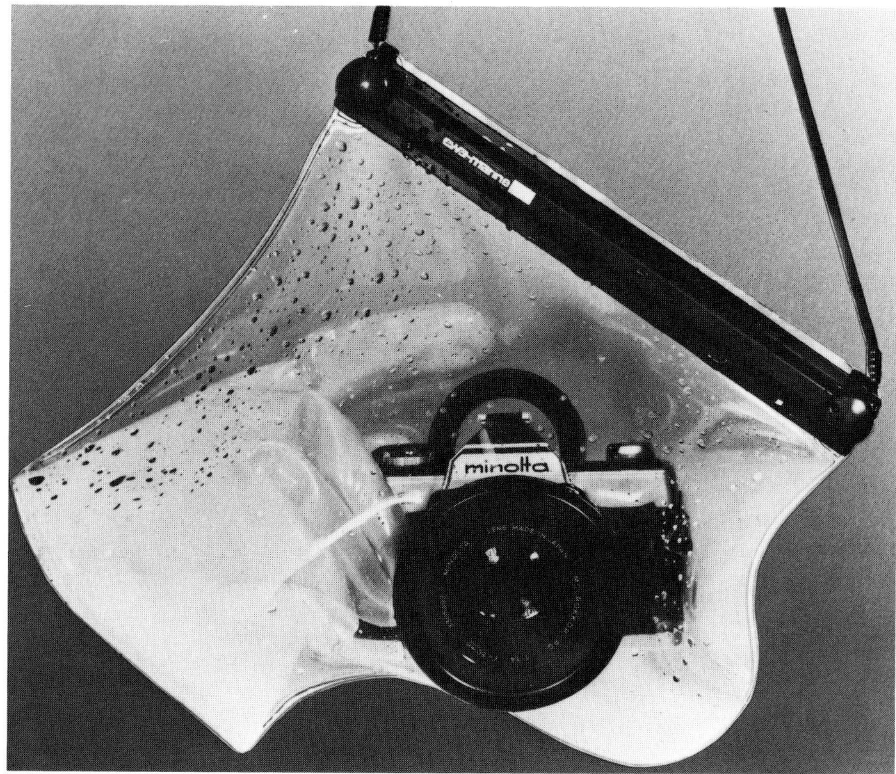

This heavy plastic bag, made by EWA, is an effective way to protect your camera against water and sand. It also can be used under water to a depth of thirty feet. Photograph courtesy of Pioneer & Co.

of the special all-weather cameras, such as the Nikonos or the Minolta 110 Weathermatic. Some photographers use surplus ammo boxes lined with foam. They make good watertight, batter-proof cases.

Telephoto lenses are a must for capturing the action of other boats. A wide angle is useful for in-camp scenes and scenery.

In the forest

When camping in a car or in an RV (recreational vehicle), be sure your equipment is in a safe place. Unfortunately theft has become a problem. Also, if you carry liquid or cream-based insect repellents, wipe the residue off your hands before handling the camera. Otherwise the camera will get oily or sticky.

Backpacking and bicycling

When backpacking or bicycling, your primary consideration should be weight. One of the lightweight camera systems will help keep the burden down. A midrange zoom is a good choice if you will be carrying only one lens, particularly if it offers close focusing. On backpack trips a long telephoto might be useful for photographing animals. Frankly, though, unless you know how to stalk animals, they will know you are coming long before you see them, and they will be almost impossible to find.

Keeping your camera safe yet ready for action is a little more difficult with these activities. Cases also add unnecessary weight. So you might want to try using a plastic bag, which offers some protection against dirt. However, be careful of condensation in damp weather.

One handy item is the clamp-pod. This device will hold your camera steady during low-light exposures. You can also mount your camera to a tree or prop it against a rock with the help of this device. It will also enable you to use the camera's self-timer and take group shots with no one left out.

At amusement parks

When photographing your family at amusement parks, try capturing their reactions to the attractions. If possible, get ahead of them on rides so you can turn around and photograph them. Be careful, however, on roller coasters and similar rides. You may get thrown against the side of the car if you're not watching ahead. Also, don't use flash in dark areas. Your photos will not have the spooky effect of the ride, and you may spoil the enjoyment of those around you.

Sometimes statues can look like funny companions for your family members. Also, costumed characters will often pose with your children. Don't be bashful about taking advantage of these opportunities.

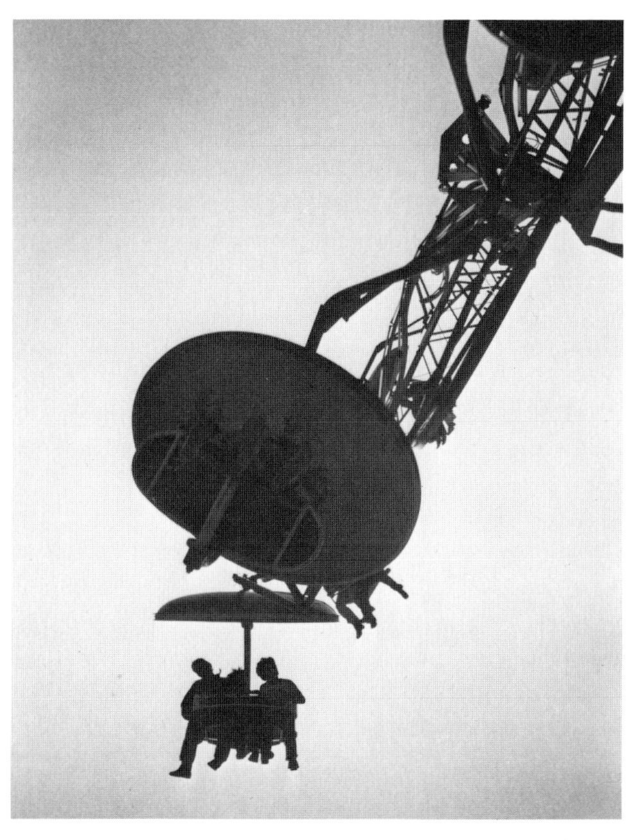

Here are two photos taken at an amusement park. The photo below is much more exciting than the photo on the left because it captures the reaction of the girls to the Scrambler ride.

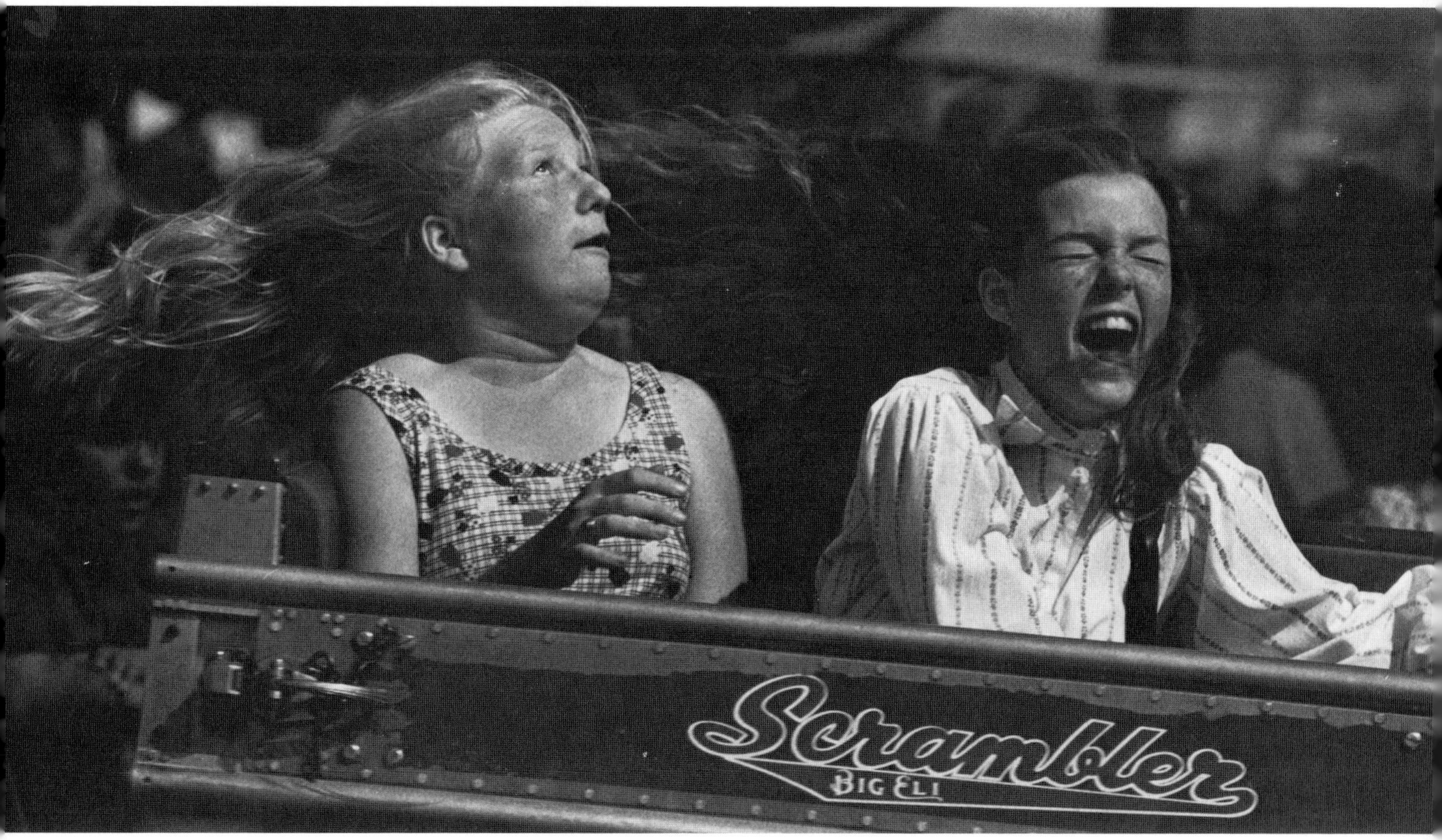

Filters can add impact to your adventure photos, and many other photos as well. These thin glass discs, which are attached to the front of your lens, can enhance certain aspects of a scene or create special effects. Several of the filters most often used will be discussed here. Once you have become familiar with their uses, you may want to try other types. And there are whole books devoted to the subject, such as the *Amphoto Guide to Filters.*

Orange and red filters

Intended for black-and-white film, orange and red filters are used to darken skies and make white clouds stand out. Since they prevent blue light from hitting the film, they also reduce haze in mountain scenes and add texture to snow.

Light-balancing filters

As previously explained, color film should be used under a specific color of light. The film you are most likely to encounter should be used in daylight or with an electronic flash or blue flashbulbs. Film balanced for tungsten light is designed to give correct color under photoflood bulbs. With the use of a balancing filter, however, you can use daylight film under tungsten light, and vice versa. The 80B filter matches tungsten light to daylight film; the 85B filter matches daylight to tungsten film.

Another light-balancing filter is the FLD, which balances fluorescent light to daylight film. You might consider carrying one and an 80B, when photographing in museums.

Polarizing filters

These filters work with both black-and-white and color film. They cut glare and reflections from shiny surfaces, darken skies, and can increase color saturation in many photos. You can see the effect of a polarizing filter by looking through it and rotating it.

Haze and skylight filters

Although these filters look clear, they remove some of the ultraviolet light to which the film is sensitive. They are good for both black-and-white and color photos, and many photographers keep these filters on their lenses at all times. They help protect the front of the lens from dirt, dust, and scratches.

Special-effect filters

There are many special-effect filters, and they can add new dimensions to family photography. Perhaps one of the most useful is the soft-focus filter. The diffused effect produced by

	Filter	Effect	Correction
COMMON FILTERS			
B&W film	Yellow	Causes slight darkening of blue, lightening of yellow, and slight haze penetration.	Open lens one stop or set shutter one speed slower.
	Orange	Causes moderate darkening of blue, particularly skies.	Open lens two stops or set shutter two speeds slower.
	Red	Causes blue skies to appear almost black, clouds stand out, and strong haze penetration.	Open lens three stops or set shutter three speeds slower.
Color film	80B (blue)	Use when shooting outdoor film under tungsten lights.	Open lens two stops or set shutter two speeds slower.
	81A (lt. blue)	Removes excess blue from electronic flash.	Open lens 1/3 stop.
	85B (salmon)	For shooting tungsten balanced film in daylight.	Open lens 2/3 stop.
B&W and Color	Neutral Density	To reduce exposure in extra bright light or permit slow shutter speeds or wide apertures.	Available in a variety of strengths. Meter through filter.
	Polarizing	Reduces glare and enhances color saturation.	Meter through filter.

this filter obscures wrinkles and adds a dreamy, romantic feeling to photos. No exposure correction is necessary.

You can make your own soft-focus filter by dabbing clear nail polish on an old skylight filter in a polka-dot pattern.

Star filters are another popular filter. These filters make candle flames, specular reflections, and exposed light sources look like stars.

There are many other effects you can create with filters, and some manufacturers have devised entire systems, complete with holders, to adapt to any camera. If you are looking for new excitement with your camera, try filters.

Filter factors

Generally when you place a filter over your lens, you must increase exposure to compensate for the light blocked by the filter. The amount of this increase is called the filter factor, and this factor can be found on both film and filter instruction sheets. Sometimes the filter factor is also engraved on the ring of the filter.

The accompanying chart shows the most common filter and the corrections you must make.

It is unwise to meter through filters because meter cells do not always respond to filters in the same way as film. Therefore, when using auto-exposure cameras, you should take your meter reading without a filter in place. Then once you have adjusted the controls for the necessary correction, place the filter over the lens. To do this, you will probably have to use the exposure system in the manual mode. Check your camera's instructions for the exact procedure.

HOW TO TEST YOUR CAMERA IN THE FIELD

While on vacation there are a few basic tests you can make to check for major malfunctions. First you should be sensitive to the feel and sound of your camera. Often, problems are discovered because the equipment doesn't feel right.

Check the aperture

On auto-exposure cameras you can be sure the aperture is closing properly by following this procedure:

Set the camera's exposure system on manual.

Set the shutter speed for one second.

Set the aperture for its smallest opening.

Look at the front of the lens and trip the shutter. You should see the aperture blades close down during the exposure. Try several aperture settings.

If your camera has no shutter-speed control, perform the test in a dimly lit room with the exposure system turned on. Since the shutter may only open for a moment, you will have to watch carefully to see the aperture stop down.

If the aperture does not stop down smoothly and consistently, the camera needs service.

Check the shutter

To check the shutter, set the exposure system on manual. Remove the lens from the camera if possible; if not, set the lens for its widest opening. Test the shutter at each speed, looking at the light as it passes through the camera. You should notice a difference between each shutter speed, however slight, at each setting.

If your camera has no shutter-speed control, leave the lens in place and the exposure system on. Open the camera's back and watch the shutter blades as you aim the camera at a light source, such as a table lamp. Fire the shutter. The shutter speeds should change as you change aperture settings.

If your camera has neither aperture nor shutter controls you can operate, look through the back of the camera. See if light is passing from the lens to the film when you release the shutter.

How to check flash synchronization

When shooting with flash, this short burst of light must go off at the precise moment the shutter is open. Sometimes the mechanisms inside the camera controlling this sequence break down. Although the flash still fires, it is a fraction of a second too early or late. The result is often blank film.

Listed below is a basic test for flash synchronization:

Attach the flash and set the shutter at the proper speed.

Set the lens at its widest opening.

Open the camera's back, aim the camera at a white surface, and fire the shutter.

Look through the camera's lens and check for a flash of light.

Repeat this test several times, checking all four corners of the frame as well as the center. If the shutter is slightly out of adjustment, you will see the flash on only part of the frame.

How to check film advance

With 35mm cameras you can easily put the film in incorrectly. You will think you are taking photos, yet the film will not be advancing. To check if the film is advancing, take the slack out of the rewind knob and see if the knob turns as you operate the advance lever. Do this test for each roll of new film.

CHAPTER EIGHT

PETS AND HOBBIES

Tips and techniques for effective photos

Pets are an important part of a family, and if you want to include them in your album, you will find tips and techniques on pet photography in this chapter. Hobbies, too, can be photographed more effectively by using a few simple techniques.

The most common pet subjects are dogs and cats. The most common mistake is shooting from an eye-level perspective while the animal sprawls on the floor or cowers in a corner. Therefore, the first rule of good pet photography is: get down to the animal's eye level. Photos from a high angle diminish the stature of any subject. If your pet is worthy of being photographed, it is worthy of a little prominence in the frame. Remember, too, most pets are smaller than people. So move in closer when photographing a pet than when photographing its master.

How to get low-angle shots

To get low-angle shots of pets, you will have to get on the floor or put the animals on a table. The table technique may not work with dogs who are not used to being far from the ground.

If you can get a 4-foot-square piece of $\frac{3}{4}$-inch plywood, you can make a sturdy, low-level platform that will not frighten an animal. Better yet, buy a periscopic attachment for your viewfinder. This device will allow you to hold the camera at a very low level without forcing you to lie on the floor. If your camera has a removable prism, you can either remove the prism and look straight down at the focusing screen or you can attach a waist-level finder.

COMPOSE CAREFULLY

Once you have the correct perspective on your pet, do not forget the compositional tips in Chapter 3. In particular, watch the background carefully. Since nature originally intended animals to blend with their surroundings, a background of mottled foliage is likely to blend with the coats of many pets. A plain background will make the animal the prominent feature in the composition.

If you need someone to hold the pet, include that person in

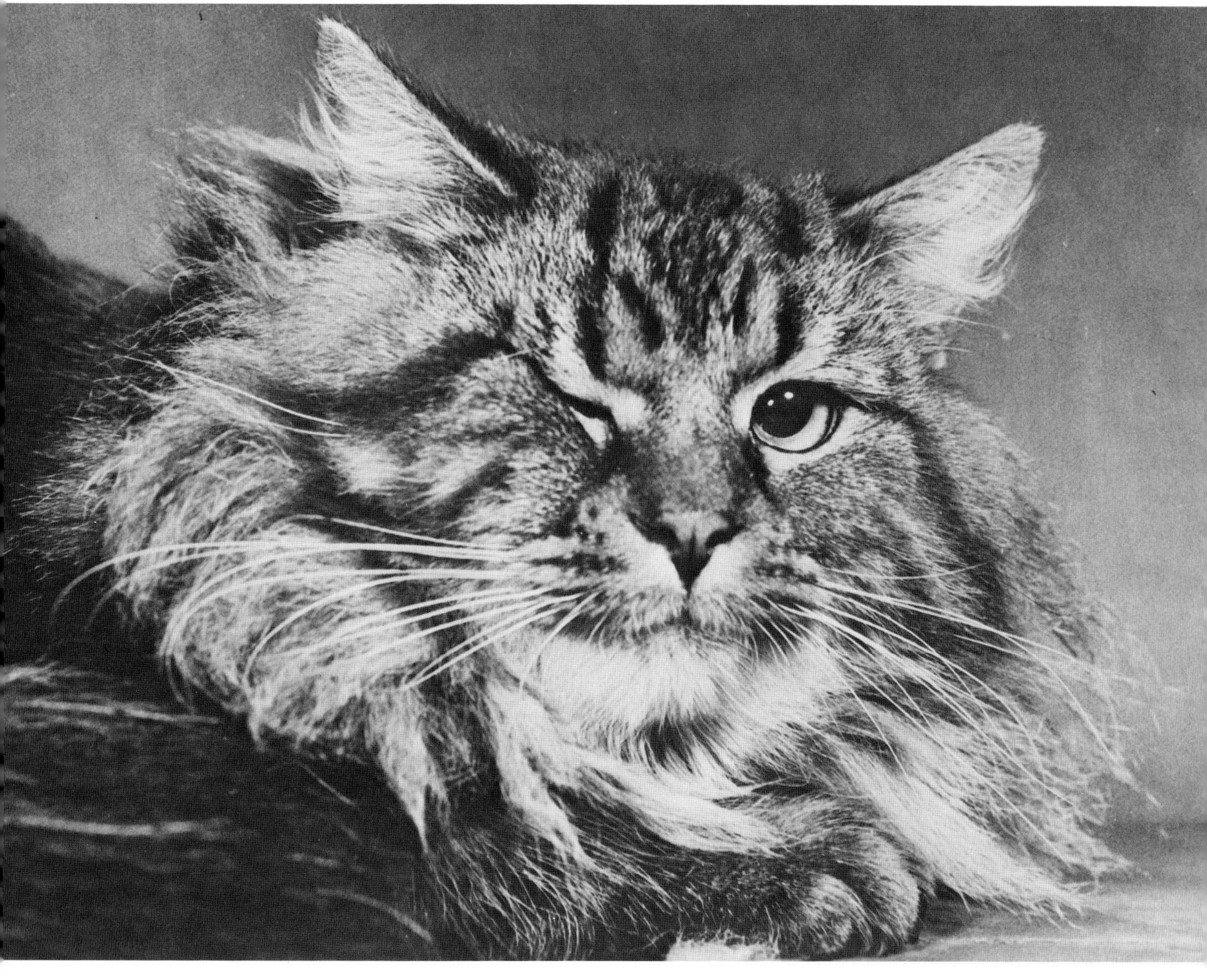

the photo. A shot of a sitting dog will look strange if there is a mysterious arm reaching in from outside the frame.

In order to get low-angle, head-on portraits of pets, you will have to get down on the floor or put the animal on a table. Photograph courtesy of Lowe's Inc.

USE FAMILIAR LOCATIONS

Animals are likely to be nervous or filled with an urge to explore if you put them in an unfamiliar environment. Therefore you will get better results if you go to the territory they're familiar with. Should you need lighting equipment or special background material, set it up in advance and give the animal a chance to examine it. Dogs always want to check out new things. Somehow it seems that as soon as you hold the camera up to your face, they come over and put their wet noses against the lens.

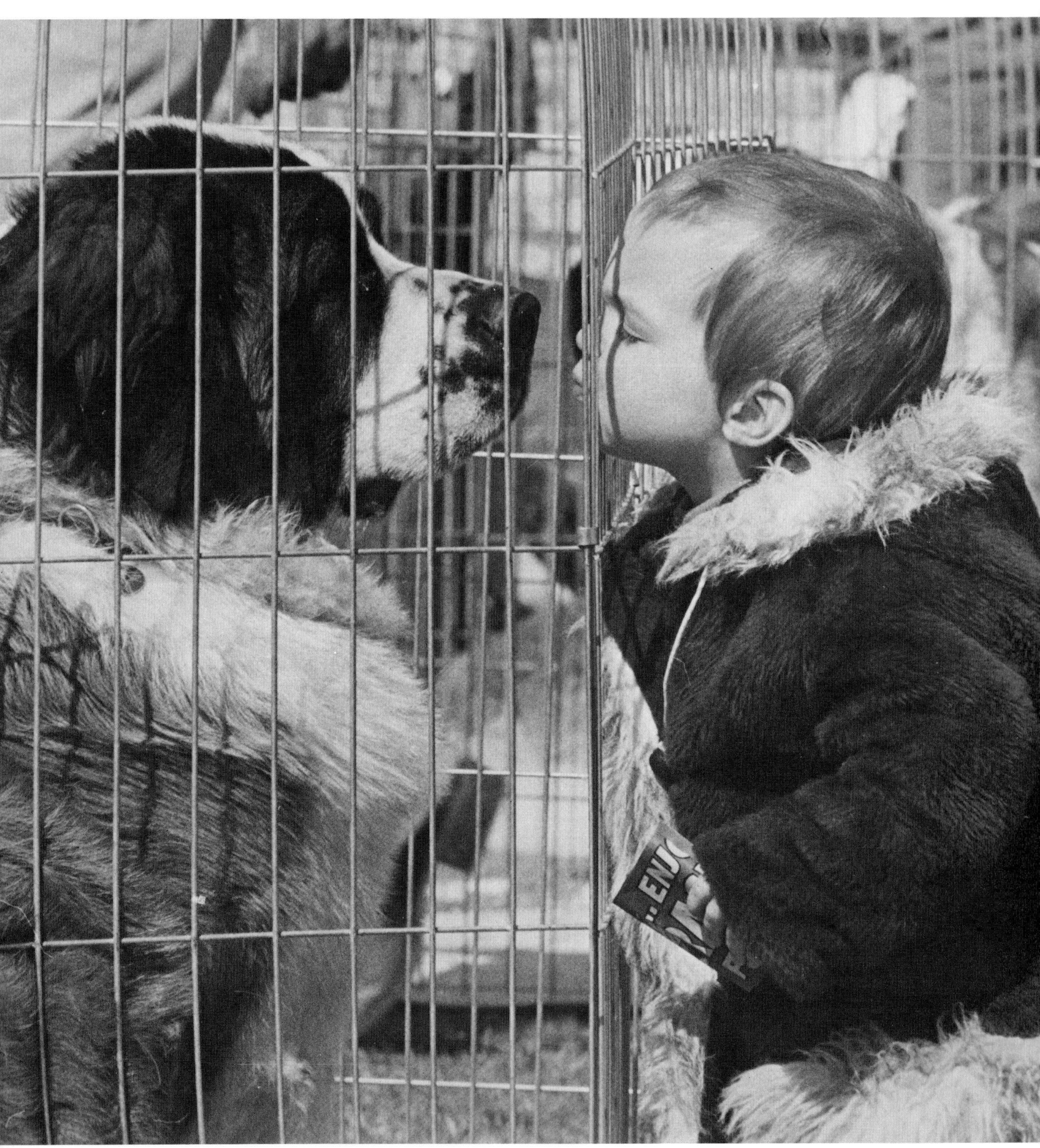

In this picture, a telephoto was used to throw the background out of focus and prevent it from interfering with the subject. Photograph by Joseph A. Frisina, Jr.

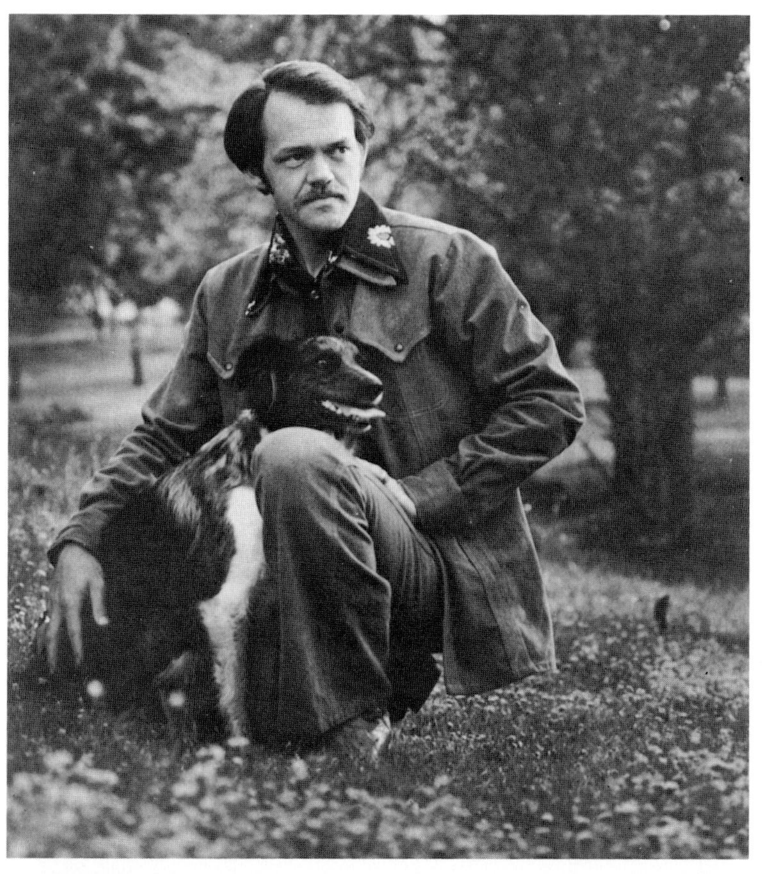

When trying to photograph a frisky dog, pose him with his master and you will have a nice portrait of both of them. Photograph by Colleen Leman Scheidt.

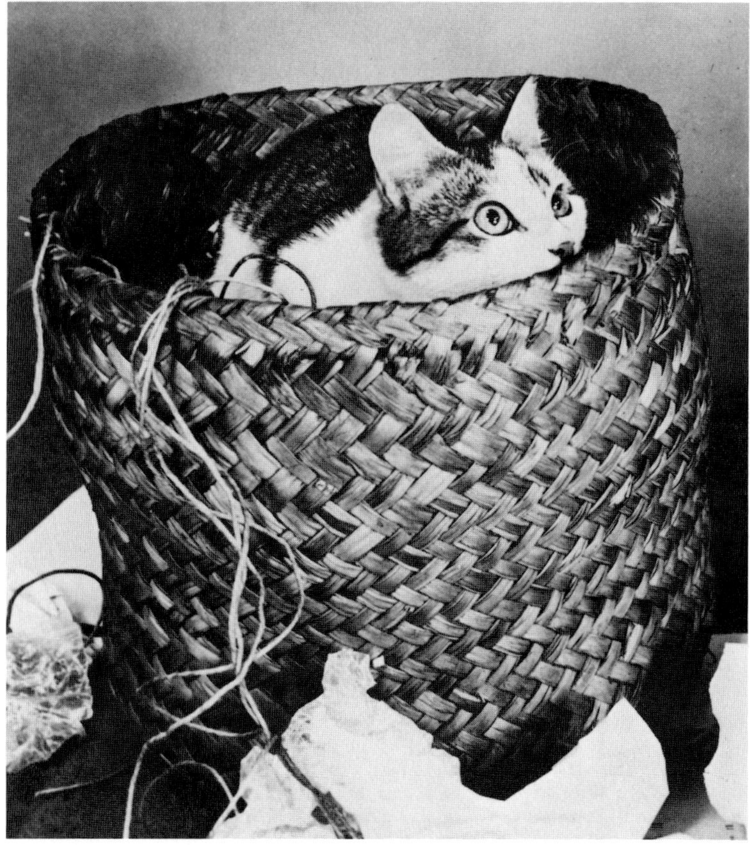

If you are using a special prop with your pet, give the animal a chance to examine the prop before you start the photo session. Photograph courtesy of Lowe's Inc.

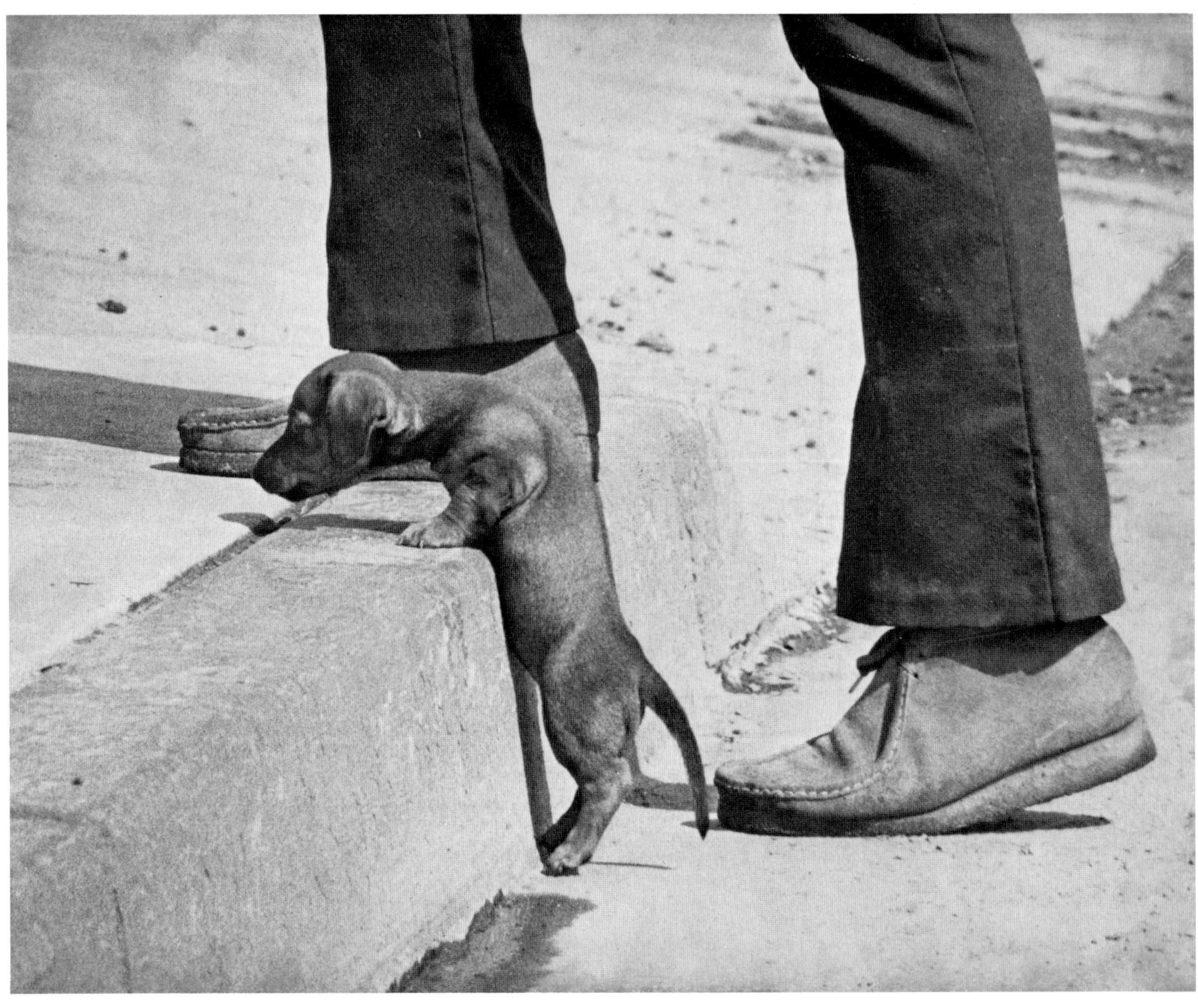

Photograph by Joseph A. Frisina, Jr.

SPECIAL EXPOSURE PROBLEMS

Light or dark fur reflects an abnormal amount of light, and this can fool the camera's light meter. A photo of a dark animal may end up being nothing more than a black mass, while a light animal can end up looking like a textureless blob. To avoid this, take a meter reading of the overall scene. Then open your aperture an additional half an *f*/stop for dark animals, close it by half a stop for light ones.

SPECIAL TIPS

Before a meal a dog will be alert and more interested in pleasing you, particularly if he thinks he'll be rewarded with a treat. After a meal, although he will be less jumpy, he will be less interested in performing. Since each pet is different, you will have to try both times to find out which is best.

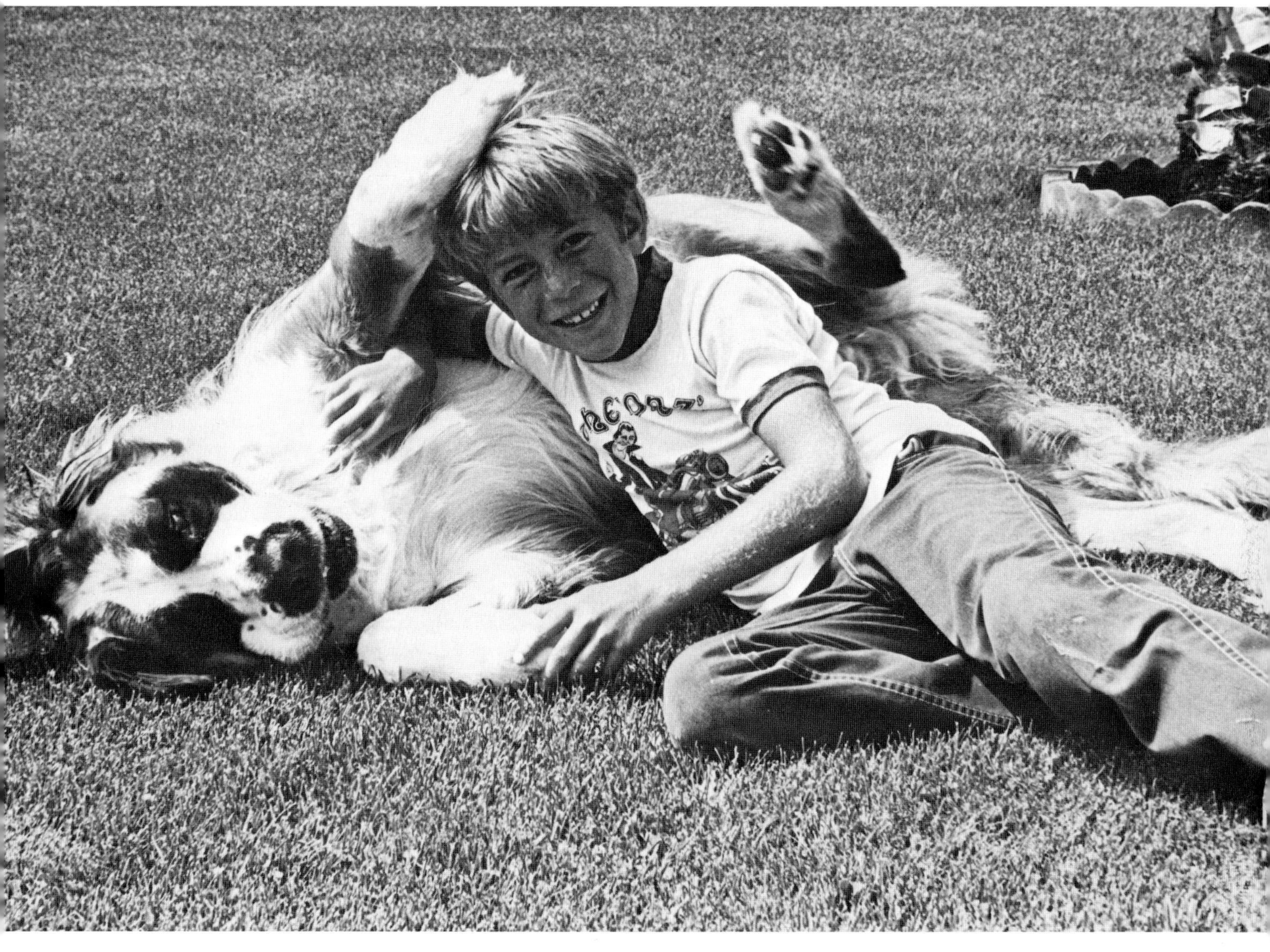

Photos like this require a patient photographer who is willing to shoot a lot of photos in order to get one successful one. Photograph by Mark Appel.

Use three-quarter or side light. Place a dog so that light falls on him from a side angle. This will accentuate the texture of his fur. Avoid using on-camera-flash, or front lighting. Both conceal texture and spoil any possible feeling of dimension.

Use a high-speed film, a small aperture, and a high-shutter speed. This combination will help you produce sharp, blur-free photos; a definite plus when working with active dogs.

Try a midrange zoom. A lens in the 35–70mm range will allow you to adjust to a situation as it changes. A lens with a single control ring is preferable because you can then control the zoom and the focusing quickly. In addition, when the zoom is used at longer focal lengths, you will be able to stand farther from the dog. This sometimes reduces a dog's nervousness. It also makes it easier to throw the background out of focus to emphasize your subject.

Work quickly without a tripod. The dog may not respond to too many calls for attention. So be prepared to shoot and compose quickly.

Expect a high shooting ratio. You must take many photos to get a few superb ones. An auto-winder will help you keep up with the animal's expressions.

Try using an electronic flash. For indoor photos many dogs are not bothered by this short burst of light. And the flashes will freeze the animal's motion for a sharper photo. Photofloods get hot too quickly and the animal may get lethargic and uncomfortable.

Of course do not force a dog to continue with a session. If you insist on prolonging the photography, you may give him a negative impression about camera equipment. Then when the next session approaches, he may remember the bad experience and head for the corner of the yard.

CATS

If you own a cat, you know that he makes all the rules. If he doesn't want to be photographed, forget it until another day. If your animal is a lap cat, try placing him in a helper's lap. This is a convenient level for taking eye-to-eye portraits. And the cat will often stay put for quite a while if his head is being scratched at the same time.

Since cats are relatively small, be sure you compose your shot carefully, taking full advantage of the negative area. If you have to do extensive cropping, it will increase the grain and decrease the sharpness of the photo. Also, focus on the eyes and use as small an aperture as possible. This will help keep the face and whiskers sharp.

Many amateur cat photos tend to be of sleeping animals. Try catching your cat washing, lapping up milk, sharpening its claws, or simply surveying the world. A nice angle for the latter is to put the cat on a wall or fence. Then photograph him from a low angle, using the sky as a plain background.

Mature cats will not always put up with special settings. So approach them calmly, setting your camera near them for a while for their examination. Kittens are easy to work with because they are attracted to almost anything that moves. Try having a helper dangle pieces of string in front of them. You might also try putting a small shoe or oatmeal box on a table to see how a kitten responds to it. Needless to say, keep a kitten away from the edges of the table.

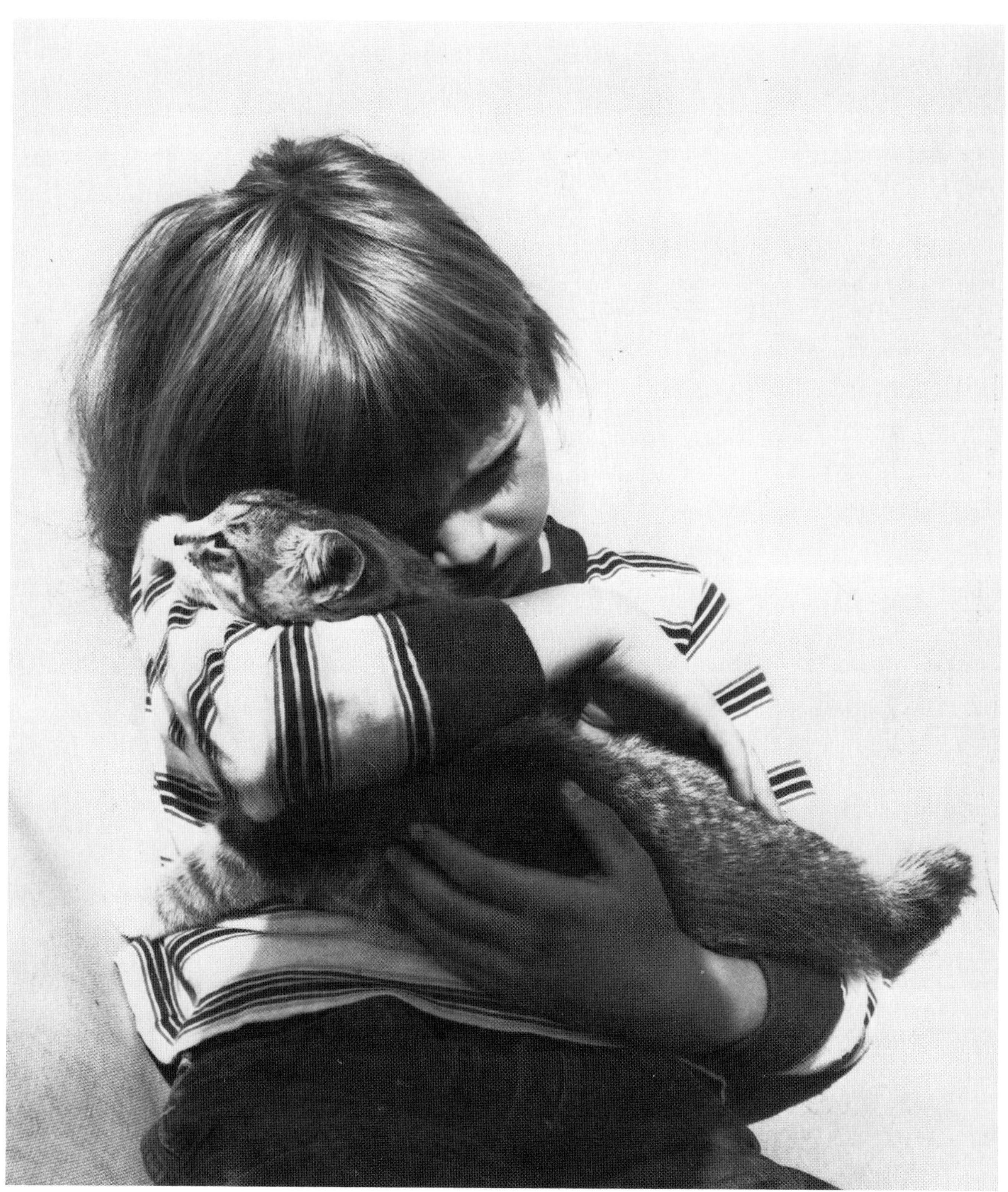

For camera shy pets, try having a helper hold the animal. Photograph by Betty Rosenzweig.

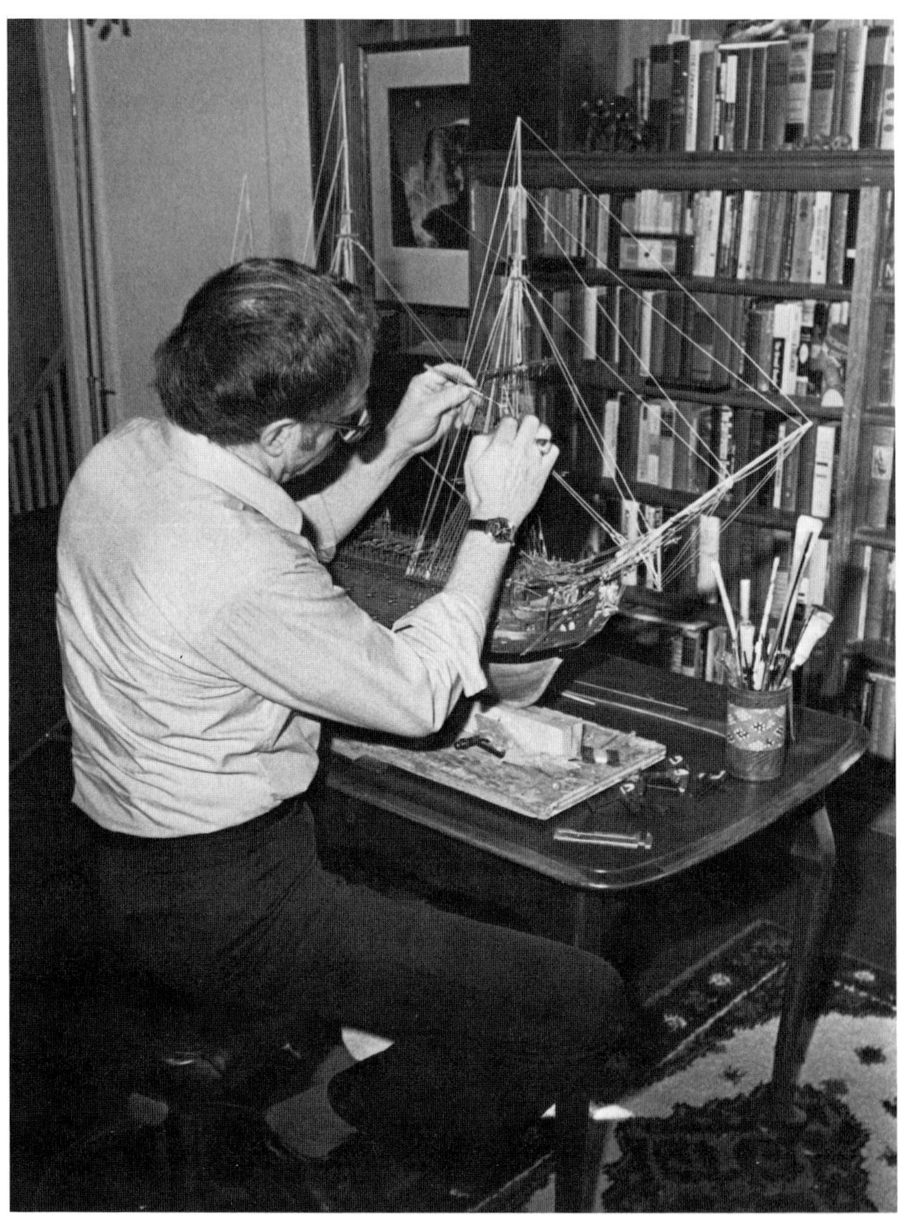

Right: *This photo does not show the model or the modeller. Photograph on opposite page is a much better approach.*

HOBBIES

Hobbies are part of family life for many people. When photographing a hobby, be sure both the person and the product or activity will be visible in the photo.

Crafts and models

When photographing crafts and models and the people who made them, you can generally use the basic lighting techniques already discussed. If a product is small, however, you might want to place the product in the foreground with the craftsperson in the background. Then use the side lighting so that both elements are illuminated with the same degree of brightness. (See the accompanying illustration for an example.)

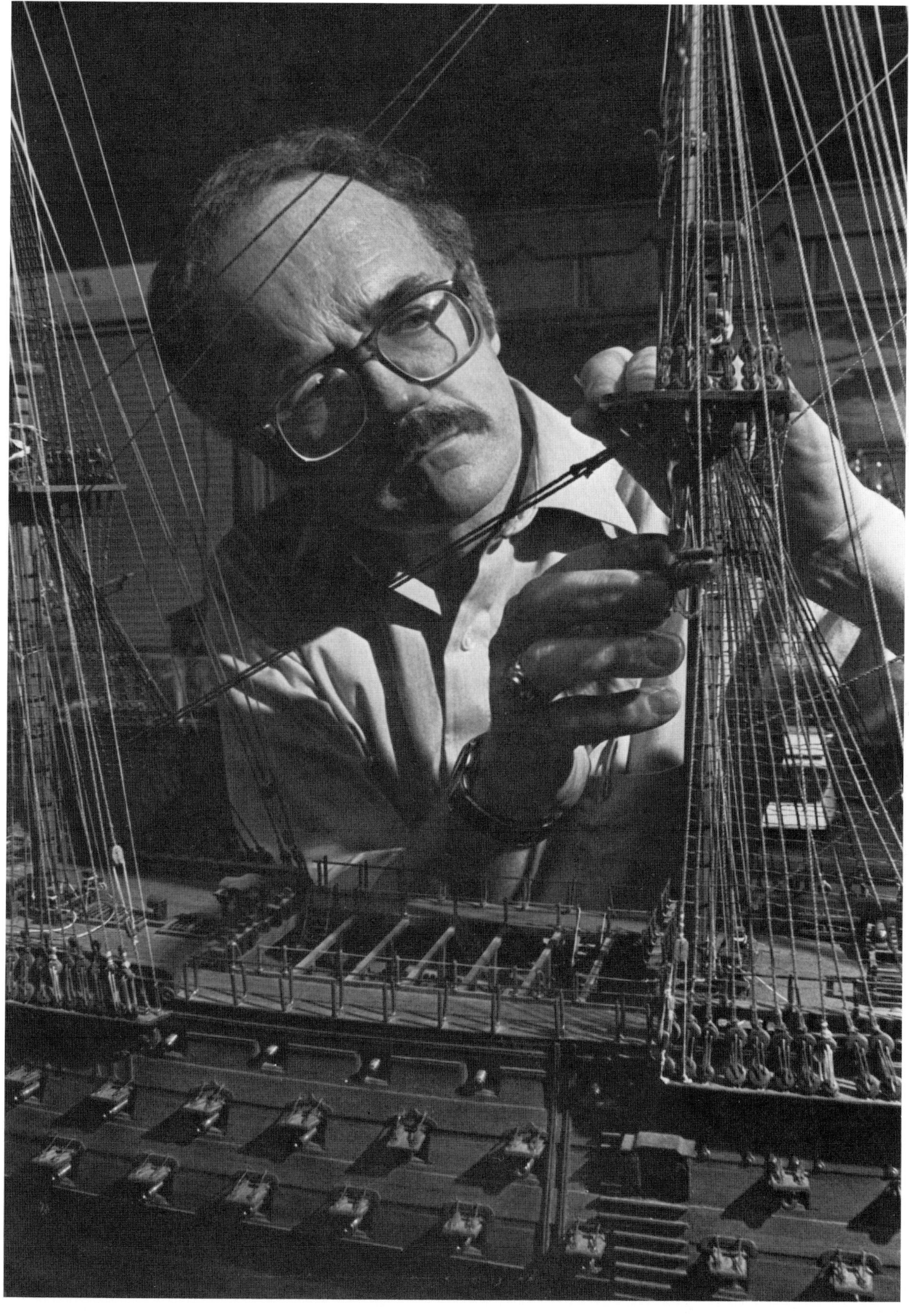

In such a situation you will need a high light level so you use a small aperture, which will keep both foreground and background sharp. Of course you can try a wide aperture, but then you will only be able to focus sharply on one element. For dramatic impact, try placing the product at eye level.

For photos of a person working on his project, be sure the situation is a real one. And beware of over-the-shoulder shots. In these photos people are bending over their work in such a way that only the backs of their heads and shoulders are visible.

Collectors

If there is a collector in your family, have him pose with some of his favorite items. If the collection is unique in terms of size, try taking a wide-angle shot that shows a huge collection almost burying its collector. If the collection has great value, take close-up photos that can be used for identification or insurance claims.

Extreme close-ups are easy to take with a zoom lens that has close-focusing ability. If you only have a normal lens, you might want to buy an inexpensive close-up attachment lens. With this lens you will be able to fill a frame with just one coin. For most collections soft side-lighting is best.

Top right: *Learn to anticipate the peak action so you can trip the shutter at the perfect moment. Do not rely on motor drives to do this for you, because the film might be advancing when the action is at its best.*

A slow shutter speed was used to capture the graceful movement of the horse and rider. When trying this effect, use a telephoto lens and shutter speeds of 1/15 or 1/60 sec. Plan on making about a half a dozen exposures in order to get one good shot.

Fish

Listed below are tips on taking fish photos:

To avoid photographing reflections from the side of the tank, either darken the room or fit the lens with a rubber hood that can be pressed against the glass.

To keep fish close to the camera, you will have to create a barrier inside the tank. To do this, obtain a sheet of glass about ½ inch smaller than the side of the tank through which you will be photographing.

Use lighting that comes from the top or the side.

Be patient. Shoot only when the fish are in a position that looks good to you.

HORSES AND OTHER COUNTRY ANIMALS

Photographing horses and their riders is similar to photographing other sports. For animals in action, you will probably want to use a telephoto lens and an auto-winder. Animals in a show ring are almost always too far away to use a normal lens. Explore different shutter speeds and their responses to action. To photograph jumping horses, it is best to fire the shutter just as the horse leaves the ground or just as he is halfway through the hurdle. The landing is usually an awkward-looking action.

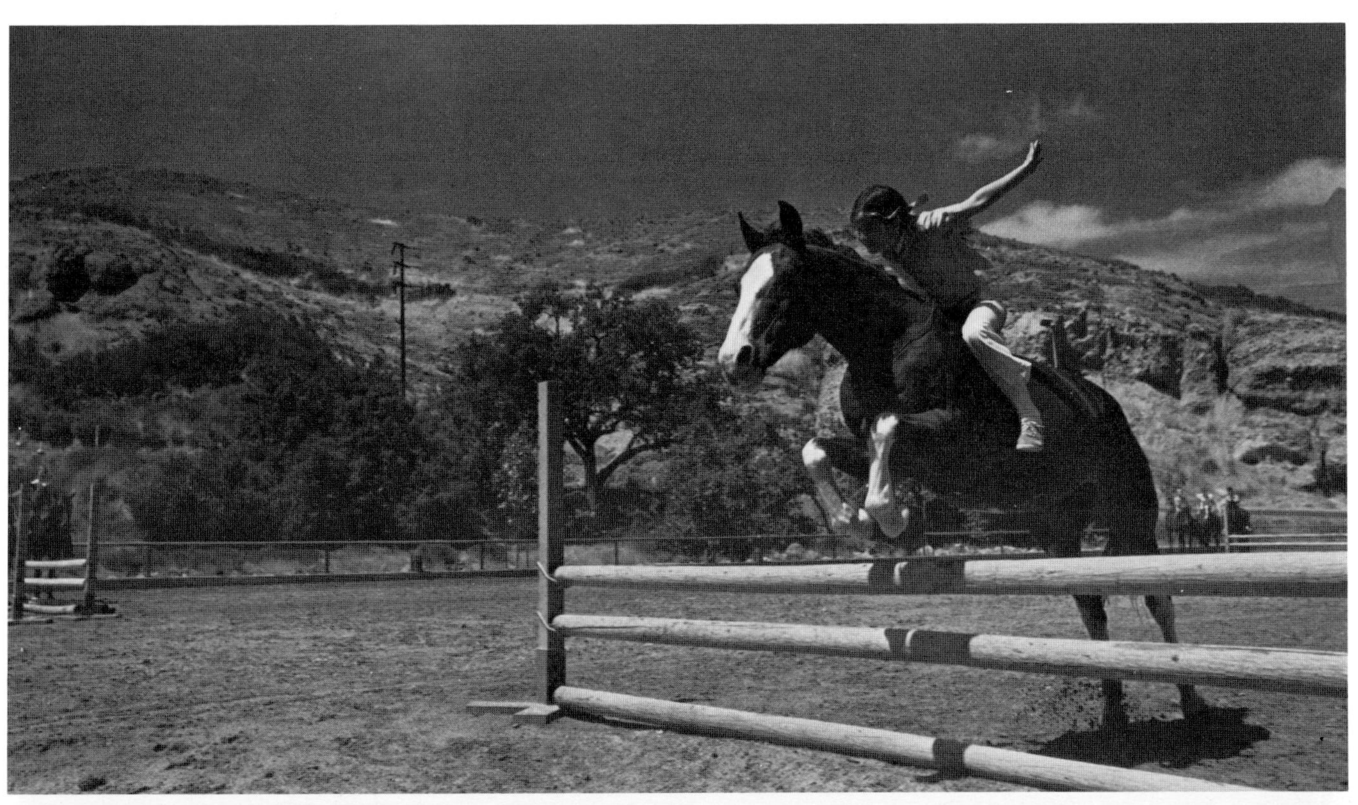

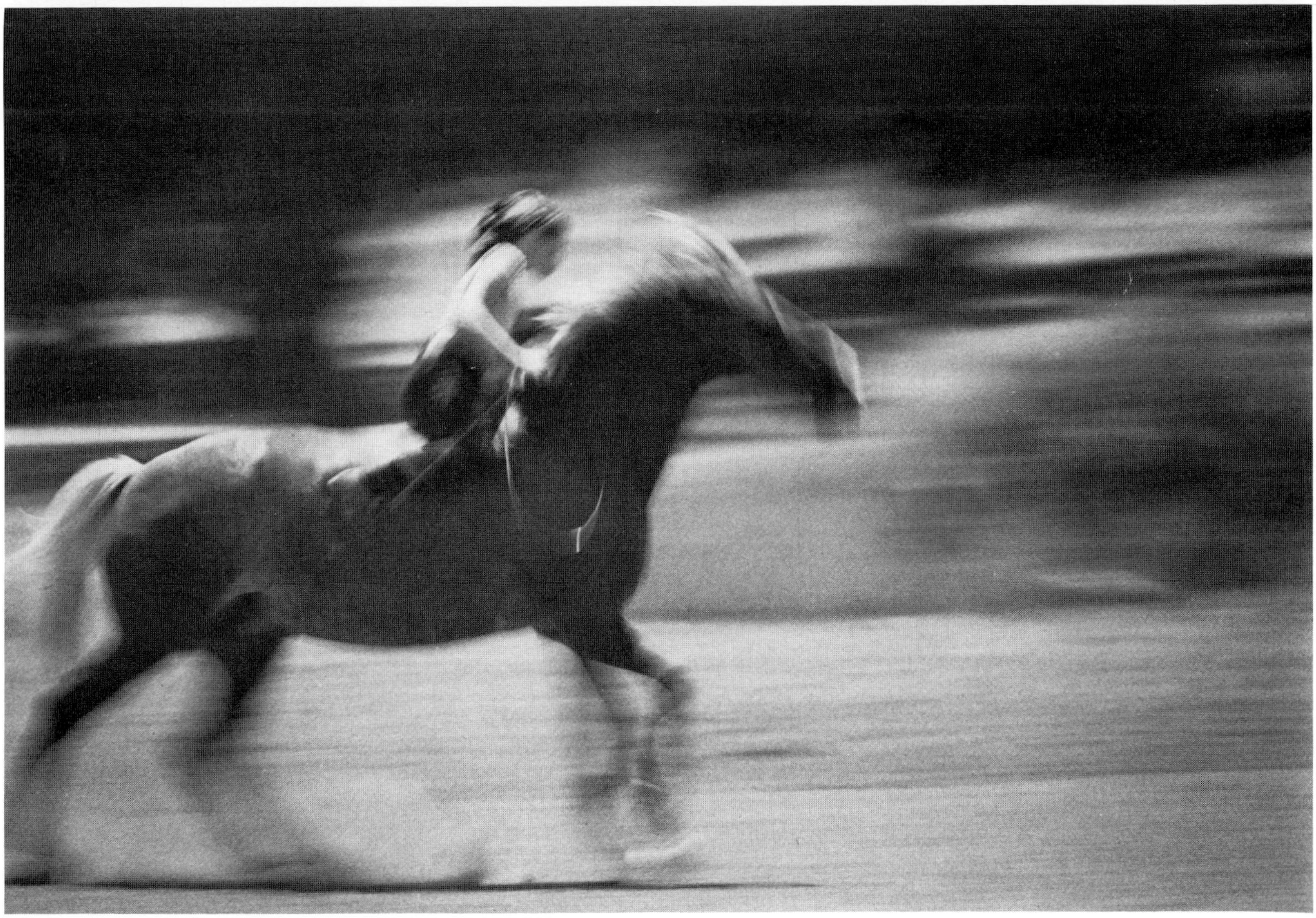

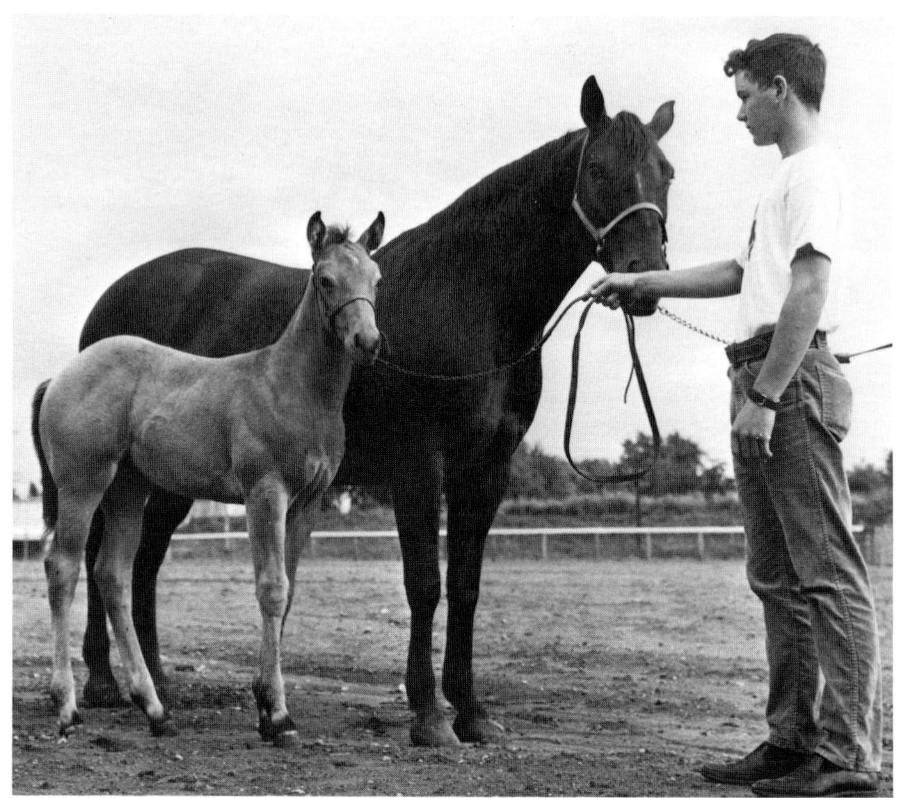

Note the pose of the horse and the colt. The colt is correctly posed to show its best qualities. Photograph courtesy of National 4-H Council.

Opposite page: *Photograph by Joseph A. Frisina, Jr.*

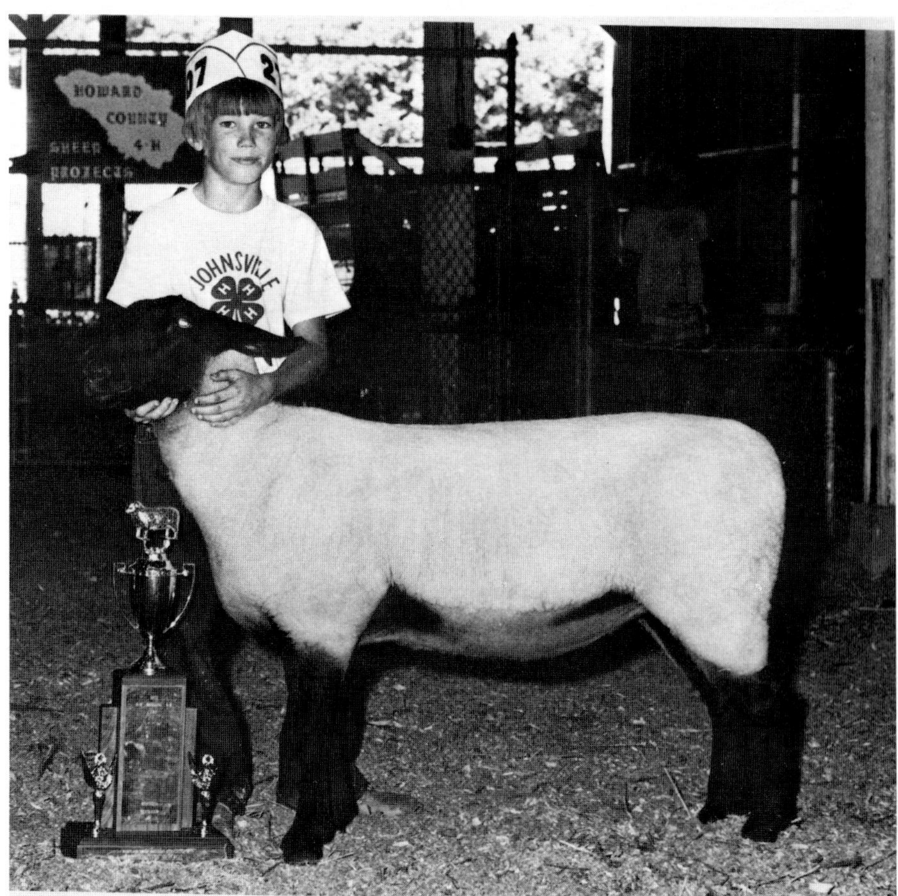

Bottom right: *If an animal is part of a youth project, include the animal's owner in the photo. Photograph courtesy of the Maryland Cooperative Extension Service.*

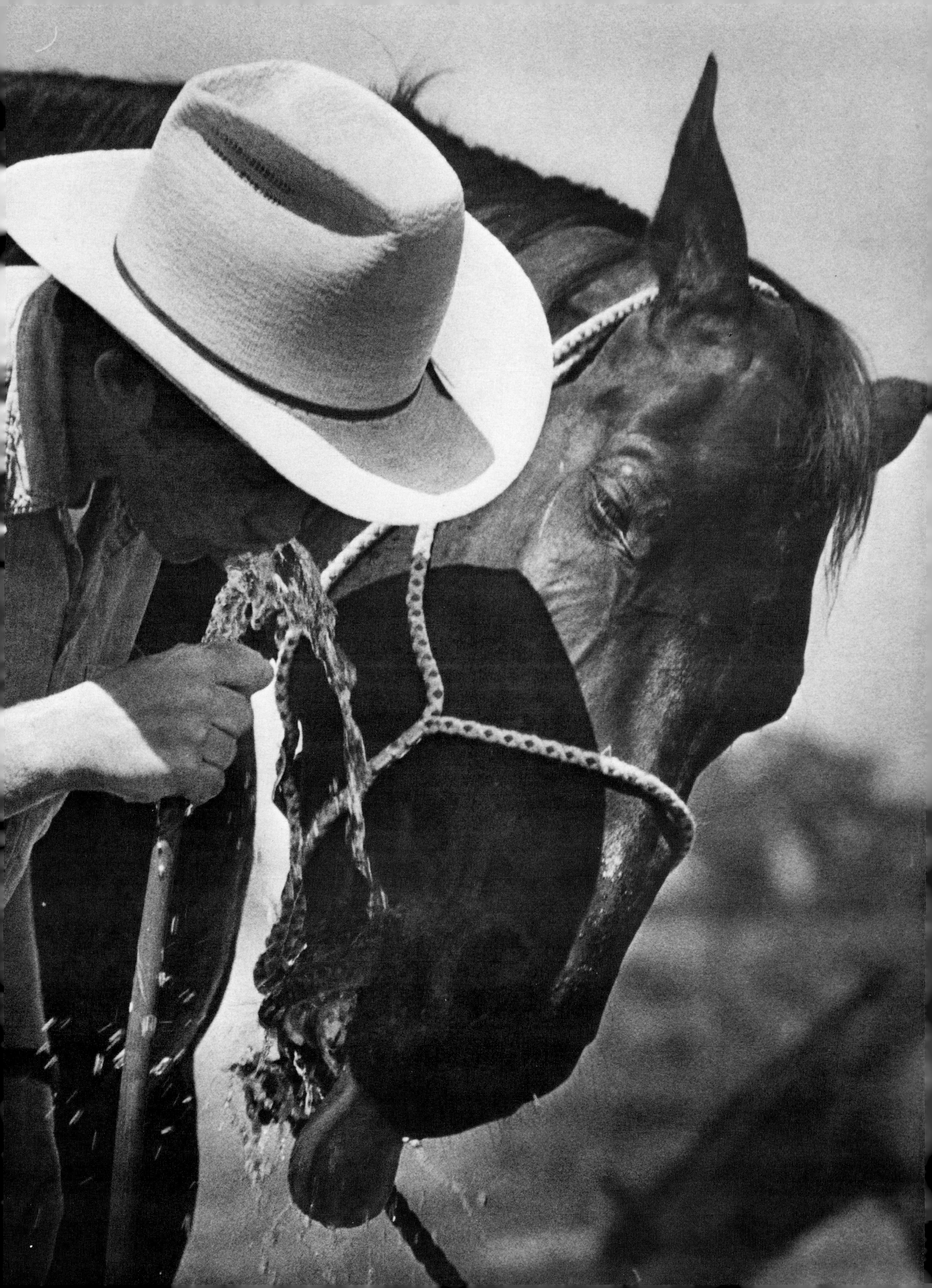

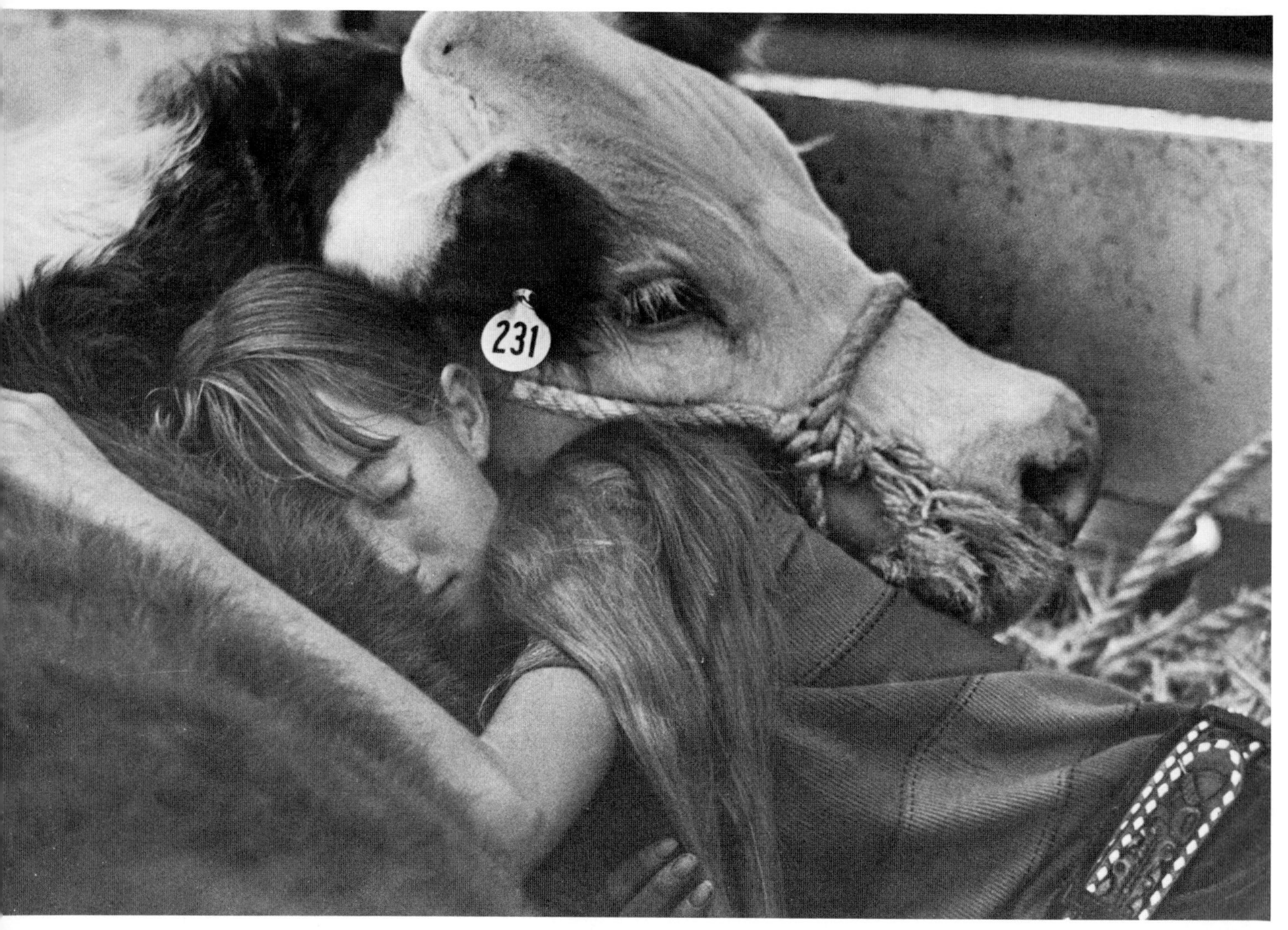

Photograph by Colleen Leman Scheidt.

Standing shots can be taken with a normal lens. But since the horse may dislike your camera, you may have to let the animal survey you and that shiny thing for a while. For a formal photograph that will show the horse's best qualities, place the animal, either with or without rider, against a plain background on a level terrain.

This type of photo is usually taken from the left side of the horse with the camera at the photographer's eye level. The foreleg nearest the camera should be ahead of the other foreleg; the hind leg nearest the camera should be behind the other hind leg. The head should be turned slightly toward the camera. The horse's ears should be straight up, and the tail should be in its normal position.

Other large animals are usually best photographed with a telephoto lens. This is because they may be suspicious of your motives if you are too close. If an animal is part of a show or project, include the animal's owner in your photo. As with horses, special stances may be necessary for formal photographs. Check photos in agricultural publications for examples and try duplicating the poses.

DOCUMENT YOUR POSSESSIONS

In addition to taking photos of your family and their activities, it is wise to take photos of the interior and exterior of your house for possible use with insurance claims. Such photos are not intended to be beautiful. They are merely a record of your possessions.

To take such photos, follow the suggestions given below:

Use a wide-angle lens for interiors.

Put the camera on a tripod and use a small aperture to ensure sharpness.

Use a fine-grained film, such as Panatomic-X or Kodachrome, for maximum detail.

Use a bounce flash or time exposure to avoid the glare from direct lighting.

Take views of each room so that all furniture and decorations can be seen.

Open drawers and take photos of their contents.

Take close-ups of special items, such as jewelry, stereo equipment, and firearms.

Do not keep the processed photos at home. If there should be a fire, your documents might be destroyed.

IN CASE OF A TRAFFIC ACCIDENT

If you should have a traffic accident, some photos from that accident would probably help your insurance agent. Of course if you are injured, you will not be concerned with photos.

To take such photos, try following the rules below:

Set your exposure on automatic. You will probably be too shaken to think about exposure settings.

Photograph each approach to the accident scene. At a normal intersection, this would require four photos, one from each direction.

Photograph any skid marks.

Photograph the damage on all vehicles.

Take the photos with a normal lens at eye level.

If the matter ends up in court, photos looking like artistic interpretations may be labeled distorted, making them useless evidence.

CHAPTER NINE

SHOWING OFF YOUR FAMILY PHOTOS

No more shoe boxes

Family photos should be looked at and enjoyed, not stored in some shoe box full of mixed-up prints and negatives. So when those shots come back from processing, waste no time in preparing them for view.

The most common way of organizing and presenting family photographs are in albums, enlargements made for wall and table display, and slide shows.

ALBUMS

Albums are available in styles to fit any taste. Some come with pages whose windows hold individual prints. Others, a more traditional type, require gummed corners to hold the photos. The most convenient type perhaps are those whose pages are coated with adhesive and then covered with clear acetate. Such albums not only allow you to arrange your photos in various designs but they also allow you to make changes in that design.

When arranging prints in an album, try to use a story-telling technique, including photos of signs and artwork you have made as titles. You can also include such mementos as news clippings, ticket stubs, and children's sketches.

Be sure to mark the photos with dates and other information. As the years go by, memories fade. And when the photos are enjoyed by future generations, they will need this information. For example, our family photo collection includes nineteenth-century portraits that have been vaguely labeled "Cousin Ed" and "Mildred's Brother." It took quite a bit of detective work to figure out who cousin Ed was. And since Mildred had three brothers, we will never know whose portrait that is.

Photographic greeting cards

A great way to display your family and your work is to send photographic greeting cards. Photofinishers offer standard

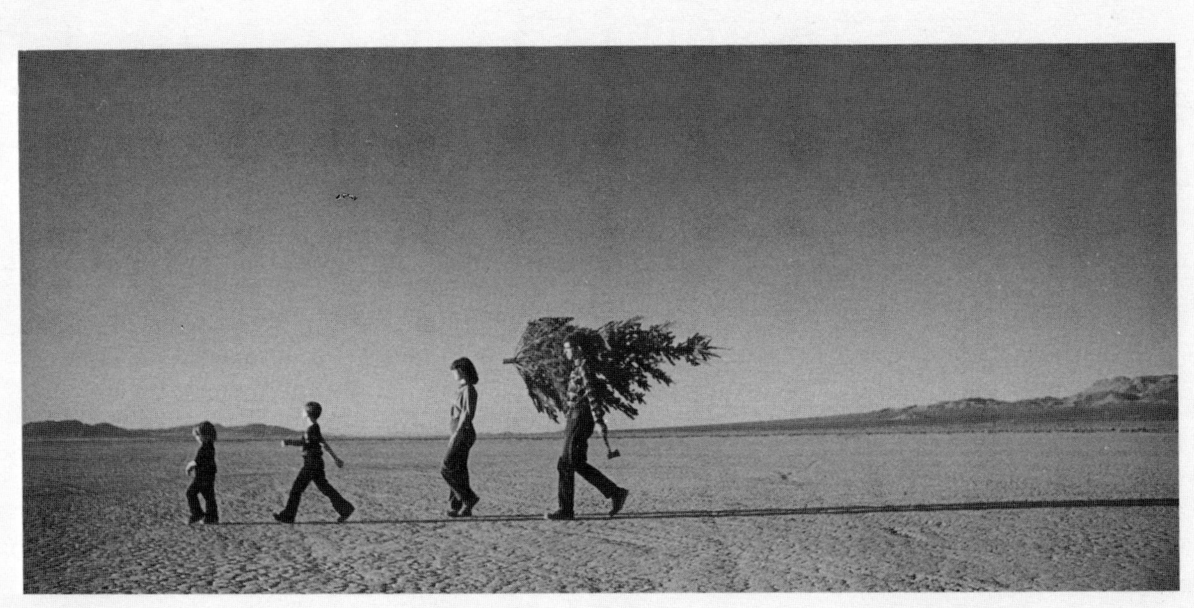

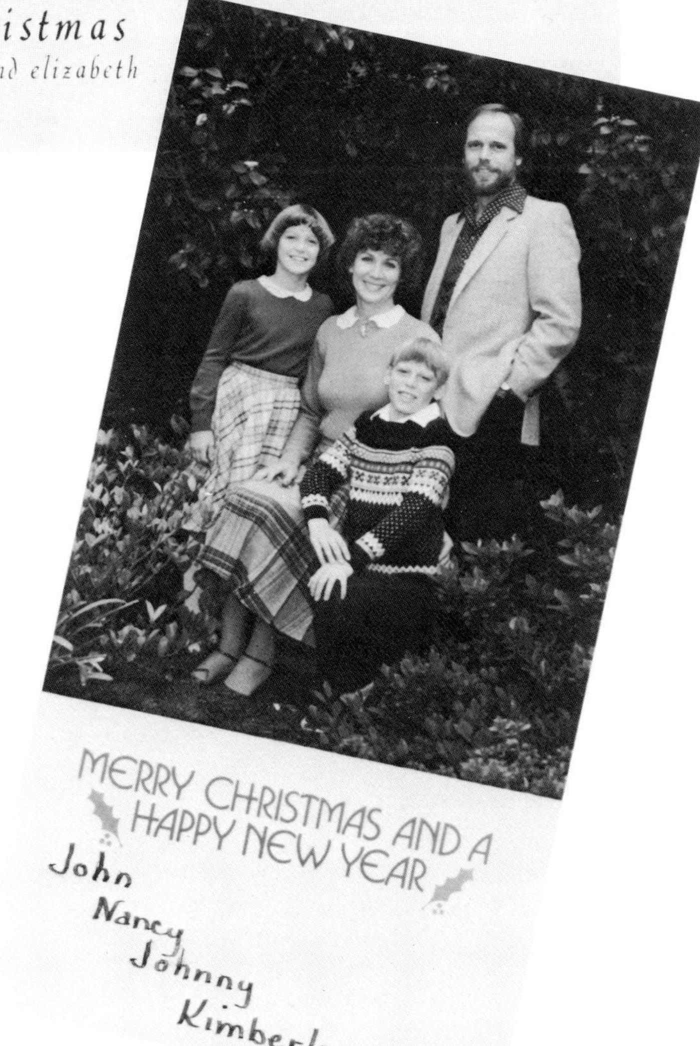

Above: *I made this Christmas card in my own darkroom.*

Right: *A custom photo lab can help you produce your own special greeting card, such as using your photo and printing your message on it. Photograph by Ed Khanoyan.*

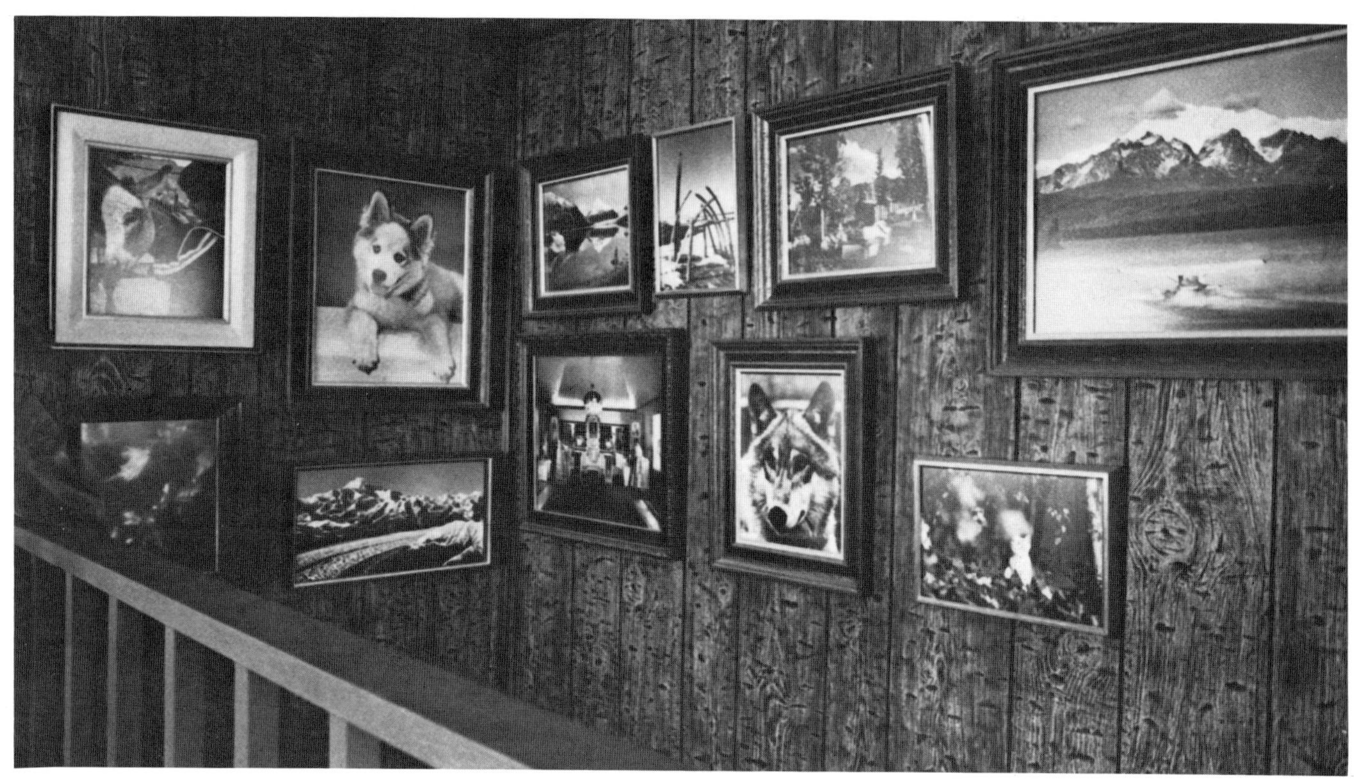

This area is at the top of a stairwell leading from a living area down to a lower level recreation room and darkroom. It can be seen from the living room and entry, and is an effective way to use both the photographs and the space. Photograph by Delores Brown.

designs that can be made from a negative. You can also design your own card.

If you have your own darkroom, the possibilities are limited only by your imagination. (The examples here show a standard-format card and a custom design.)

You need not limit your cards to holiday greetings. You can also have a local printer make up some general-purpose cards or stationery from one of your favorite photographs.

WALL DISPLAY

The best place to put your family photos is on the wall where you can enjoy them every day. A family wall should include photos of ancestors and relatives as well as your immediate family. You can also use photos in other decorative ways throughout the house.

When ordering prints for your wall, be sure you choose only from your best work. Fingerprints, dirt, and scratches on negatives or slides will be enlarged along with the image. Fingerprints are a particularly serious problem because skin oil can permanently damage film emulsion. Be sure the shot is sharply focused, too. A large print from a fuzzy negative can be very hard to live with.

Design your display

You will have a more effective display if you vary the size of your prints. To help you decide on sizes, plan your design ahead of time. Cut scrap wrapping paper to the intended print sizes and tape the pieces to the wall with masking tape. Make changes until you have just the effect you want. Then order your prints.

Remember to consider viewing distance when planning this design. An 8- × 10-inch enlargement placed in the middle of a large wall looks quite small when viewed from a distance. Yet it may be just the right size for a hallway where viewers are apt to be only a few feet away. For a family wall you might want to include a couple of large prints for impact—perhaps 16 × 20 or 20 × 24 or larger—as well as smaller prints to balance out the presentation.

Another factor to consider when designing your wall is color. Keep in mind the scheme of the room and the general trend of the photos. For example, a large photo in which the dominant color is bright orange could either conflict with the rest of the setting or add just the right counterpoint to the decor.

ORDERING PRINTS

You will probably get better quality work from a custom lab than a high-volume photofinisher, and some large sizes are only available from specialty houses. Check the phone book or the ads in photo magazines for custom labs.

When ordering prints, you will probably like matte finishes better than glossy. The shiny surface of a glossy print reflects light and makes viewing difficult.

Prints from slides

Remember that prints can be made from slides as well as negatives. When you take your slide to the lab, they may ask you which type of print you prefer, type C or type R. A type C print is made from an internegative of your slide. There may be a charge for this internegative, but if the photo needs major color corrections, this method gives the lab a few more ways to improve the image. Type C prints seem to be a little softer, both in color and sharpness, than type R prints. And this can be a plus for some moody or delicate subjects.

Type R prints are made directly from the slide, without an internegative. Contrast tends to build in these prints, although recent improvements in reversal-print materials have controlled contrast quite well.

Cibachrome prints are also made directly from a slide, and it is said that these prints have a higher resistance to fading than others. Cibachrome is a brand name for a specific reversal-print system.

You can easily determine the type of print you like best by sending a slide to a lab and asking them to print it two or three ways. Send a slide that is properly exposed and representative of the scenes you photograph.

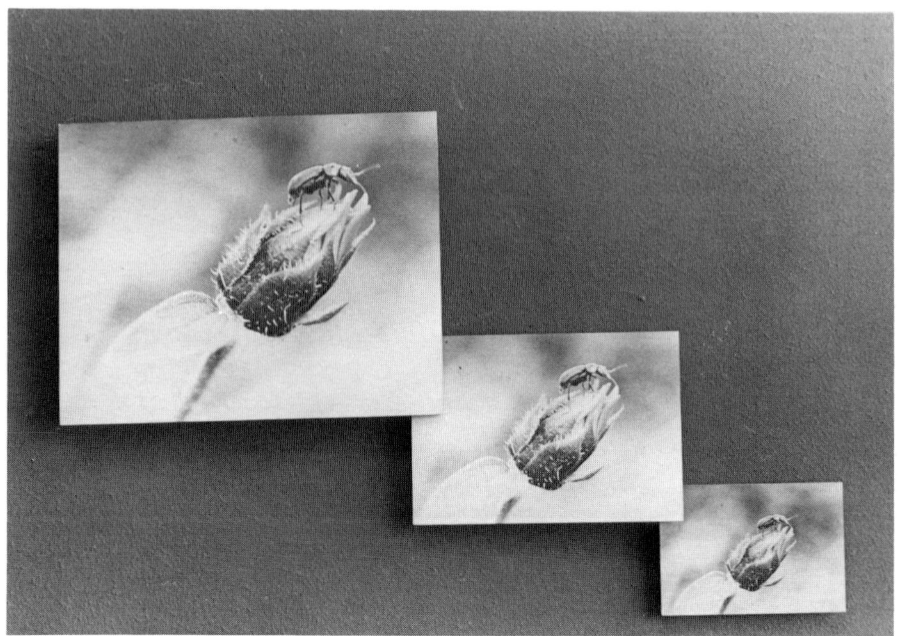

One effective way to mount a print is to attach the print to a piece of foam-core board sprayed with adhesive. Then trim the print and board edges so they are even with each other. Photograph by Jan B. Miller.

FRAMING

When it comes to framing your prints, you can be as simple or as elaborate as you choose. There are many inexpensive, easy-to-use mounting devices in art supply and frame shops.

One effective way to mount your work is to spray a piece of foam-core board with adhesive. Attach the print to it, then trim the board and print edges so they are even with each other. This is known as a flush mount. Next, glue small blocks behind the board to make it stand out from the wall. Foam-core board is available in art and frame shops.

By the way, do not use rubber cement for mounting photos. It will not hold permanently. Use special adhesives intended for mounting. Also, do not frame photos behind nonglare glass. It prevents you from seeing the full color saturation and detail of the print.

If you intersperse your permanently framed works with those that can be easily changed, you can update your wall as your family grows and changes.

Include your family heritage

When designing your family wall, don't forget to include photos from your family's past. Ancestral portraits as well as snapshots add an important piece of history to the collection.

Photos that are damaged can be taken to a professional photo studio where they can be copied and restored. Be very cautious about mounting and framing old prints. Do nothing that will prevent the print from being removed and remounted again. You don't want these heirlooms to be lost to future generations because of crumbling matte board, decaying adhesive, or other physical problems.

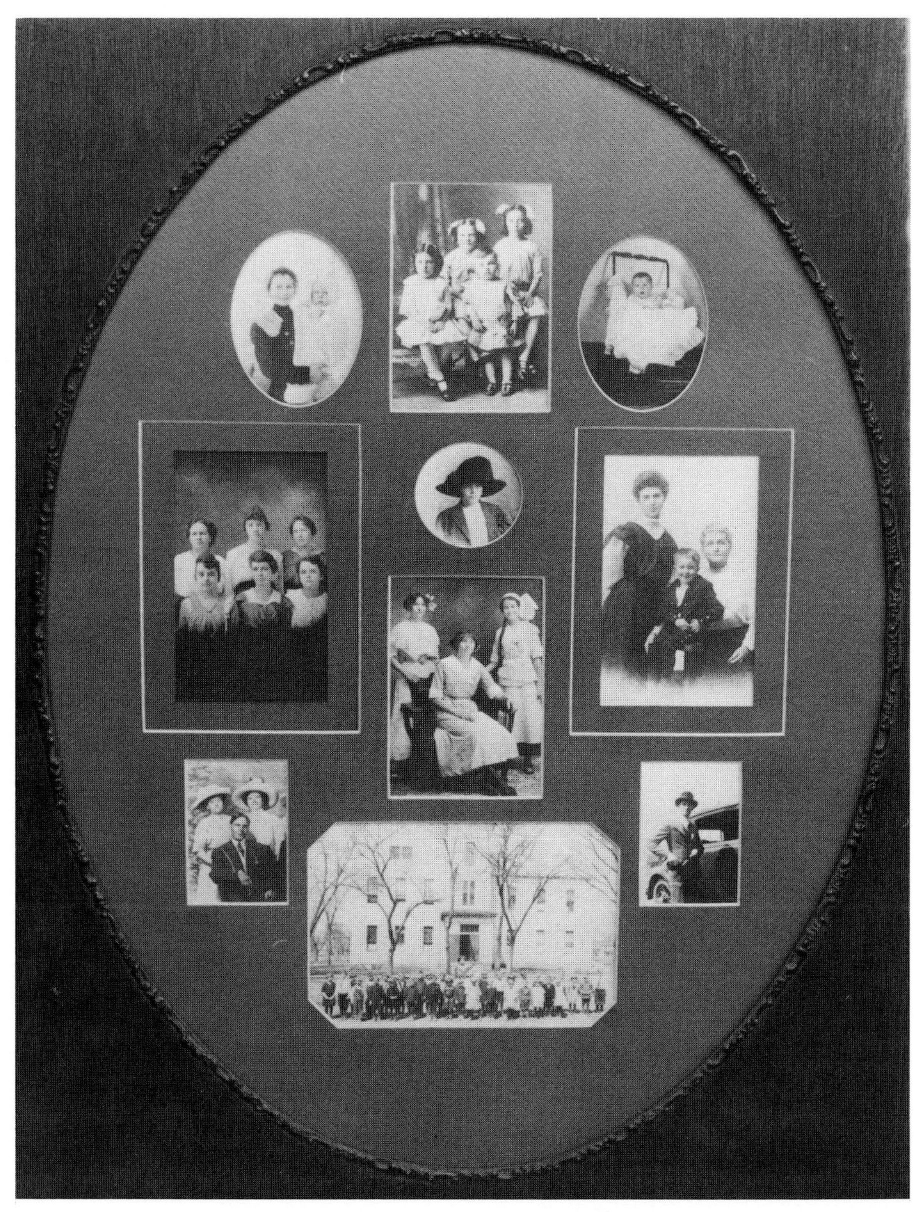

When designing your family wall, don't forget to include photos from your family's past. Photograph by Jan B. Miller.

HOW TO PRODUCE A SLIDE SHOW

If you like shooting slides, you will soon have many little boxes in your drawer or file. For some people, showing slides is quite an ordeal. They insert slides into the projector upside down and out of order, and they show the bad along with the good. If you are one of these people, don't inflict this treatment on your family and friends. Take some time to check the slides and arrange them into shows.

To arrange a show, you must first do some editing. Show only your best work. You should never have to make excuses for the photos. Don't show photos that are unduly repetitious, out of focus, or poorly exposed. These should go in the trash. If you just can't bear to part with them, establish an outtake file for personal perusal when the mood strikes.

Next, put your photos into some sort of logical order. Although you may not have a chronological story to tell, such as one about a vacation trip, at least try to group the images by subject and date. Shoot title slides for the beginning and end of your show. If you have young children, photos of their artwork can make interesting title slides.

Finally, control the pace and length of your show. Try to vary the amount of time each image is on the screen, and schedule an intermission before your audience shows signs of strain. Leave your audience wanting more rather than having had too much.

Tips for better slide projection

Use a projection screen or smooth white wall. Wrinkled bedsheets don't compliment your work.

Try to avoid keystoning. This is the effect produced by an image when the projector is tilted up at a steep angle. The top border of the projected image is wider than the bottom, and the two sides tilt outward. Correct the problem by placing the projector on a higher platform.

Avoid flashing the white light from the projector on the screen. This can be quite jolting to your audience after a series of slides.

Be sure everyone is seated comfortably and can see the screen without neck strain.

Clean the projector lens and condensers occasionally.

Clean your slides when necessary with a static brush or gun and a large ear syringe.

Be sure the slides are in order and inserted correctly. Slides should enter the projection gate upside down with the dull side of the film toward the screen.

FILES FOR PRINTS AND SLIDES

I know a photographer who uses the shoe-box method of filing negatives. He simply piles them into a shoe box until it is full. Then he buys another pair of shoes and starts filling another box. Although this system is certainly easy for him, he sometimes spends several hours looking for negatives or slides. There are other ways of filing negatives that don't take inordinate amounts of time.

Negative files

I file negatives separately from slides. After contact sheets are made of each roll, the negatives are placed in an envelope and stapled to the contact sheet. The sheets are then

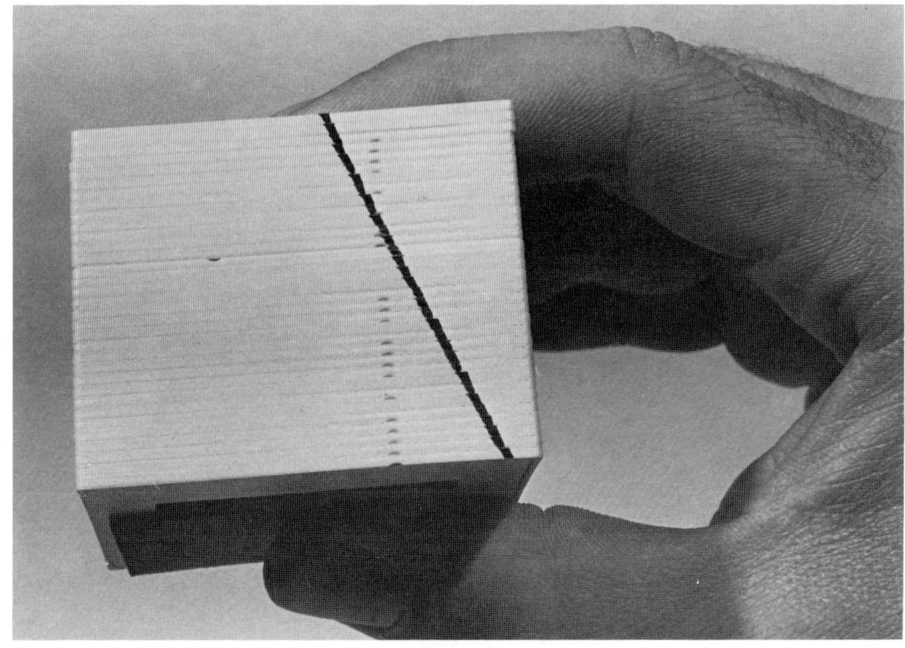

Draw a diagonal line across a stack of slides like this and you can quickly tell if they are in order. Note the small piece of scrap card protecting the end of the slide from fingerprints.

filed in manila folders by subject. General family snapshots are labeled by month and year and filed under the heading *Family*. Specific trips and events each have their own file folders, such as *Disneyland* or *Seattle Trip 1980*.

Transparency files
Transparencies, or slides, can be filed in their original boxes after editing or in plastic see-through pages. I use both methods. The see-through pages are great for miscellaneous subjects or sets of slides that don't make up a show.

Slides arranged for a show should be kept in boxes. The reason for this split system is that it is much faster to find a single slide when the images are in pages. But it is very tedious to pull several dozen slides out of pages for a show.

For shows you use frequently, it is convenient to keep the slides in projector trays. But don't keep all of your slides in projector trays or you'll end up with storage problems.

How to clean a slide
If your slides become dirty or fingerprinted, you must clean them with care. Remember, they are the original images and there are no negatives to fall back on for new prints.

First use an antistatic brush or gun to neutralize any charge that may be attracting dust. Then blow off the dirt and dust with a large ear syringe. If there are fingerprints on the slide, do the following:

Remove the slide from the mount. Carefully slit open the edge of the mount and peel back the two thin layers of cardboard. (If the slide is in a plastic mount, carefully pry the two halves apart with a small, sharp knife.)

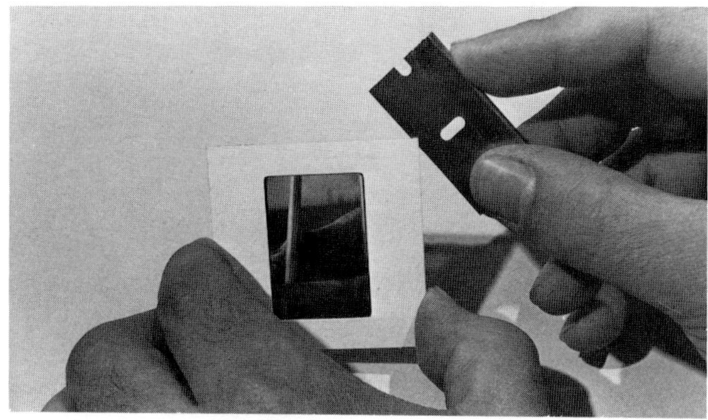

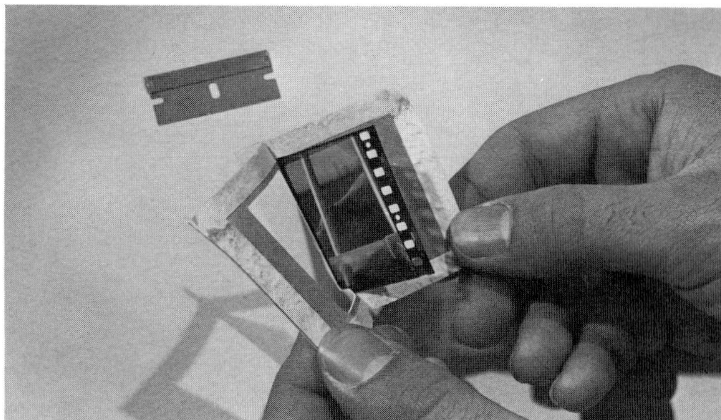

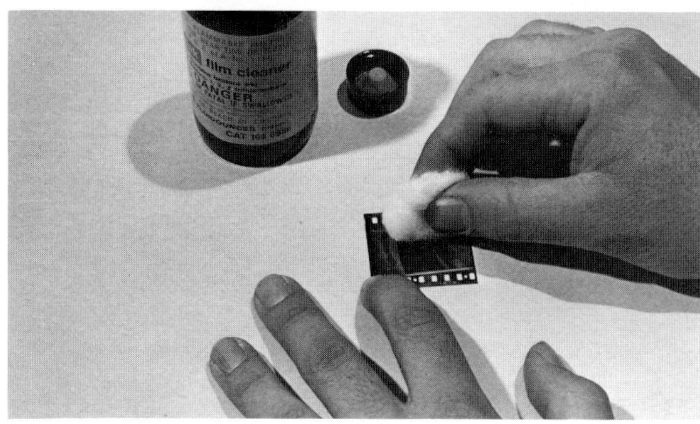

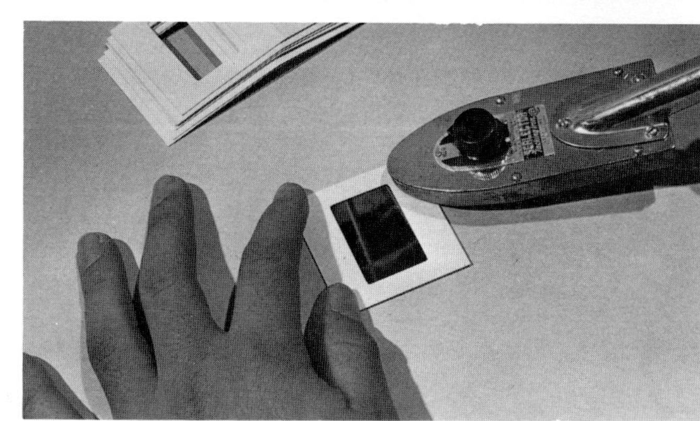

Top left: *To clean a slide that has been marked with fingerprints, first slit into the edge of the mount with a razor blade or very sharp knife.* Top right: *Then peel apart the slide mount and remove the slide.* Bottom left: *After dust and grit are blown off with a large ear syringe, gently rub the slide with a piece of cotton lightly moistened with film cleaner. (Make sure that there is not any grit on the slide before you start to rub it or you will scratch the slide.)* Bottom right: *Then remount the slide. Empty mounts are available at camera shops.*

Remove the film and place it on clean typing paper.

Lightly moisten a cotton ball with film cleaner and gently wipe the film.

Grab a dry piece of cotton as quickly as you can, and dry the film.

When the slide is clean and dry, remount it.

Film cleaner is available at camera stores. Also, be sure you use only genuine cotton. Synthetic materials can scratch the slide. Also, use only light pressure when wiping the film. Any scratches caused by dirt picked up by the cotton will permanently damage the film. For remounting, empty mounts are available at camera shops.

ONE FINAL THOUGHT

I hope that the ideas in this book will help you enjoy family photography. Be sure to take lots of photos as carefully as you can, but don't lose a special moment because you are thinking about composition or other technical matters.

Remember, newer cameras, more accessories, and advanced technical knowledge are not prerequisites for good family photography. You will be successful if you photograph with feeling and love.

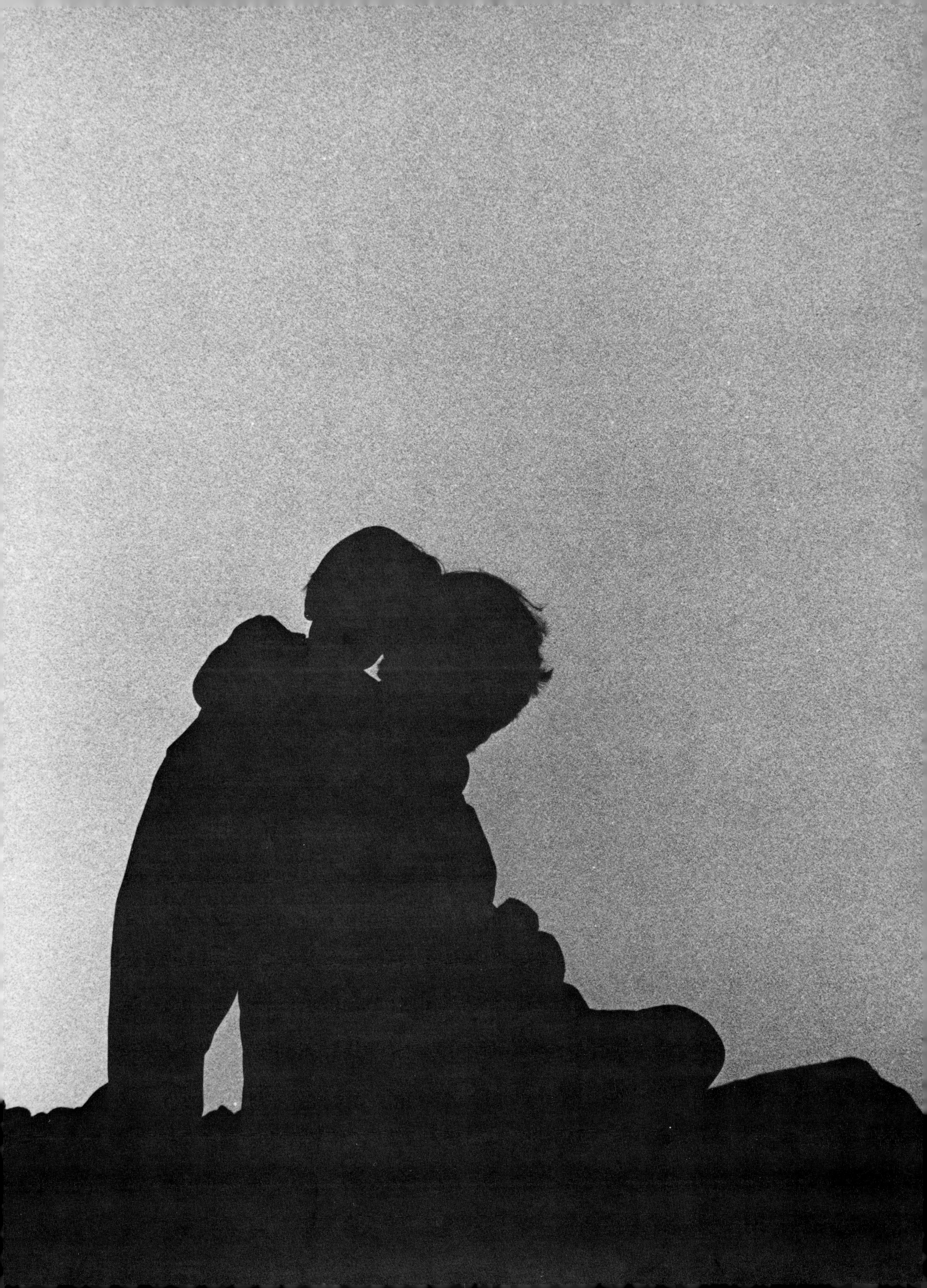

Edited by Michael O'Connor and Lynn Burrasca
Designed by Jay Anning
Graphic production by Hector Campbell
Set in 12 pt. Memphis Light